Nightmare

‡ THE BIRTH OF HORROR ‡

Nightmare

✦ THE BIRTH OF HORROR ✦

CHRISTOPHER FRAYLING

BBC Books

Dedicated to the memories of Angela and Theo

This book accompanies the television series *Nightmare – the birth of horror* first broadcast in 1996
Producer/Director Derek Towers. A Wall to Wall Production

First published in 1996 by BBC Books, an imprint of BBC Worldwide Publishing
BBC Worldwide Ltd., Woodlands, 80 Wood Lane, London W12 0TT

ISBN 0 563 37198 6
Designed by Martin Hendry
Picture research by Deirdre O'Day
Set in Garamond 3
Printed and bound in Great Britain by Butler & Tanner Ltd, Frome and London
Jacket printed by Lawrence Allen Ltd, Weston-super-Mare

ACKNOWLEDGEMENTS

Grateful thanks, first of all, to Derek Towers, the producer/director of the BBC television series *Nightmare – the birth of horror* which this book accompanies; it is in large measure thanks to Derek that the series looks and feels like a *series* rather than a collection of individual films. Thanks, too, to executive producer Alex Graham (of Wall to Wall Television), production manager Letitia Knight, cameraman David South, sound recordist Anthony Wornum, camera assistant Eric Fever and series co-ordinator Polly Magraw. Mons. Jolie (on behalf of the Washer family) kindly arranged for us to film in the Villa Diodati overlooking Lake Geneva; Catherine Santschi helped us re-open the Genevan police files of summer 1816; Stephen K. Urice and Wendy Van Wyck Good – of The Rosenbach Museum and Library, Philadelphia – made it possible for us to reveal on film the secrets of Bram Stoker's notes for *Dracula*; Jean Pateman allowed us to film the 'closed' section of Highgate Cemetery; and Lord Gowrie got his teeth firmly into the role of his villainous ancestor Lord Ruthven, the founding vampire of English literature; Robin Smith, of the Department of Manuscripts National Library of Scotland, allowed us to resurrect the long-buried treasure of the Graham Balfour archive. Dracula specialist Bernard Davies, Holmes specialists Peter Blau, Anthony Howlett and Catherine Cooke (of Marylebone Library) and dogs-in-poetry specialist Karen Chester (of the Poetry Library) all helped to clear up some thorny research problems: Richard Lancelyn Green was especially generous with his time, and his insights into the meaning of those footprints of a gigantic hound. My thanks to Sheila Ableman, Martha Caute and Deirdre O'Day of BBC Worldwide Publishing; and to Barbara Nash who was an inspired editor special thanks. Gill Plummer processed the text, from my semi-decipherable handwriting, with her characteristic efficiency, good humour and speed. And my wife Helen put up with, and shared, an obsessive work-programme which should have been two summer holidays.

But my greatest debt is to two dear friends who are no longer with us. The late Theo Brown, who was honorary research fellow in British folklore at Exeter University, had an encyclopedic knowledge of 'black dogs' and 'entrances to the other world' in the West Country. The late Angela Carter, novelist and critic, with whom I used to chat about the 'cybernetic birth' of the creature invented by Mary Shelley, was so amused at the thought of my travelling around Transylvania in search of vampire lore that she wrote a story about it in her marvellous collection *The Bloody Chamber*. They would both – I hope – have enjoyed this book, the fruit of 'many and long conversations' twenty years ago.

As a result of those conversations, I wrote to Bath City Council in the mid-1970s, suggesting that they put a metal plaque 'Frankenstein was created here by Mary Shelley, 1816-17' on the wall of what used to be 5, Abbey Churchyard. The Council remained unconvinced. Jane Austen, Richard Brinsley Sheridan and even Georgette Heyer seemed more in keeping with their image of the City: *Frankenstein* would surely lower the tone. Since then, interest in – and appreciation of – the literature of horror has developed worldwide beyond all recognition, thanks to the creative contributions of writers such as Angela and the insights of critics listed in the bibliography. Maybe it is time for Bath City Council to think again; to accept that nightmares can lead to great art.

CHRISTOPHER FRAYLING
Bath, London and Galway

FRONTISPIECE: *The vampire in the drawing room; an adapted Victorian steel engraving by the Surrealist artist Max Ernst.*

Contents

Prologue: The Nightmare   6

Introduction: The Birth of Horror   13

FRANKENSTEIN   14

DRACULA   66

DR JEKYLL AND MR HYDE   114

THE HOUND OF THE BASKERVILLES   162

Epilogue: The Horror…   215

Select Bibliography   216

Picture Credits   221

Index   222

Prologue:
The Nightmare

I N THE SPRING of 1782, the Zurich-born painter John Henry Fuseli (or Johann Heinrich Füssli) first exhibited *The Nightmare* at London's Royal Academy. The picture showed a young girl sleeping on her back, an incubus or mara squatting on her stomach and looking out at the viewer, and the head of a wall-eyed horse – staring blankly through the red bed-curtains. On a wooden bedside table, at the girl's feet, was a tray, two jars and a mirror – a mirror which *could* have reflected the incubus, but didn't.

Henry Fuseli, who later wrote that 'one of the most unexplored regions of art are dreams', and who was said to have supped on raw pork chops specifically to induce his nightmare, made his name with this painting. And engraved versions, produced in 1782, 1783 and 1784, distributed the image across Europe, until Fuseli's masterpiece became *the* way of visualising bad dreams.

When in the 1930s Universal Studio Hollywood sought a ready-made design for nasty nocturnal visitations its art department automatically turned to Fuseli. More recently, Swiss artist Hans Rudi Giger made reference to the painting when he created *Alien*. Fuseli's *Nightmare* is *Alien*, without the special effects.

Although *The Nightmare* was painted just before the Romantic craze in Western Europe – which revelled in peeling back the veneer of rational civilisation to reveal the 'natural' being or the raw sensations beneath, sometimes through the gateway of dreams – it was well known to the writers and painters of the early nineteenth century. One of them wrote that 'it was Fuseli who made real and visible to us the vague and insubstantial phantoms which haunt like dim dreams the oppressed imagination'.

The Nightmare was fascinating – and scary – because it operated at so many

*J*ohn Henry Fuseli's painting The Nightmare, *first exhibited 1782, was* the *way of visualising bad dreams in the Romantic era.*

different levels at once. It was set in the present (the stool and bedside table are 'contemporary' in style), and it was concerned not so much with an individual's nightmare – the usual subject-matter of dream paintings, often involving famous individuals and their prophecies – as with nightmares in general. It was not *A* Nightmare, but *The* Nightmare; not a vision but a sensation. This gave it a direct impact, unmediated by history, which put a lot of critics off.

In the painting, the victim is sleeping on her back, turned to her left side, with her head lower than her legs and a pressure just below her chest – all of them rational, 'enlightened', explanations of why nightmares occurred. Dr John Bond, who wrote *An Essay on the Incubus, or Nightmare* in 1753, had concluded his study with the thought:

The Nightmare generally seizes people sleeping on their backs, and often begins with frightful dreams, which are soon succeeded by a difficult respiration, a violent oppression of the breast, and a total privation of voluntary motion.

Sometimes, added Bond, this was caused by bad circulation of the blood, or a weight on the chest, or by too many stimulants at bed-time (maybe *that* is what is contained in the glass jar on the table).

When the Romantics started using dreams as gateways into the darkness (so that, as the German poet Novalis put it, 'world becomes dream; dream becomes world' – provided you could then snap out of it and write a poem about the experience), they began – like Fuseli – deliberately to induce nightmares. Southey used laughing gas, Anne Radcliffe ate indigestible food late at night, while others opted for portions of undercooked meat after prolonged periods of vegetarianism. But not all these had the desired result. The 'romantic agony' sometimes took the form of serious indigestion!

Dr Bond was at pains to distance himself from 'anything that did not appear serious or probable': so, he wrote in his *Essay*:

I have therefore omitted an enquiry into the origins of many old epithets and quaint names, commonly given to this Disorder: such as Hag-riding, Wizard-pressing, Witch-dancing, and etc.

But in *The Nightmare* Fuseli decided to include two of these 'superstitions' – the mara which sits on the victim's chest looking like a thoughtful penis while the girl lies back in a post-coital pose, and the wild, blind horse.

The mara was, according to Dr Johnson's *Dictionary*, 'a spirit that, in the northern mythology, was related to torment or suffocate sleepers' and Fuseli depicted it as a mixture of Gorgon-figure and fertility fetish. The horse, another folkloric symbol of male sexuality often associated with the devil, was the mara's mode of transport and *not* intended to be the nightmare. The confusion in the English language between nightmare (or mara) and nightmare (or female horse) in fact seems to date from printed versions of Fuseli's painting. The edition of 1783 included some explanatory lines from Erasmus Darwin's poem *The Loves of the Plants*:

So on his NIGHTMARE through the evening fog
Flits the squab fiend o'er fen, and lake and bog;
Seeks some love-wildered maid with sleep oppress'd,
Alights, and grinning sits upon her breast.

The poem went on:

On her fair bosom sits the Demon-Ape,
Erect, and balances his bloated shape;
Rolls in their marble orbs his Gorgon-eyes
And drinks with leathern ears her tender cries.

*M*ax Klinger's engraving Dead Mother *(1898), a version of* The Nightmare *where the demon has become a confused baby and the victim has become a woman lying on a funeral bier – a link between Fuseli's painting and the researches of Sigmund Freud.*

he Hollywood version of Frankenstein *(1931) explicitly referred to Fuseli's image of* The Nightmare; *since then, many horror films have used the same visual source.*

Darwin was right to use the word 'erect', but quite wrong to associate Fuseli's blind horse with 'his NIGHTMARE'. The horse in the painting is, by the way, derived from a classical sculpture, complete with marble eyes, which Fuseli had observed in the Piazza Quirinale, Rome.

Edmund Burke, in his influential *Philosophical Enquiry into the origin of our ideas of the Sublime and Beautiful* (1757) had defined 'the sublime' – the most satisfying aesthetic principle/experience of all – as a confrontation between the viewer and extreme natural phenomena, which triggers the emotion of terror. In his list of useful stimuli, he included ruined temples, dark landscapes, howling wildernesses, gloomy forests, vicious animals, raging storms, gaping chasms and rough seas – a list which could almost be a menu for the horror novels of the time.

Fuseli would no doubt have added goblins and figures of folklore to Burke's list. The point, Burke had said, was to create terror out of the sense of 'there but for the grace of God go I'; to identify with the *victims* of natural catastrophes and thus scare oneself stiff. But once the Romantics had taken up Burke's ideas and run with them – jettisoning the morality but keeping the terror – 'the sublime' turned into something simpler: just nasty things which happen to turn you on. Fuseli was uncomfortable with this development and wrote in his fifth *Lecture on Painting* (1802):

> We cannot sympathise with what we detest or despise, nor fully pity what
> we shudder at or loathe … mangling is contagious, and spreads aversion
> from the slaughterman to the victim.

In other words, the *shlocky* approach to horror was less effective than shadows, suggestions and symbols. It is, of course, an argument which is still going strong today.

Where the symbolism of *The Nightmare* was concerned, the female is clearly intended to be the victim of a fantastical sexual predator. Fuseli's paintings tend to be about muscular, larger-than-life men, often in classical poses, and submissive or provocative women with strange hair-dos, and he usually casts the viewer in the role of male *voyeur*. This particular image, it has been suggested, represents his own frustrated longing for a woman he had met in Zurich a couple of years before (and whose portrait is painted on the back of the canvas). The mirror, which does not reflect the mara, suggests that the nightmare-penis is a figment of the victim's imagination: a case of wishful thinking on Fuseli's part. So in addition to the levels of the rational, the folkloric and the philosophical, *The Nightmare* is – within late eighteenth-century conventions – about the sexual as well.

Maybe it was this aspect which attracted Sigmund Freud to the picture. For, although he never wrote about it, he had a print of Fuseli's *Nightmare* hanging in his waiting-room at Berggasse 19, Vienna (next to a print of Rembrandt's *Anatomy Lesson*), and he later transported them both to his house in Hampstead.

By the time Freud wrote his *Interpretation of Dreams* (1901), it had become unfashionable to study nightmares as examples of actual visitations, or the result of indigestion, or the product of stimuli external to the sleeper. And the folkloric explanation, which had been in *vogue* again during the Romantic period, had been consigned to fairyland.

For Freud, dreams were the 'guardians of sleep', the carriers of waking wishes or repressed desires which could not emerge in any other way. As a rule, these were 'erotic wishes … and sexual desires', and they emerged through the freedom of the dream state in *displaced* or *symbolic* forms. So in nightmares, these wishes and desires were 'transformed into anxiety', and the more forbidden the desire the greater the anxiety. Later, Freud added that nightmares could also be attempts, in dream, to take control of events which had got the better of the victim in the waking state. The important thing was that nightmares embraced in some way the terrors which the sleeper feared the most.

At precisely the same time that Freud was researching dreams and nightmares, the German artist Max Klinger was preparing his extraordinary cycle of prints called *On Death, Part II*. One of the final images in the set was an engraved transcription of Fuseli's *Nightmare* called *Dead Mother* (1898). This showed a young woman lying on a funeral bier with flowers in her hair, a baby squatting on her chest and looking out at the viewer, and through an arched doorway a dark forest with a sea beyond.

Originally, Klinger intended the child's face to be elderly and demon-like (a human version of Fuseli's mara) – an example of 'the child as murderer'. Later, he decided that the child's face should be beautiful, in contrast with the mother's which should be under-nourished or withered. In the end, the print showed panic on the face of the child, peace on the face of the mother and added the punch-line 'the individual dies – the species lives'. The young sapling just behind the child, in a forest of majestic old trees, makes a similar point.

Klinger's *Dead Mother* harks back to German Romantic painting of the late eighteenth to early nineteenth century: Fuseli's *Nightmare*, the landscapes of Caspar David Friedrich, the nature-studies of Philipp Otto Runge. It is also very much of its own time, in its *fin de siècle* obsession with love and death, and re-working of the idea of *The Nightmare* from a psycho-sexual point of view. *Dead Mother* had a profound effect on the Norwegian artist Edvard Munch, who in turn transformed it into an image of a predatory vampire. Some have argued that this was 'a forerunner of surrealism'.

In this painting, instead of the Gorgon-figure, a confused baby; instead of the supine victim, a dead mother; instead of the horse peering through the curtain, a forest appearing through the arched doorway (based, by the way, on the Roman church of St Paul's Outside the Walls). Has the birth of the child killed the mother? Or has the child drained the mother of her vitality? Or are we supposed to conclude that the death of the mother is simply part of the natural cycle of things? The individual dies – the species lives on. If so, why does the child have such a panic-stricken look on its face, and why is it looking straight out at *us*?

However we react, Fuseli's painting – a mixture of enlightenment ideas, classical figures, and folklore – has been transformed by Max Klinger into a modern image of desire, anxiety and biology. The space between *The Nightmare* and *Dead Mother*, between the way-of-seeing of the late eighteenth century and the way-of-seeing – several nightmares later – of the late nineteenth century, is the subject of this book.

The Birth of Horror

THE NINETEENTH CENTURY, and especially the Victorian age, saw the birth of the great horror stories which still play a huge part in global culture. In some ways, a more significant part than ever before. They have even become absorbed into the English language – a Frankenstein monster, a vampire-like relationship, a Jekyll and Hyde character, a Baskerville hound – a sure sign that they have become an accepted feature of everyday life. These stories are among the most significant contributions by British writers of the last century, to the mass culture of this century – and I mean 'mass': films, videos, books, poems, toys, games, computer software, comics, advertisements, theme-restaurants, everything from novels to breakfast cereal products.

In the process, the great horror stories have been re-created again and again: Frankenstein has become confused with his own creation, who has in turn become a thing of nuts and bolts, stitches and sutures; Dracula has become an attractive lounge-lizard in evening dress; Mr Hyde has become a simian creature who haunts the rookeries of Whitechapel in East London; and Sherlock Holmes, dressed in his obligatory deerstalker and smoking a meerschaum pipe, says 'elementary, my dear Watson' whenever he exercises his powers of deduction. Not one of these re-creations came directly from the original stories on which they were based: successive publics have re-written them – filling in the gaps, re-directing their purposes, making them easier to remember and more obviously dramatic – to 'fit' the modern experience.

The great horror stories began as fantasies by gaslight, personal nightmares – of 'desire with loathing strangely mix'd' in the poet Coleridge's words – experienced and recounted by sensitive individuals: today, they have not only become de-personalised, they have long ago left the literary world to which they originally belonged; they are read and studied all over the world for reasons which their authors would probably not even have recognised – let alone understood. Even the circumstances of their creation – the nightmares themselves – have become the stuff of folklore and legend.

The long-term origins of these stories go back to the legends of Greece and Rome, or even earlier; the serpent in the Garden of Eden, Prometheus the fire-bringer, the bride of Corinth, the hellhound Cerberus – guardian of Hades. But the birth of *modern* horror begins in summer 1816, in the unlikely, well-manicured setting of the shores of Lake Geneva.

Frankenstein

I saw — with shut eyes, but acute mental vision — I saw the pale student of unhallowed arts kneeling beside the thing he had put together. I saw the hideous phantasm of a man stretched out, and then, on the working of some powerful engine, show signs of life, and stir with an uneasy, half-vital motion ... His success would terrify the artist; he would rush away from his odious handiwork, horror-stricken. He would hope that, left to itself, the slight spark of life which he had communicated would fade; that this thing, which had received such imperfect animation would subside into dead matter; and he might sleep in the belief that the silence of the grave would quench forever the transient existence of the hideous corpse which he had looked upon as the cradle of life. He sleeps; but he is awakened; he opens his eyes; behold, the horrid thing stands at his bedside, opening his curtains and looking on him with yellow, watery but speculative eyes.

MARY SHELLEY

The first Frankenstein *illustration, from the popular edition of 1831: it shows the nightmarish moment after the birth of the 'beautiful' creature, when the terrified young scientist rushes out of the laboratory.*

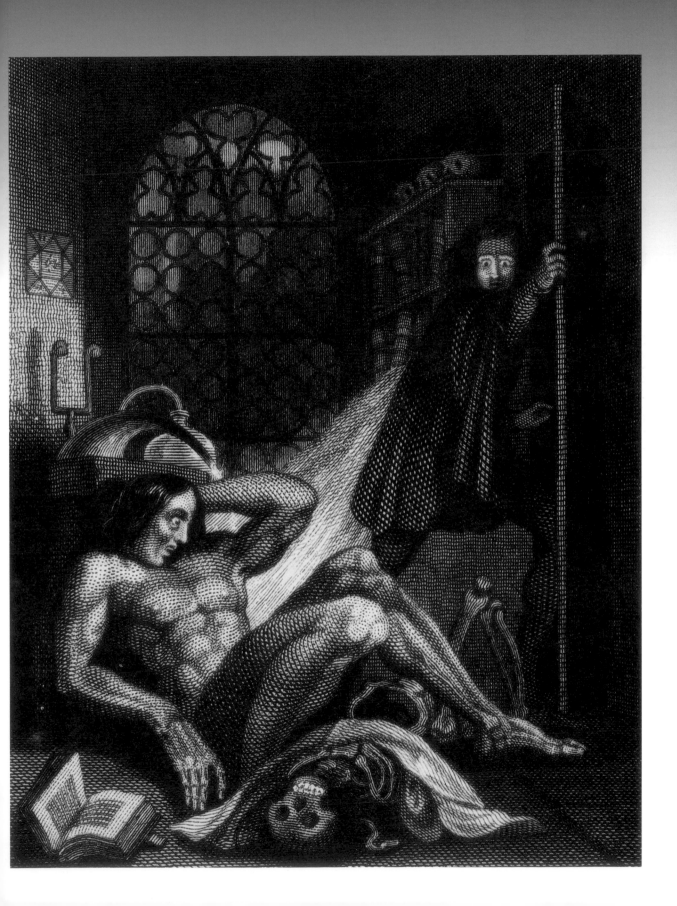

O N 13 MAY 1816, Percy Shelley, eighteen-year-old Mary Wollstonecraft Godwin, their five-month-old son William and Mary's stepsister Clare Clairmont (who was eight months younger than Mary) checked into Monsieur Dejean's fashionable Hôtel d'Angleterre facing the Alps on the north side of the lake, just outside the city of Geneva. They were tired out. Mary had been sea-sick and coach-sick for most of the ten-day journey from London.

The Hôtel d'Angleterre, a large three-storey stone building set back from the lakeside, with a park leading to the road from Geneva to Lausanne, was a stop-over favoured by the British starting on their grand tours. It was the first coaching inn on the way out of the austere walled city which shut its gates at 10 p.m. sharp.

The hotel's main building was demolished in 1845 – its site now houses the Department of Parks and Environment of the City of Geneva – but a sur-viving pavilion near the Lausanne Road, just beyond the Parc Mon Repos, still bears a plaque which says *ici s'elevait une Hotelerie où Byron et Shelley ... ont séjourné autrefois*. And parts of the little harbour, where Monsieur Dèjean used to hire out boats, still exist.

After they had had time to settle in, Mary Godwin wrote to her half-sister Fanny:

> From the windows of our hotel we see the lovely lake, blue as the heavens which it reflects, and sparkling with golden beams. The opposite shore is sloping and covered with vines, which however do not so early in the season add to the beauty of the prospect. Gentlemen's seats are scattered over these banks, behind which rise the various ridges of black mountains, and tower-ing far above, in the midst of its snowy Alps, the majestic Mont Blanc, highest and queen of all ...

Mary Godwin was fond of lakes and mountains: the happiest time in her childhood had, she said, been spent in the more picturesque parts of Scotland. But on the whole she liked her landscapes tranquil and soothing. Shelley, on the other hand, preferred to revel in the extremes and dangers of the sublime.

A week later, Lord Byron and his travelling companion/personal physician Dr John Polidori, accompanied by a *valet de chambre*, two servants and two drivers, arrived at Sécheron. Before he left England at the end of April, Byron had given Jane Clairmont (then known as 'Clara') his address as 'Milord Byron, Poste Restante, Genève', which was why she had managed to persuade Percy Shelley and Mary Godwin to go to Geneva (rather than to Italy, which Percy had originally preferred). For, in April 1816, Clare briefly – in a charac-teristically impetuous move which, she later wrote, gave her ten minutes of pleasure and a lifetime of pain – had become Byron's mistress.

Unknown to his noble employer, twenty-year-old Dr Polidori, who had recently graduated in medicine from the University of Edinburgh, had been offered 500 guineas to produce a publishable journal of their adventures, so he noted the Byron party's movements in some detail. He was, in the words of his acquaintance Harriet Martineau, 'a handsome, harum-scarum young man'. He also had ambitions to be a poet rather than a medical man. But, as his *Journal* amply shows, he was not a very gifted writer:

> May 26 – Went to the house beyond Cologny that belonged to Diodati. They ask five-and-twenty louis for it a month … The view from this house is very fine; beautiful lake; at the bottom of the crescent is Geneva. Returned …
>
> May 27 – … LB met M Wollstonecraft Godwin, her sister [in fact stepsister] and Percy Shelley. I got the boat into the middle of Leman Lake, and there lay my length, letting the boat go its way … Dined; PS, the author of Queen Mab came; bashful, shy, consumptive; twenty-six [in fact only twenty-three]; separated from his wife; keeps the two daughters of Godwin, who practise his theories [of the emancipation of women, and of open marriage; evidently Byron had been gossiping]; one LB's [Clare Clairmont] …

A few days after, the Shelley party – now with a Genevan nursemaid called Louise Duvillard but known as 'Elise' – moved across the lake to the smaller of two secluded properties owned by a M. Jacob Chappuis. The address was 'Maison Chappuis, Montalègre', but Mary Godwin referred to it as 'Chapuis'. The square, stone-built, two-storey 'cottage' set among vineyards near the winding lake road (which in those days hugged the hillside rather than the edge of the lake), had access to a small harbour which belonged to Chappuis.

From a portrait of Mary Wollstonecraft Shelley by Richard Rothwell. She married Percy Shelley in December 1816, a fortnight after hearing of the death of Shelley's wife Harriet.

The Maison Chappuis was demolished in 1883, and all that remains of the surroundings is the stable next door (converted into a small house) – which can be seen from today's main road – a cellar with an ornamental iron door, and a stone stairway in the garden. Mary Godwin wrote to her half-sister on 1 June, from 'Campagne C, near Coligny':

> Unfortunately we do not now enjoy those brilliant skies that hailed us on our first arrival to this country. An almost perpetual rain confines us principally to the house; but when the sun bursts forth it is with a splendour and heat unknown in England. The thunder storms that visit us are grander and more terrific than I have ever seen before. We watch them as they approach

Frankenstein or The Modern Prometheus

THE STORY

Captain Robert Walton, an English explorer in the Arctic, takes the Genevan scientist Victor Frankenstein on board his ice-bound ship, and listens to his sad life story. Frankenstein, it transpires, has discovered the secret of giving life to dead tissue while researching medieval and modern chemistry at the University of Ingolstadt. After carefully assembling the various parts of a male human body – found in graveyards and dissecting rooms – he makes an eight-foot creature and gives him the spark of life; but the sight of the creature's 'watery eyes' causes Frankenstein to flee in a deep depression. The scientist tries hard to shut the blasphemous deed out of his mind, but the violent death of his little brother William (and subsequent, wrongful, execution of the family servant Justine Moritz for murder) convinces him that the 'filthy daemon' is at large. They eventually meet on the Mer de Glace, in the Alps, and his creature tells of his rejection by all the people he has encountered, of his education in language, literature and emotion – by observing an impoverished family in a country cottage, and discovering a portmanteau full of books – and of his need for a female partner.

Victor Frankenstein at first agrees to create one for him, on condition the creature 'quits Europe forever'; and travels with his close friend Henry Clerval via the Rhine and Rotterdam to the remote north of Scotland in order to perform the operation. But he has second thoughts and aborts his female creature, causing the 'daemon' to threaten 'I will be with you on your wedding night' and to strangle Clerval (a crime for which Frankenstein himself is almost convicted).

Despite the threat, Frankenstein goes ahead and marries his cousin and childhood sweetheart Elizabeth Lavenza, and that night the creature murders her in the bridal bed. The scientist chases his creature across Europe and the Black Sea to the Frozen Ocean and the Arctic, where he dies of exhaustion after finishing his story. The creature, who by now resembles 'a mummy' (because of decomposition), pays his last respects and floats on an ice-raft into the darkness. Captain Walton decides to abandon his explorations, and return home to England.

from the opposite side of the lake, observing the lightning play among the clouds in various parts of the heavens, and dart in jagged figures upon the piny heights of Jura, dark with the shadow of the overhanging cloud …

Mary Godwin was beginning to share Shelley's 'enjoyment' of storms, though she still preferred 'sunshine and gentle breezes'. Byron, too, was busy exploring the impact of the increasingly extreme weather conditions on his emotions. In Canto the Third of *Childe Harold's Pilgrimage* (92 & 3), which he wrote at this time, he described a heavy storm he had experienced on 13 June:

Thy sky is changed! – and such a change! Oh night,
And storm, and darkness, ye are wondrous strong,
Yet lovely in your strength, as is the light
Of a dark eye in woman!

Lord Byron had moved into the Villa Diodati several days before. This villa, which had belonged to the family since Gabriel Diodati supervised its construction in the early eighteenth century, was not occupied: Edward Diodati and relatives lived in a smaller house near the village of Cologny, and rented out the main house to visitors. It was, and is, a two-storey grey stone villa with a substantial porticoed basement, surrounded on three sides – at first-floor level – by a large balcony with an elaborate iron balustrade.

Today, Diodati is the best-conserved of all the grand lakeside villas of the period. It boasts a memorial plaque 'Lord Byron English poet wrote ... Canto III of *Childe Harold's Pilgrimage*'. The Byron party seem to have been under the impression that John Milton once stayed there. He didn't, for the simple reason that the villa was not built in his lifetime.

In early June, Clare Clairmont discovered that she was pregnant, but waited a while before breaking the news to Byron. His response was: 'Is the brat mine?' In the meantime, he continued to have sex with her, and used her to copy out Canto the Third of *Childe Harold's Pilgrimage* (which he had finished by 27 June) for despatch to his publisher in London.

Mary Godwin also copied verses – a job she enjoyed, since she, too, evidently felt an attraction for Byron (though not always for his behaviour) and was impressed by his staggering 'intellectual energy': but gossip among the English tourists at Sécheron claimed that she did the other thing as well!

When Byron later made an announcement to Clare Clairmont and Percy Shelley that his relationship with her was over, he specifically asked that Mary should *not* be present to hear the news. This confused but did not surprise her, for Byron had made it abundantly clear, since their meeting on 27 May, that he preferred to have conversations about important matters with men rather than women. As Mary was to recall, in October 1822:

> I do not think that any person's voice has the same power of awakening melancholy in me as [Byron's] – I have been accustomed when hearing it to listen and to speak little – another voice, not mine, ever replied ... Since incapacity and timidity always prevented my mingling in the nightly conversations of Diodati – they were as it were entirely tête-a-tête between my Shelley and [Byron] ...

Polidori's journal also makes it clear that Byron preferred to dine and talk with Shelley alone – 'Dined with S ... ', 'Then to see Shelley ... ', 'Thence to Shelley ... ', 'To Shelley in boat ... ', and so on – and that the ladies were expected to amuse themselves with less grown-up pursuits.

Being excluded from these intimate *têtes-a-têtes* was a new disturbing experience for Mary Godwin. From her earliest conversations with Percy Shelley in June 1814 – in front of the tomb of her mother Mary Wollstonecraft in St Pancras cemetery – she had come to expect her

The Villa Diodati overlooking Lake Geneva, built in the early eighteenth century and rented by Lord Byron in June 1816.

relationship with him to be a communion of equals, a meeting of like-minded individuals who had freely chosen to live together outside the conventions of society. She was the daughter of Shelley's two favourite political philosophers – 'a child of love and light' he called her – and the most impressive scholar of any woman he had ever encountered.

On the sound Godwinian principle that 'to read one book without others beside you to which you may refer is mere child's work', they read and talked and studied languages together; they ate vegetarian food and travelled everywhere together (except when Shelley was on the run from debt-collectors or visiting lawyers, or hiding from bailiffs); they discussed 'the cardinal article of his faith, that if men were but taught to treat their fellows with love, charity and equal rights, this earth would realize Paradise'; and they both did without sugar, which they reckoned was politically incorrect because it was produced by slaves on West Indian plantations.

In her *Journal* for October 1822, Mary wrote that Percy brought out the best in her: 'I thought how superiorly gifted I had been in being united to one to whom I could unveil myself, and who could understand me'. He was the *only* person who could achieve this: she tended to feel much less 'natural' with his friends, and sometimes felt upset when he discussed their intimate affairs with them. In other words, her life had become sharply focused on his. So when she found herself excluded from the 'nightly conversations of Diodati', it must have come as a shock. It told her a lot about Lord Byron, and maybe a little about Percy Shelley as well.

he earliest published account of the circumstances in which *Frankenstein* was written, comes from Percy Shelley's preface to the first (anonymous) edition of the novel, dated September 1817. This was presented 'as if' by Mary, but was in actual fact subtly diminishing of her efforts (in comparison with those of her two better-known friends):

> … this story was begun in the majestic region where the scene is principally laid, and in society which cannot cease to be regretted. I passed the summer of 1816 in the environs of Geneva. The season was cold and rainy, and in the evenings we crowded around a blazing wood fire, and occasionally amused ourselves with some German stories of ghosts, which happened to fall into our hands. These tales excited in us a playful desire of imitation. Two other friends (a tale from the pen of one of whom would be far more acceptable to the public than any thing I can ever hope to produce) and myself agreed to write each a story, founded on some supernatural occurrence. The weather, however, suddenly became serene; and my two friends left me on a journey

among the Alps, and lost, in the magnificent scenes which they present, all memory of their ghostly visions. The following tale is the only one which has been completed.

But a fuller and better-known account comes from Mary Shelley's introduction to the 1831 popular edition – written fourteen years after Shelley's, and fifteen years after the events it purported to describe:

But it proved a wet, ungenial summer, and incessant rain often confined us for days to the house. Some volumes of ghost stories translated from the German into French, fell into our hands. There was the History of the Inconstant Lover, who, when he thought to clasp the bride to whom he had pledged his vows, found himself in the arms of the pale ghost of her whom he had deserted. There was the tale of the sinful founder of his race whose miserable doom it was to bestow the kiss of death on all the younger sons of his fated house, just when they reached the age of promise ... I have not seen these stories since then; but their incidents are as fresh in my mind as if I had read them yesterday.

'We will each write a ghost story', said Lord Byron; and his proposition was acceded to. There were four of us. The noble author began a tale, a fragment of which he printed at the end of his poem of Mazeppa. Shelley, more apt to embody ideas and sentiments in the radiance of brilliant imagery, and in the music of the most melodious verse that adorns our language, than to invent the machinery of a story, commenced one founded on the experiences of his early life. Poor Polidori had some terrible idea about a skull-headed lady, who was so punished for peeping through a keyhole – what to see I forget – something very shocking and wrong of course ... The illustrious poets also, annoyed by the platitude of prose, speedily relinquished their uncongenial task.

I busied myself to think of a story – a story to rival those which had excited me to this task. One which would speak to the mysterious fears of our nature, and awaken thrilling horror – one to make the reader dread to look round, to curdle the blood, and quicken the beatings of the heart. If I did not accomplish these things, my ghost story would be unworthy of its name. I thought and pondered – vainly. I felt that blank incapacity of invention which is the greatest misery of authorship, when dull Nothing replies to our anxious invocations. Have you thought of a story? I was asked each morning, and each morning I was forced to reply with a mortifying negative ...

Many and long were the conversations between Lord Byron and Shelley, to which I was a devout but nearly silent listener. During one of these, various philosophical doctrines were discussed, and among others the nature of the principle of life, and whether there was any probability of its ever

Chapter 7th

21 45

It was on a dreary night of November
that I beheld ~~the form on whic~~ my man compleated, ~~and~~
with an anxiety that almost amount
ed to agony, I collected ~~y~~ instruments of life
around me ~~and endeavour~~ that night to infuse a
spark of being into the lifeless thing
that lay at my feet. It was already
one in the morning, the rain pattered
dismally against the window panes, &
my candle was nearly burnt out, when
by the glimmer of the half extinguish
ed light I saw the dull yellow eye of
the creature open — It breathed hard,
and a convulsive motion agitated
its limbs.

~~But how~~ How can I describe my
emotion at this catastrophe, or how deli
neate the wretch whom with such
infinite pains and care I had endeavoured
to form. His limbs were in proportion
and I had selected his features & as
beautiful
~~handsome~~ ~~Handsome~~ — *beautiful* Handsome; Great God! His
yellow ~~skin~~ skin scarcely covered the work of
muscles and arteries beneath; his hair
of a lustrous black, &
was flowing and his teeth of a pearly white
ness but these ~~were~~ luxuriances only ~~formed~~
formed a more horrid contrast with
his watry eyes that seemed almost of
the same colour as the dun white
sockets in which they were set,

𝕿he manuscript draft of Frankenstein, *in Mary Godwin's handwriting, shows the*
opening words of the 'creation' scene originally to have been 'It was on a dreary night
of November that I beheld my man completed …'

being discovered and communicated. They talked of the experiments of Dr Darwin (I speak not of what the Doctor really did, or said that he did, but, as more to my purpose, of what was then spoken of as having been done by him), who preserved a piece of vermicelli in a glass case, till by some extraordinary means it began to move with voluntary motion. Not thus, after all, would life be given. Perhaps a corpse would be reanimated; galvanism had given token of such things: perhaps the component parts of a creature might be manufactured, brought together, and endued with vital warmth. Night waned upon this talk, and even the witching hour had gone by, before we retired to rest. When I placed my head on my pillow, I did not sleep … On the morrow I announced that I had thought of a story. I began that day with the words, It was on a dreary night of November, making only a transcript of the grim terrors of my waking dream.

At first I thought of but a few pages – of a short tale; but Shelley urged me to develop the idea at greater length. I certainly did not owe the suggestion of one incident, nor scarcely of one train of feeling, to my husband, and yet but for his incitement, it would never have taken the form in which it was presented to the world. From this declaration I must except the preface. As far as I recollect, it was entirely written by him.

And now, once again, I bid my hideous progeny go forth and prosper …

The dramatic events had all started with a two-volume collection of ghost stories, *Fantasmagoriana ou Recueil d'Histoires d'Apparitions, de Spectres, Revenans, etc.*, translated into French from the original German by Jean Baptiste Benoit Eyriès. A copy of the book was found in Geneva, and Lord Byron read it aloud while they sat around the ornate fireplace, and – taking his cue from the second story in the collection – suggested in a playful spirit that they should each have a go at writing a tale of terror: 'Everyone is to relate a story of ghosts, or something of a similar nature', said a character in the story *Les Portraits de Famille*, 'it is agreed amongst us that no one shall search for any explanation, even though it bears the stamp of truth, as explanations would take away all pleasure from ghost stories'.

If we compare Polidori's *Journal* written at the time, with Mary Shelley's version, there are significant variations in their accounts of what happened next. Mary's is a much better read. It successfully promotes the book it is prefacing and contains a thrilling cliff-hanger ('Have you thought of a story?'), but the events it describes probably did not happen like that at all.

'There was', she says, 'the *History of the Inconstant Lover* … [and] the tale of the sinful founder of his race' – these were, in fact, called *La Morte fiancée* and

Les Portraits de famille, and Mary's summaries of them are not strictly accurate; it is interesting, though, that she remembered them as stories about a) a man who is pursued by the ghost of his deserted wife and b) a family whose 'younger sons' are doomed to die, because she was troubled by the fate of Harriet Shelley – Percy's deserted wife – who was to drown herself in the Serpentine later that same year; and, as we shall see, she had personal experience of what it was like to lose her baby. Evidently, these distressing incidents which were 'as fresh in my mind as if I had read them yesterday' had chimed with her own deepest concerns, and subsequently became confused in her mind with the stories.

'There were four of us' – in fact there were *five* people present: as usual in her reminiscences, Mary omits Clare Clairmont.

'Poor Polidori had some terrible idea about a skull-headed lady … ' In fact, the doctor told the story which was to become his *Ernestus Berchtold* (1819) about the love-affair between a Swiss patriot and a lady who turns out to be his sister and which, in the published version, he referred to as 'the one I began at Cologny, when *Frankenstein* was planned'. Maybe this was thought by participants to be too near the knuckle, given the (perhaps) malicious rumours circulating in England at the time about Byron's incestuous relationship with his half-sister. The story Mary refers to, about a lady who peeps through the keyhole and sees something she shouldn't, was probably told by Clare. It is, sad to relate, the sort of story she might have told.

'The illustrious poets … speedily relinquished their uncongenial task' – in fact, Lord Byron and Percy Shelley took a lot longer to become bored with the game than she suggests. Mary also implies that they disliked the prospect of sitting indoors and chatting (when they could be out in the boat exploring Rousseau territory): in Canto the Third (98) of *Childe Harold* though (which was completed about ten days after the ghost-story session), Byron felt that 'confinement' might stimulate them all to 'find room/And food for meditation, nor pass by/Much, that may give us pause, if pondered fittingly'. According to Moore's *Letters and Journals*, Byron said to Mary about the ghost-story session: 'you and I will publish ours together'.

Mary's account of what happened next – 'Many and long were the conversations between Lord Byron and Shelley, to which I was a devout but nearly silent listener' – may not be strictly accurate: the conversation in question was almost certainly between *Polidori* and Shelley.

The *atmosphere* that Mary creates around the family ghost-story game also seems to have been far less genial and playful than she recalls. Polidori was at his most pretentious. Clare had just announced that she was pregnant. Mary was uneasy about the amount of time Clare was spending with Percy. Byron, feeling competitive and sensitive to the slightest criticism, was making his views about intellectual women more and more apparent. Percy was feeling highly strung. On the night of 18 June, all these factors turned the ghostly talk into a bizarre encounter group: the 'tempestuous loveliness of terror' was getting seriously out of hand. Polidori noted:

> June 18 … Shelley and party here … Began my ghost-story after tea. Twelve o'clock, really began to talk ghostly. L.B. repeated some verses of Coleridge's Christabel, of the witch's breast; when silence ensued, and Shelley, suddenly shrieking and putting his hands to his head, ran out of the room with a candle. Threw water in his face, and after gave him ether. He was looking at Mrs S, and suddenly thought of a woman he had heard of who had eyes instead of nipples, which, taking hold of his mind, horrified him. – He married; and, a friend of his liking his wife, he tried all he could do to induce her to love him in turn. He is surrounded by friends who feed upon him, and draw upon him as their banker. Once, having hired a house, a man wanted to make him pay more, and came trying to bully him, and at last challenged him. Shelley refused, and was knocked down; cooly said that would not gain him his object, and was knocked down again …

The lines from Coleridge's *Christabel* that had pushed Shelley over the edge and sent him shrieking from the room were these:

> Then drawing in her breath, aloud,
> Like one that shuddered, she unbound
> The cincture from beneath her breast:
> Her silken robe and inner vest
> Dropped to her feet, and full in view,
> Behold! her bosom and half her side,
> Hideous, deformed, and pale of hue -
> A sight to dream of, not to tell!
> And she is to sleep by Christabel!

This horrifying image, confused with a fantasy that was already on his mind, was the one that Shelley projected on to 'Mrs S'.

Mary had informed him, the previous year, that Coleridge's concept of the 'hideous, deformed' bosom had originally been more specific: 'two eyes in her bosom'. The image had evidently stuck, as well it might. And so he put his hands to his head, thinking perhaps that he had gone mad, shrieked, and rushed out of the room. The image of Mary as a harpy – 'hideous, deformed and pale of hue' – was too much for him. What *she* thought of the attribution, neither Polidori nor Mary recorded. And why Shelley should suddenly have imagined her as 'a sight to dream of, not to tell' remains a mystery.

And all *this* happened on the very evening which Mary blandly referred to as the one when 'Shelley … commenced [a story] founded on the experiences of his early life'.

Throughout the short-story evenings, Polidori also seems to have been kept busy dispensing ether or laudanum to Shelley (for his nervous headaches and hyperactivity) and Black Drop – a popular compound, which contained opium – to Byron. These were not thought to be *stimulants*; there was enough stimulation going on already – they were tranquillizers.

n the introduction to her book, Mary Godwin externalizes these extraordinary tensions and turns them into the stage-effects of a Gothick melodrama: rain and thunder and lightning, witching hours and stories to 'curdle the blood and quicken the beatings of the heart', the kiss of death and the skull-headed lady.

Just before describing the events of June 1816, she confesses in the same essay that she feels much more at home with 'airy flights of my imagination' than with attempts to describe everyday life and people – 'Life appeared to me too common-place an affair as regarded myself': instead of turning lived experience into prose, she preferred, she says, 'the formation of castles in the air – the indulging in waking dreams … My dreams were at once more fantastic and agreeable … '

And this may provide a clue as to the *real* reason why she re-wrote the story of the ghost-story session. She had to contend with notions of feminine literary decorum – readers of the popular edition of *Frankenstein* would have been *truly* shocked if she had been more than 'a devout but nearly silent listener' in such august male company. It would not have been seemly to delve into, and write about, *their* deepest fantasies. The trappings of the Gothick – where sexuality became a matter of drawbridges and moats and castles – were just about okay, but lived

he radical poet Percy Bysshe Shelley, who was separated from his wife and living in Geneva with Mary Godwin in the summer of 1816.

experience was not. She also lacked confidence where writing was concerned, and may even have agreed with Shelley that a tale from the pen of Lord Byron 'would be far more acceptable to the public than anything I can ever hope to produce' – even though, as her introduction implies, it might have been better if she had said so herself, rather than publicly admitting it in a 'preface … entirely written by him'.

So perhaps the key phrase is 'Life appeared to me too common-place an affair as regarded myself'. It was obviously *not* commonplace where Byron and Shelley were concerned. But she couldn't possibly write about that. It was not at all 'commonplace' where she was concerned either, but, for all sorts of personal and social reasons, that's the way it appeared to *her*.

None of this explains why she wrote Clare Clairmont and John Polidori out of the ghost-story sessions: apart from adding 'my readers have nothing to do with these associations'. It may be that she saw herself as one of the keepers of the flame of Shelley's and Byron's posthumous reputations. But another important reason why she re-wrote the events – as well as the purpose of introducing the cheap edition of *Frankenstein* and the obvious one of marketing her work to a new generation of readers at a time when she had to rely on her earnings as an author – was that she needed publicly to establish the motherhood of her own 'progeny'.

The first edition had been anonymous. Percy Shelley had, in fact, helped her with the writing style (and made it more rhetorical – for better or worse), acted as her copy-editor and corrected most of the proofs. Some readers of the first edition, however, thought that *Frankenstein* was *by* Percy Shelley. It certainly attracted more public attention, and was better received, than anything he had written up until then. So, quite rightly, she felt that she had to state loud and clear that she was in fact the mother.

She makes it clear that the pressure on her, in that august company, was intense. Shelley and Byron were being competitive. Byron had offered to share a publication – a fantastic offer, for an apprentice writer. 'As the daughter of two persons of distinguished literary celebrity' – Mary Wollstonecraft and William Godwin – Mary Wollstonecraft Godwin was *expected* by all who knew her to be a writer of significance. This, however, did not come easily: 'In [my early writings – and she *was* only eighteen] I was a close imitator – rather doing as others had done than putting down the suggestions of my own mind'. To increase the pressure, 'my husband … was from the first, very anxious that I should prove myself worthy of my parentage, and enrol myself on the page of fame'.

Lord Byron would not have had much time for her as a writer even if she *was* able to prove herself worthy of her parentage: where he was concerned, she was better occupied in copying out the manuscript of *Childe Harold*. Shelley was highly supportive, but his kind of Promethean genius tended to unsettle her: her views on over-reachers who aimed to steal the fires from heaven without taking responsibility for the consequences were made abundantly clear in the character, and fate, of Victor Frankenstein. Or maybe, when Shelley supported her, he was just being nice. He was 'always most earnest and energetic in his exhortations that I should cultivate any talent I possessed, to the utmost', but maybe his encouragement – she thought – was 'not so much with the idea that I could produce anything worthy of notice, but that he might himself judge how far I possessed the promise of better things hereafter'. And the pressure of that 'promise' made her frightened of failure, and frightened of not living up to his high expectations of her.

In this atmosphere, Mary busied herself, according to her account of the events of mid-June 1816, to find her own voice – crucially, to think of 'a story to rival those who had excited me to this task'. But it just wouldn't come. Only 'that blank incapacity of invention which is the greatest misery of authorship'. *Have you thought of a story?*, she was asked each morning. And each morning the answer was 'a mortifying negative'.

Eventually, following a late-night discussion with Byron and Shelley – and it was important for what she was trying to say that it *had to be* with Byron and Shelley, the illustrious poets who had excluded her from their *têtes-à-têtes* about 'the nature of the principle of life', the experiments of the poet-scientist Dr Erasmus Darwin and of Luigi Galvani – she had her waking nightmare. And, much to everyone's surprise, came up with the creation sequence of *Frankenstein* in short-story form.

Again, it didn't happen like that, but – where the motherhood of the text is concerned – that may not be the point. Polidori's *Journal* reveals that Mary was almost certainly the *first*, not the last, to tell her story. She had evidently been mulling it over in her mind for some time. But it *was* triggered by that principle-of-life chat at 'the witching hour' – the chat which finally released her writer's block. As Polidori wrote:

> June 15 – … Shelley etc. came in the evening; talked of my play etc., which was worth nothing [Polidori had written a drama called *Cajetan,* which had already caused much hilarity]. Afterwards Shelley and I had a conversation about principles – whether man was to be thought merely an instrument.
>
> June 16 – Laid up. Shelley came, and dined and slept here, with Mrs. S and Miss Clare Clairmont. Wrote another letter.
>
> June 17 – … Dined with Shelley etc. here … The ghost-stories are begun by all but me.
>
> June 18 – … Shelley and party here …

So the conversation about 'the nature of the principle of life' (or, in Polidori's version, about 'principles – whether man was to be thought merely an instrument') took place on the evening of 15 June. Two days later 'the ghost stories are begun by all but me'. If the conversation was the immediate stimulus to Mary's waking nightmare, the dream must have happened either on the night of the 15th or 16th – most probably the 16th when the Shelleys slept at the Villa Diodati. In this case the ghost-story session happened on 17 and 18 June (when Polidori told *his* story, and Shelley lost control of himself).

Byron's uncompleted story – later published with his *Mazeppa* (1819) – was indeed dated 17 June 1816. And, when Mary described the physical surroundings of her nightmare – 'the dark *parquet*, the closed shutters … the glassy lake and white high Alps' – she was describing her room in the *Villa Diodati*, rather than in the Maison Chappuis. The description still fits.

From the point of view of the history of literature, it is unfortunate that Mary Godwin surrounded the events of 17 and 18 June 1816 with Gothick stage-effects and tacky stories about skull-headed ladies, because thereafter this tended to associate Frankenstein with the bandits and necromancers who had been fashionable since the late eighteenth century, and which Jane Austen was about to satirise in *Northanger Abbey* (published just three months before *Frankenstein*).

In collections of 'Gothic novels', *Frankenstein* is still referred to as an example of 'female Gothic', and Mary Shelley's approach is still described as something called 'the Gothic imagination'. This, despite the fact that Percy Shelley wrote that his wife's novel was far more than 'a mere tale of spectres and enchantment'. It raised much more interesting issues, and was based on Mary's lived experience. For, whatever she subsequently wrote Mary's nightmare, her 'hideous progeny', was both personal to her and based on many years' gestation. Her *Introduction*, though, makes *Frankenstein* sound like just another horror story, born in a thunderstorm. It was, and is, much more than that. And when she began that morning (17 June), reading aloud the words *It was on a dreary night of November* – 'making only a transcript of the grim terrors of my waking dreams' – she was going well beyond the bounds of female literary decorum. These words were to become the opening of Chapter IV of the 1818 edition, and of Chapter V of the 1831 edition.

In the longest surviving manuscript of *Frankenstein* (part of the Abinger Shelley Collection at the Bodleian Library Oxford) – perhaps a draft, since it has additions and corrections by Percy Shelley, perhaps a fair copy – the words appear, in a slightly different form, as the opening of 'Chapter 7th'. The manuscript of the original short-story version has disappeared. Dr Polidori seems to have made his own 'outline' of it – together with Lord Byron's and his own – and turned himself into something of a social celebrity at Genevan dinner parties by re-telling the stories for the rest of that summer.

The 'outline' of the story told by 'Miss M.W. Godwin' found its way to the editor of the *New Monthly Magazine* (together with *The Vampyre*), having been sent on some time later by one of Polidori's hosts. But this, too, has since disappeared. So the Abinger manuscript is the earliest version we have, and there is no way of checking whether the words 'It was on a dreary night of

November … ' really *were* the exact opening words of Mary Godwin's short story, as she was to recall in 1831.

The passage she started reading aloud on 17 or 18 June could not have been identical with the printed version (which went through at least one draft stage, before finalisation), but it was near enough. They have since become the most famous 'moment' in the whole of *Frankenstein*. The draft version goes like this:

> It was on a dreary night of November, that I beheld my man completed and with an anxiety that almost amounted to agony, I collected instruments of life around me, and endeavoured to infuse a spark of being into the lifeless thing that lay at my feet. It was about one in the morning; the rain pattered dismally against the window panes and my candle was nearly burnt out, when by the glimmer of the half extinguished light I saw the dull yellow eye of the Creature open – it breathed hard, and a convulsive motion agitated its limbs.

It is likely that Mary Godwin's nightmare would have been visualised in similar ways to Fuseli's painting *The Nightmare*. She had met Fuseli, knew something of his background, and would certainly have been familiar with the picture. In *Frankenstein* (volume 3, chapter VI of the 1818 edition) she based the chilling scene of the creature fulfilling his prophecy 'I shall be with you on your wedding-night' directly on the design of the painting:

> Great God! [says Victor Frankenstein when he discovers what has happened to his new wife Elizabeth,] why did I not then expire! She was there, lifeless and inanimate, thrown across the bed, her head hanging down, and her pale and distorted features half covered by her hair. Every where I turn I see the same figure – her bloodless arms and relaxed form flung by the murderer on its bridal bier. Could I behold this, and live? Alas! Life is obstinate, and clings closest where it is most hated.

This scene, which a recent scholar has described as 'straight out of Fuseli's *Nightmare*', harks back to the strange and revealing dream which Frankenstein experiences immediately after seeing the consequences of his creation. It involves another nocturnal visit – again linked to the death of the female, and to erotic desire:

> I thought I saw Elizabeth, in the bloom of health, walking in the streets of Ingolstadt. Delighted and surprised, I embraced her; but as I imprinted the first kiss on her lips, they became livid with the hue of death; her features appeared to change; and I thought that I held the corpse of my dead mother in my arms; a shroud enveloped her form, and I saw the grave-worms crawling on the folds of the flannel. I started from my sleep with horror; a cold dew covered my forehead, my teeth chattered, and every limb became convulsed; when, by the dim and yellow light of the moon, as it forced its way

through the window-shutters, I beheld the wretch – the miserable monster whom I had created. He held up the curtain of the bed; and his eyes, if eyes they may be called, were fixed on me. His jaws opened …

So in the novel – as in life – the creation scene is linked to a nightmare. Mary was to recollect it as a half-waking half-sleeping nightmare of a 'vividness far beyond the usual bounds of reverie'. A nightmare which *included* Frankenstein's dream, as a dream-within-a-dream (see page 14).

When *she* awoke, Mary tried to blot out this terrifying succession of images by concentrating hard on the physical realities of her bedroom at the Villa Diodati: the *parquet* floor, the wooden shutters, perhaps the stone urn-shaped washbasin in the corner (which is still there), the reassuring sense that the lake and white high Alps were outside in the rain. But she could not get the nightmare out of her mind. It was only at *this* stage, according to her recollection, that she thought of the competition with the illustrious poets and of 'my tiresome, unlucky ghost story'. Maybe she could turn the terrors of the night *into prose*. Maybe *this* would give her the confidence to write. And it was this thought – 'swift as light and as cheering' – which finally exorcised the demon, which turned it from nightmare into *material*.

There had been five main components to the nightmare: 'the pale student of unhallowed arts kneeling beside the thing he had put together'; the creation itself, on the 'working of some powerful engine' (another sexual reference?); the artist-scientist 'rushing away' when he sees what he has done (in the hope that it will just *fade*); the sleep of the creator and fantasy about 'the silence of the grave'; and the 'horrid thing opening his curtains', waking him up and staring at him.

But at the heart of the nightmare, in Mary's account, was the moment of rejection – simultaneously an artist-scientist not taking responsibility for his actions *and* a father looking at his new-born baby, horror-stricken, then rushing out of the room to a troubled post-partum sleep: the modern Prometheus confronted by the full implications of stealing the fire from the gods *and* at the same time, as a critic has suggested 'all the dread, fear, guilt, depression and excitement of birthing'.

Both were subjects about which Mary Godwin knew a great deal, despite her relative youth. She had read a copy of 'Ovid's *Metamorphosis* in Latin' (book 1) the previous autumn which contained a classic account of the Prometheus myth. In 1816, she supplemented this with 'Prometheus of Eschylus-Greek'. She had no doubt heard the poets talking about the myth's romantic attractions, as they together contemplated *Prometheus Unbound* and *Prometheus* respectively. The Prometheus myth took two main forms: the

Greek version, which has the young Titan stealing fire from the gods and being punished for it; and the Latin version, which has him 'metamorphosing' earth into man. Mary was equally fascinated by both of them.

And she certainly knew about the traumas of birthing. Her own mother Mary Wollstonecraft had died just twelve days after giving birth to her.

More recently, on 22 February 1815, Mary Godwin herself had given birth to an illegitimate and premature baby girl – a traumatic event (for all parties) which was recorded by both Percy and herself in her private *Journal*:

> [Shelley]: Maie is in labour, and after very few additional pains she is delivered of a female child – 5 minutes afterwards Dr Clarke [brother of the physician who had attended Mary's mother at her birth] comes. All is well. Maie perfectly well and at ease. The child is not quite 7 months. The child not expected to live. S. sits up with maie. much agitated and exhausted …
>
> Monday 6th March
>
> [Mary] find my baby dead … Send for Hogg [Shelley's close friend, to whom Mary wrote on the same day] "… It was perfectly well when I went to bed – I awoke in the night to give it suck it appeared to be sleeping so quietly that I would not awake it – it was dead then but we did not find that out till morning – from its appearance it evidently died of convulsions" … I am no longer a mother now – talk – a miserable day …
>
> Monday 13th
>
> … stay at home and think of my little dead baby – this is foolish I suppose yet whenever I am left alone to my own thoughts and do not read to divert them they always come back to the same point – that I was a mother and am so no longer …

And on Sunday 19 March Mary added a postscript:

> Dream that my little baby came to life again – that it had only been cold and that we rubbed it by the fire and it lived – I awake and find no baby – I think about the little thing all day – not in good spirits – Shelley is very unwell.
>
> Monday 20th
>
> Dream again about my baby ——

In future, Percy Shelley would experience lung and chest pains, or spasms in his side, whenever Mary had a baby. On this occasion, however, he consulted a Dr Pemberton who diagnosed that 'he was dying rapidly of consumption'. Pemberton then introduced his patient to Dr William Lawrence, who could discover none of the usual symptoms of the disease and eventually made Shelley feel 'much improved', which was either a miracle or evidence of a false alarm. Mary never quite believed the consumption theory.

Mary had become pregnant round about the time she eloped with Percy in summer 1814. The birth, traumatic enough in itself, was firmly associated in her mind with Shelley's illness and Clare's silliness — both of which were to recur, with a vengeance, in June 1816. Her dream about re-animating the child's corpse in front of the fire is a dream which strongly resembles her *Frankenstein* nightmare.

She was pregnant again two months later and, on 24 January 1816, her son William was successfully born: illegitimate, of course, but this time after the full term of nine months.

The next volume of her *Journal* (21 July 1816 onwards) contains some references to her anxieties about William's health. And, perhaps to get these anxieties out of her system, when she came to expand her short story into the full-length *Frankenstein*, she made Victor's beautiful little brother William the first of the creature's victims — strangled in a field on the outskirts of Geneva. It has to be remembered, however, that William was not only the name of Mary's baby son — it was also the name of her father. And it may be that her nightmare of birthing and rejection was in part, as another critic has put it, about 'Mary Godwin's sense of guilt for having caused her mother's death and her rage at her father's remarriage [to Mary Jane Clairmont, in December 1801]'.

Certainly, her ambivalent feelings about her father William Godwin were to be strongly expressed in her *Journal* later that summer. She had hoped that William's birth would lead to a reconciliation: that, as Shelley wrote to Godwin on 6 March 1816 the couple would no longer be 'confounded with prostitutes and seducers' in his eyes. But he stubbornly refused.

Many critics these days see *Frankenstein* as Mary Godwin expressing her nausea at the very *idea* of childbirth. More likely, the book expressed her views about rejection and responsibility and her *anxieties* about childbirth.

The nightmare was about a motherless child, and the father's rejection of it: not because the baby was misshapen, or wrinkled, or disappointing-looking (the usual reasons), but because the father realises that his 'odious handiwork' — the result of about nine months of candle-lit labour in 'my workshop of filthy creations' — has been *against nature*. Nature is active, alive: he has treated it as inert and dead, something to breathe life into. He realises, at last, where his Promethean longings have taken him. And, in describing the father, Mary Godwin resorts to Gothick-medieval language: he was a 'pale student of unhallowed arts', a latter-day occultist. One reviewer, in fact, was to express surprise that the book was not *set* in the Middle Ages.

Mary certainly knew about Dr Faust, and his pact with Lucifer (knowledge in exchange for a soul) in late medieval Nuremberg: in autumn 1815, she had read '*De l'Alemagne* by Madame de Stael', which contained a section on the Faust legend (1808). From de Stael she would also have learned about some current German researches into 'the principle of life'.

y the beginning of July 1816, it appears that she had settled on the name 'Frankenstein' for her over-reacher: the trigger for this choice probably being Percy Shelley's observation that some of the ruined chateaux he had seen during his promenade sur le lac with Lord Byron reminded him of the castles he had seen with Mary, on the Rhine, two years before (in late August and September 1814). At that time, he and Mary had made their way home from a madcap overseas jaunt by the cheapest possible form of transport, a slow-moving public boat on the Rhine. Most self-respecting British tourists observed the romantic excitements of the river from the relative comfort of a private coach: Mary was later to pride herself on the fact that she was:

> ... nearly the first English person, who many years ago made a wild ventur-
> ous voyage, since called hackneyed – when in an open flat-bottomed sort of
> barge we were borne down the rapid stream ... and what uncouth animals
> were with us, forming a fearful contrast between their drunken brutalities
> and the scene of enchantment around.

The latter was an observation she had made at the time, in her *Journal*, too: only in August 1814 she added 'Twere easier for god to make entirely new men than attempt to purify such monsters as these'. The heat, the food, the midges and the behaviour of the 'uncleansable animals' who accompanied them – especially two inebriated students from Strasburgh University – seem seriously to have got on her nerves. Evidently, 'the Rhine experience' was spoiled by *people*.

Percy and Mary described the scenery, though, as if it had come straight out of the paintings of Caspar David Friedrich – all ruined towers, plunging ravines and river sunsets.

As Mary Shelley was to recollect the experience through twilight-tinted spectacles:

> Each tower-crowned hill – each picturesque ruin – each shadowy ravine and
> beetling precipice – was passed and gazed upon with eager curiosity and
> delight. The very names are the titles of volumes of romance; all the spirits
> of Old Germany haunt the place ...

One of these names was Frankenstein. On the leg of their journey which took them from Mannheim to Mainz (September 2-3), they looked in at the town of Gernsheim. And from there – looking east and upwards towards the northern foothills of Magnetberg – they could see the outer tower and bridge tower of Castle Frankenstein. Mary and Percy went for a 'walk for three hours' around the region. They could not possibly have reached the Castle in that time (I've tried it), but they could certainly have gazed from a distance upon its ruined walls and fortifications – constructed in their original form in the 1250s – with their 'usual eager curiosity and delight'.

aspar David Friedrich's quintessentially romantic painting The Wanderer Over the Sea of Clouds *(1818).*

The castle was not a grand medieval construction: it had domesticated turrets, a wood-and-brick structure with half-timbering, and it resembled a fortified manor house rather than a fully-blown Gothick Castle. But it had a terrific name, meaning castle or rock of the Franks, and a legend associated with it – the legend of the alchemist and necromancer Johann Konrad Dippel who was born a refugee in the castle in 1673 (and thus signed himself 'Frankensteiner').

Neither Mary Godwin nor Percy Shelley mentions the castle or its legendary inhabitant. But they could well have seen it, and Mary at least could equally well have recollected the name.

he nightmare of 'the pale student of unhallowed arts' was, however, about the present, not the Middle Ages. The science in *Frankenstein* is – as Mary recalls in her *Introduction* – about debates which were current in 1816. We know that the immediate stimulus to her nightmare was a conversation about 'the nature of the principle of life' or 'principles – whether man was to be thought merely an instrument'. And we know Mary had been reading the latest German researches into the subject. But there was another connection nearer to home.

In the years just before the writing of *Frankenstein* – around 1814-16 – the big scientific debate in London, which had been the subject of several public lectures at the Royal College of Surgeons, was about the origin of the life-principle itself.

On the one hand, the traditional view was that life began, and begins with a vital spark that was 'analogous to electricity', some 'subtle, mobile, invisible substance' – a vital spark which jump-started the soul and which ultimately came from God. Like in Michelangelo's fresco of the creation of Adam: the current which passes through the fingers. On the other hand, the new view – an early version of what was to become the theory of evolution – was that life was 'an assemblage of all the functions of the body', a strictly material thing which had to have a new label to describe it, the word 'biology'. No vital spark, no soul – just parents. And instead of being an inert thing to which God gave life, nature was active, responsive to environment – and (to use the 'buzz' word of the day) 'perfectible'.

The main contributors to this debate were two professors at the Royal College, and one of them – Dr William Lawrence, who proposed the radical argument – was the man whom Mary called 'an eminent physician', the man who was treating Percy Shelley for his supposed consumption.

Lawrence was shortly to be suspended from his Professorship, and to be dismissed from his position at the Bethlehem Hospital in Lambeth. But, in March 1816, he fuelled the debate by giving two public lectures on the subject of 'vitalism' (which were published three months later). It is very likely that *this* was the topic of conversation at the Villa Diodati. A modern Prometheus was stealing the electric current from the gods, for the use of people on earth – and explaining it away in the process.

Mary Godwin had been brought up in a household which enjoyed hearing about – and discussing – the latest technological developments, while despising the institutions which manipulated them. The chemist and natural philosopher Humphry Davy sometimes came to dinner. Mary had been taken by her father to watch the very first successful parachute landing in England when André-Jacques Garnerin jumped off a balloon and reached the ground just behind what is today St Pancras railway station. And the pioneering work of the Garnerin brothers must have stuck in her mind, for over ten years later on 28 December 1814 she noted in her *Journal*:

> ... go to Garnerin's lecture – on Electricity – the gasses – and the Phantasmagoria – when return at half past nine Shelley goes to sleep.
>
> Thursday 29th
>
> ... in the evening S and Clary go to Garnerin's lecture ... S and C return a little before tea – there was no lecture tonight.

Shelley had evidently missed something special: the 'Phantasmagoria' was a mixture of magic lantern slides, optical illusions, and – as a climax – big displays of electric current with spectacular sparks. This would have upset him, because he had been interested in the more spectacular forms of experimental physics and chemistry ever since his schoolboy days at Eton.

But, in her retrospective account of the genesis of *Frankenstein*, Mary included some more specific and sophisticated references – to 'the experiments of Dr Darwin ... who preserved a piece of vermicelli in a glass case', and to 'galvanism' which perhaps could endue a corpse with 'vital warmth'.

We know that Mary was reading the 'Introduction to Davy's *Chemistry*' (probably Humphry Davy's *Elements of Chemical Philosophy*, 1812) when she wrote the chapters on Victor Frankenstein's curriculum at the University of Ingolstadt in October and November 1816. From her other reading, she would have discovered that Ingolstadt (in Upper Bavaria) was a centre of radical Enlightenment thought, and the latest physiological researches.

Victor Frankenstein's education is like the whole history of western science in microcosm: he begins with 'the search of the philosopher's stone and the elixir of life', using medieval masters such as Albertus Magnus and Paracelsus as his magi; then, after he has seen a lightning-bolt strike an old oak tree, he moves on to modern experimental science and the study of nature. His Professor of natural philosophy urges him to be less intellectually ambitious, to study what Victor scornfully comes to call 'realities of little worth' even if they do contain 'sound sense'. But his Professor of Chemistry, M. Waldman, promises not only knowledge but power as well:

> The ancient teachers of this science promised impossibilities and performed nothing. The modern masters promise very little; they know that metals cannot be transmuted, and that the elixir of life is a chimera. But these philosophers, whose hands seem only made to dabble in dirt, and their eyes to pore over the microscope or crucible, have indeed performed miracles. They penetrate into the recesses of nature, and shew how she walks in her hiding places.

Victor is thrilled by this lecture, because, although he has gone through a succession of 'scientific revolutions' in his own quest for knowledge, he is still asking the same old questions and still wants power and glory.

O̶ne of the restored towers of Castle Frankenstein, originally built in the 1250s in the foothills of Magnetberg: Percy Shelley and Mary Godwin visited the region in summer 1814, and may well have seen the castle from a distance.

The charismatic Professor Waldman's lectures seem, at some level, to be a parody of Professor Davy's famous subscription lectures at the Royal Institution (which started in 1801 with 'The New Branch of Philosophy, Galvanism' and climaxed with the publication of his wide-ranging survey and history of the discipline of chemistry, the *Elements* of 1812). Davy was undoubtedly a brilliant lecturer. His annual series were said to have given 'fashion to science' (among his privileged fee-paying audiences) and to have put the Royal Institution, founded in 1799, on the social and financial map.

In his youth, Humphry Davy had written a hymn of praise to the modern chemist – in verse – which he had published in the poet Robert Southey's *Annual Anthology* (1799-1800). It was called *Sons of Genius*:

> To scan the laws of Nature, to explore
> The tranquil reign of mild Philosophy;
> Or on Newtonian wings sublime to soar
> Through the bright regions of the starry sky ...
>
> Like you proud rocks amidst the sea of time,
> Superior, scorning all the billows' rage,
> The living Sons of Genius stand sublime,
> Th'immortal children of another age.

Mary Godwin, then, may have had Davy in mind, as she dreamed of her scientist-hero. If so, the comparison was less than just. For Humphry Davy usually prefaced his remarks by saying that 'the first step towards the attainment of real discovery was the humiliating confession of ignorance'. He had a healthy cynicism about system-builders of all denominations.

Maybe Mary was concerned that the 'living Sons of Genius' would, in all their excitement about 'the bright regions of the starry sky', forget their humility and their sense of responsibility.

As the character of Victor Frankenstein developed, he came to embody the central ambiguity of Percy Shelley's poetic quest – an ambiguity he himself likened to Ariel and Caliban in *The Tempest*: Ariel, the aspiration, the flights of fancy, the intellectual experimentation, the other-worldly, the voyage towards the infinite, the belief in new knowledge; Caliban, the darker side, the rough clay of the creature, the delving into the occult, the rude awakening after the euphoria of preparation, the fearful result of mocking – heedlessly – 'the stupendous mechanism of the Creator of the World'.

In the 1818 edition of *Frankenstein*, the Faustian theme – which today we would call 'the social responsibility of the scientist or artist' – is not particularly emphasised. There are no devils, and, as one critic has put it the story is, surprisingly, 'acted out in the absence of God'. The story is more about *personal* responsibility and matters arising.

But, as *Frankenstein* entered the bloodstream of popular culture – through language and through plays – godlessness was to become its central theme. People began to refer to 'the Frankenstein monster', transferring the name from creator to creature: and, of course, the nameless creature *is* in a sense the son of Frankenstein, and he *does* turn into a monster after everyone has rejected him. But he was in no sense a 'monster' when he was born. He evolved into one.

In the work of the poet-botanist-physician Erasmus Darwin – sometimes in verse, sometimes in prose – Mary Godwin would have discovered an early theory of (almost) evolution 'from microscopic specks in primeval seas to its present culmination in man', a theory which would be developed some sixty years later by his grandson Charles. Whether or not Darwin kept alive a piece of vermicelli in a glass case (Mary herself doubted it), he had a lot to say in his *Zoonomia* (1794 edition) on the subject of 'creation' and 'generation'.

The female's role in the reproductive process was apparently to provide 'nutrient and oxygenation' to the embryo; the embryo's *characteristics* came from the male. What was more, Darwin had added, these characteristics depended on *what was going on in the male's mind* during 'the act of generation'.

If, as in the case of Victor in *Frankenstein*, the man was thinking monstrous thoughts, the resulting offspring would be monstrous: and, whatever the man was thinking about, it was not a good or efficient idea, from the point of view of the generation of the species, to have motherless children.

To illustrate these and other proto-evolutionary concepts, Darwin invented what he called a 'factitious spider' which walked around on a metal salver by means of rotating magnets hidden underneath, and an artificial bird with flapping wings propelled by a bottle of compressed air.

Mary had read most of Erasmus Darwin's poetical works, so it is likely that her modern Prometheus, who dared to challenge thousands of years of evolution by creating 'a new species' all by himself, owed something to him.

Erasmus Darwin's 'factitious' creatures may also have chimed with Mary Godwin's thinking in summer 1816 because one of the books she read and enjoyed, as she prepared *Frankenstein,* was Madame de Genlis's *Nouveaux contes moraux et nouvelles historiques* (1802), which contained a dramatic interlude about Pygmalion and Galatea. In this interlude, a beautiful sculpture is animated into life – and, pure and untainted as she is, discovers what a nasty place the world can be.

Some of the more extreme thinkers of the French Enlightenment had written of human beings as merely soft machines – in works such as La Mettrie's *L'Homme machine* (1747) – 'thrown down by chance at a given point on the earth's surface' by God-the-clockmaker. And this had led to explorations of whether the behaviour of living beings could be simulated by artificial means — which, in the mid-eighteenth century, meant mechanical devices. One of the most celebrated of these was Jacques Vaucanson's wooden digesting duck, which caused a sensation at Versailles by waddling across the floor and excreting pieces of biscuit from within its brass digestive system.

But perhaps the most advanced of these automata, were the three that came from the workshop of the Neuchâtel clock-maker, mechanic and theology graduate Pierre Jaquet-Droz, and his son/assistant Henri-Louis.

The Scribe, an automaton constructed in 1769 by Neuchâtel clock-maker Pierre Jaquet-Droz, which still writes various messages with a goose quill pen, including 'I think therefore I am'.

Je pense donc Je suis

The first to be made – called 'The Scribe' (1769) – represented a small child, sitting on a Louis XV style stool: his right hand held a goose quill pen, which he dipped into an ink-well and carefully wrote *Les automates Jaquet Droz à neuchatel* or *Jaquet Droz mon Inventeur* while his glass eyes followed the tracing of each letter. The scribe's *pièce de résistance*, which raised most of the big issues in the 'man as machine' debate, was the phrase *Je pense donc Je suis*.

The second, made in 1774, was 'The Draughtsman', another small child who drew a pencil portrait of Louis XV or a cartoon of a dog called 'Mon Toutou' while holding down the paper with his right hand and blowing away the excess lead power with his breath, powered by bellows in his chest.

The third, which was considerably larger, was 'The Musician' – a teenage girl in a brocade dress who played a selection of Henri-Louis' compositions on a pipe organ in the shape of a wooden harpsichord. Unlike less complex robots, she really *did* touch the keys to produce the notes and, at the end of each piece, gave what seems like a self-satisfied sidelong glance at the audience with her glass eyes.

All three automata – in full working order – are now in the Musée d'Art et d'Histoire de la Ville de Neuchâtel.

The Shelley party may have seen them when they visited 'Neufchatel' on 19-21 August 1814, although if they did they made no mention of the fact in their *Journal*. Or they may have read about these 'mechanical puppets' whose performances were widely reviewed in the press. German Romantic writers such as E.T.A. Hoffman were, in 1815-16, just beginning to exploit the imaginative possibilities of automata – as outward projections of inner states of mind, as obsessions. For example, Hoffman's *The Sandman*, written in 1815 and published a year later, told the story of Dr Coppelius, Professor Spalanzani and the divine Olympia – who 'played the piano with great accomplishment', 'performed a bravura aria in an almost piercingly clear, bell-like voice' and danced like an angel. The hero's fellow students, however, notice something odd about her:

> She might be called beautiful if her eyes were not so completely lifeless, I would even say sightless. She walks with a curiously measured gait; every movement seems as if controlled by clockwork. When she plays and sings it is with the unpleasant soulless regularity of a machine and she dances in the same way … it seems to us that she is only acting like a living creature…

In her nightmare, Mary Godwin's 'hideous phantasm of a man' seems dead behind the eyes as well. It is his eyes which betray him. But he is no automaton, or mechanical doll. He is an organism, pieced together from 'materials' found in graveyards, slaughter-houses and dissecting rooms – a piece of biological rather than mechanical engineering. And, most disturbingly, a creature with the full range of human feelings and emotions. His creator has somehow found a way of preventing his raw materials from decomposing, and has chosen them with great care:

> His limbs were in proportion, and I had selected his features as beautiful. Beautiful! – Great God! His yellow skin scarcely covered the work of muscles and arteries beneath; his hair was of a lustrous black, and flowing; his teeth of a pearly whiteness; but these luxuriances only formed a more horrid contrast with his watery eyes, that seemed almost of the same colour as the dun white sockets in which they were set ...

At this stage, he is still 'the creature': only later will Victor Frankenstein call him Demon, Monster and Fiend. And, apart from those eyes – which have not yet learned to focus, and which resemble the unseeing white orbs of the blind horse peering through the curtain in Fuseli's *Nightmare* – he is physically beautiful: skin taut over muscles and arteries, thick black hair, perfect teeth, like one of Fuseli's neo-classical studies of the male anatomy: larger-than-life, in the way that Greek sculptures are larger than life. The trouble is that as a complete organism, he is considerably less than the sum of his parts: individually, his limbs and features are 'beautiful'; together they do not quite work.

In Hollywood films 'the creature' was to become not a new Adam, but a thing of scars and stitches and skewers – based on an image of the madhouse entitled *The Chinchillas* from Goya's series of prints *Caprichos/Caprices* (1799). His huge dome-like forehead and big feet made him resemble, as did Goya's print, someone with an acromegalic condition and a serious pituitary problem: an image of disability (like most 'monsters' in popular culture) rather than of beauty.

Universal Studio's make-up artists briefly toyed with the idea of making their monster look like a robot, or mechanical man: but, in the end, the only remnant of that design idea was the steel bolt through Karloff's neck, something to plug him into.

Mary Godwin never once mentioned the exaggerated forehead, the stitches *or* the steel bolt. And, when describing her nightmare, she referred too casually to 'the working of some powerful engine' which made the creature 'show signs of life, and stir with an uneasy, half vital motion'. In the book, she was even less specific:

> I collected the instruments of life around me, that I might infuse a spark of being into the lifeless thing that lay at my feet.

Hollywood, in 1931, was more than ready to fill the gap (films *have* to be literal about these things) with pieces of technology which had not been invented by 1816: lightning-arc generators, bakelite dials and an adjustable metal hospital bed. Plus some pieces which had: among them, a huge Voltaic battery. Result: 'It's moving – it's alive – it's alive – it's alive – it's alive. IT'S ALIVE … Now I know what it feels like to be God!'

The main influence here was not *Frankenstein* at all, but Fritz Lang's film *Metropolis* (1926) – with its climactic transformation of a human being into a robot at the hands of the evil designer/necromancer Dr Rottwang.

ary Godwin's 'spark of being' seems to refer to the vitalist controversy, and ally her scientist-creator with those who argued that the vital spark of life was 'analogous to electricity' – again, *against* the evolutionists. It also refers to her speculation of 1831: 'perhaps a corpse would be re-animated; galvanism had given token of such things'.

The German physicist Johann Wilhelm Ritter had said almost the same thing at the turn of the century: 'Galvanic phenomena seem to bridge the gap between living and non-living matter'. He was referring to the doctrine of 'animal electricity' which emerged in 1791 when his Italian counterpart Luigi Galvani published the results of a series of experiments involving dissected frogs' legs, under the title *Commentary on the Effects of Electricity on Muscular Motion*. Since the legs, when hanging from a piece of string or displayed on a table, began to twitch if the exposed nerves were prodded with a metal rod – even more dramatically if the legs were displayed on a *metal* table and prodded with a rod made of a different metal – Galvani concluded that *the nerve* was the source of electricity rather than the rod. The rod simply 'released' the animal electricity, a form of 'vital force' produced by the animal's brain and transmitted to its nerves and muscles. This conclusion appealed to scientists in Romantic Germany, who joined frog-hunting parties all over the enchanted countryside: searching for the soul.

Two years later, Alessandro Volta repudiated Galvani's conclusions by claiming that the source of electricity resided, after all, in the metal rather than the animal – so it was just an example of 'electricity' – and that in the more dramatic experiment the change happened through the contact of two different metals, one plus and one minus. In 1796-7, building on this claim Volta developed the Voltaic (or Galvanic) pile made up of copper and zinc discs separated by damp cardboard – the first electric battery.

The Galvanists and the more down-to-earth Voltaists battled it out for some years – and the word 'galvanism' continued to be used for *all* forms of experiment involving electricity and organic matter – but in practice, Volta was to win the day.

Luigi Aldini, Galvani's nephew and champion, in January 1803 wired a huge Voltaic pile (240 metal plates) to the ear and mouth of the corpse of one

The Monster's make-up, for the 1931 Hollywood version, strongly resembles an image of the mad-house called Los Chinchillas *from Goya's series of prints* Caprichos/Caprices *(1799). Mary Godwin described the Creature as 'beautiful': yet his best-known incarnation remains Boris Karloff as the Monster, complete with steel bolt through his neck, exaggerated forehead, stitches and sutures.*

47

Thomas Forster, a murderer who had been hanged at Newgate just one hour before. The result, reported in the appendix to Aldini's *Account of the Late Improvements in Galvanism* (1803), was that 'the jaw began to quiver, the adjoining muscles were horribly contorted, and the left eye actually opened'; later, when the late Mr Forster's thumb was wired up, the electrical charge 'induced a forcible effort to clench the hand'. All in all, this public demonstration at 'Mr. Wilson's Anatomical Theatre' almost gave 'an appearance of re-animation'; it was even possible that 'vitality might have been restored, if many circumstances had not rendered it impossible'.

No wonder Percy Shelley wrote in his *Preface* to Mary's novel that 'the event on which this fiction is founded has been supposed, by ... some of the physiological writers of Germany, as not of impossible occurrence'. It is probable that experiments like Aldini's – which were picked up by the press – became part of that conversation about 'the nature of the principle of life'.

n the days following Mary Godwin's nightmare at the Villa Diodati, rumours of bizarre goings-on were beginning to circulate among the English tourists on the other side of the lake at Sécheron. The maitre d'hôtel M. Déjean began to hire out telescopes, so that his guests at the Hôtel des Anglais could get a closer look. One tourist – Sylvester Douglas, Lord Glenbervie – picked up some juicy stories while dining at Sécheron on 3 July. He wrote in his diary:

> Among more than sixty English travellers here, there is Lord Byron, who is cut by everybody. They tell a strange adventure of his, at Déjean's Inn. He is now living at a villa on the Savoy side of the lake with that woman, who it seems proves to be a Mrs Shelley, wife to the man who keeps the Mount Coffee-house.

This gives some idea of the kind of gossip which was circulating among those 'sixty English travellers'. The final sentence gets every single detail hilariously wrong. Byron was *not*, of course, living with 'a Mrs Shelley', who in any case was still Mary Godwin at the time. The man who kept the Mount Coffee-house was John Westbrook, father of Harriet Westbrook, who was Shelley's first (and only, in 1816) wife. So Lord Glenbervie had succeeded in confusing Mary Godwin with both Clare Clairmont *and* Harriet Westbrook, Percy Shelley with Harriet's father, and Shelley with Lord Byron. Never mind; there was obviously *something* nasty going on in the Villa; probably group sex and/or a league of incest involving Percy, Mary, George and Clare. When tablecloths were seen drying on the iron balcony, they were rumoured to be the girls' knickers.

One reason the gossip then proceeded to spread from English tourists to

Citizens of Geneva was that the behaviour of the tenants of the Villa Diodati had come to the attention of the local police. In the Genevan police records (among the Archives d'Etat), I have found ample evidence that Lord Byron and Dr Polidori, at least, were well known to the local constabulary.

On one occasion, Byron reported that his boat's anchor and some fixtures and fittings had been stolen from the harbour near the Maison Chappuis, and then took the law into his own hands by noisily threatening some completely innocent local residents. On another, Polidori roughed up a local apothecary – breaking his spectacles and throwing his hat into the gutter – because he had supplied him (or rather Lord Byron) with some substandard drugs: this resulted in a warrant for the Doctor's arrest. But the most interesting case was a bungled breaking-and-entering attempt at the Villa Diodati itself: which, according to the *rapports de police*, resulted in a lieutenant suggesting that the neighbouring cabarets should be placed under observation to see if any 'étrangers et gens suspects' (foreigners and suspicious-looking people) were hanging around: the Genevans do not seem to have been keen on foreigners; it had not occurred to the lieutenant that the culprits might be *citizens*.

In summer 1816, Geneva seems from the documents to have been swarming with upmarket English tourists. Some of them were associated with the allied troops who had recently defeated Napoleon, others stopping over on their Grand Tours, others still coming to see the latest discovery (or invention) of the Romantics – the magnificent Alps. This was, after all, the first time for fifteen years that tourists could travel freely around the continent. Tourism and Switzerland were beginning to become as synonymous as Lord Byron and scandal.

A t 8.30 a.m. on 21 July, following Percy Shelley's promenade sur le lac with Byron, Percy, Mary and Clare decided to escape the oppressive atmosphere of the villa and visit the Alps themselves. There had been weather reports of flooding and avalanches, but – for Percy Shelley at least – that was probably part of the attraction. Byron did not join them. They followed the swollen river Arve to Bonneville and Cluses, Shelley enthusiastically noting that the flooded scene was assuming 'a more savage and colossal character' by the minute. Mary reckoned that the 'mountainous and rocky path' – and particularly 'alpine bridge over the Arve' (where Shelley was inspired to write his poem Mont Blanc) – represented 'one of the loveliest scenes in the world'. She was less struck with the savagery:

> … as we went along we heard a sound like the rolling of distant thunder
> and beheld an avalanche rush down a ravine of the rock – it stopped midway
> but in its course forced a torrent from its bed which now fell to the base of

the mountain. We had passed the torrent here in the morning – the torrents had torn away the road and it was with difficulty we crossed – Clare went on her mule – S. walked and I was carried. Fatigued to death we arrived at seven o clock [on July 22] at Chamounix.

They checked in at the recently rebuilt Hôtel de Londres (on the corner of today's Rue des Moulins near the Musée Alpin), the most substantial building in the village. It had been extended from three to five storeys in 1810, by the proprietor Victor Tairraz, to cope with demand.

At some stage on the journey, Mary was encouraged by Shelley to turn her transcription of the nightmare into a full-length novel: the first reference to the book in her *Journal* was on 24 July; 'Write my story'. If the 'waking dream' itself had been strongly influenced by the environment and atmosphere of the Villa Diodati, the subsequent development of *Frankenstein* would be equally strongly shaped by her impressions of the wasteland of the Alps: the *Journal,* kept by Mary and Percy in July 1816, would find its way almost *verbatim* into volume II, chapters 1 & 2, of *Frankenstein*. The story she told at the ghost-story session had been written up while Shelley was away with Byron: the next section – the meeting of Victor and his hideous progeny – began now.

On the morning of 23 July, after breakfast, they mounted their mules to reach the source of the Arvéron, and to visit the desolate *Mer de Glace*, the sea of ice, in the shadow of Mont Blanc. The last part of the journey, on a very steep and treacherous path, was 'on foot over loose stones many of which were of an enormous size'. Shelley had been reading about the 'sublime but gloomy theory, that this earth which we inhabit will at some future period be changed into a mass of frost', which must have made the ascent towards an advancing glacier – and the absence of vegetation – seem particularly frightening: for this was, to them, *the* most dramatic example of global freezing. Mary wrote:

> Nothing can be more desolate than the ascent of this mountain – the trees in many places have been torn away by avalanches and some half leaning over others intermingled with stones present the appearance of vast and dreadful desolation … when we had mounted considerably we turned to look on the scene – a dense white mist covered the vale and tops of the scattered pines peeping above were the only objects that presented themselves. The rain continued in torrents – we were wetted to the skin so that when we had ascended more than half way we resolved to turn back … I write my story.

The following day, 25 July, they finally reached the Mer de Glace: Victor Frankenstein's ascent along precisely the same route combines the two days into one. Mary wrote in her *Journal*:

*T*he *desolate Mer de Glace in the shadow of Mont Blanc, which Mary Godwin visited in July 1816 and where – in her novel – she set the great confrontation between Victor Frankenstein and his creature.*

> We get to the top at twelve and behold le Mer de Glace. This is the most desolate place in the world – iced mountains surround it – no sign of vegetation appears except on the place from which we view the scene – we went on the ice – It is traversed by irregular crevices whose sides of ice appear blue while the surface is of a dirty white – We dine on the mountain ...

The vast Mer de Glace, the result of the confluence of three glaciers, resembled a freeze-dried blue sea at the end of the world. They dined in the wooden 'temple of nature', built in 1778 (and still there), overlooking the southern tip of the Sea. Mary decided there and then that this was a most suitable location for the climactic meeting between the scientist and his creation. Rejected by society, the creature seeks the most remote place imaginable – just as, at the end of the story, he makes for the land of mist and snow, the unexplored regions of the North Pole:

> I suddenly beheld the figure of a man, writes Victor Frankenstein, at some distance, advancing towards me with superhuman speed. He bounded over the crevices in the ice, among which I had walked with caution; his stature also, as he approached, seemed to exceed that of man. I was troubled: a mist came over my eyes, and I felt a faintness seize me; but I was quickly restored by the cold gale of the mountains. I perceived, as the shape came nearer (sight tremendous and abhorred!) that it was the wretch whom I had created. I trembled with rage and horror ...

At last, Victor is forced to confront the 'accomplishment of my toils'. In a hut next to Mer de Glace, the creature pours out his sad life story and demands that Victor, his single parent 'create a female for me, with whom I can live in the interchange of those sympathies necessary for my being ... I demand it of you as a right which you must not refuse'.

Even when on her journey to and from 'the most desolate place in the world', Mary Godwin managed to read avidly every evening (her reading-matter included Madame de Genlis's *Nouveaux Contes*). Mary and Percy took a travelling library with them wherever they went, and, according to the *Journal*, she read at least one book a day, often two, either before or after Percy had read them, so they could discuss their latest discoveries together before they went to bed.

Frankenstein has sometimes been called an example of 'bibliogenesis' – birth by books – a living piece of literary tissue pieced together from key passages from other books, as filtered through Mary Godwin's imagination. This is only partly true. Her sense of place, and her response to the social and natural environment in which she found herself, were equally strong. But there is no doubt that her insecurities as a writer, and her intellectual curiosity, combined to make her very dependent on her printed sources – a process which, like most Romantic writers, she made part of the subject-matter of her book. So for the creature's autobiographical account of his traumatic birth and upbringing as an outcast – most of volume II of *Frankenstein* – she made full use of the books she had been reading since she left England. The birth was the first section to be written; the creature's upbringing came second.

Most importantly, she used the key works written by her parents: *An Enquiry Concerning Political Justice* by William Godwin and *The Vindication of the Rights of Woman* by Mary Wollstonecraft. In the case of the Godwin text, the *Enquiry* seems to have provided her with some point of contact with her father – in his younger, more radical days – who disapproved so strongly of her elopement with Percy.

In the case of the *Vindication*, which she devoured over and over again, reading was the only possible way she could get to know her mother. *Political Justice* would have told her about the dangers of being alone too much, the importance of thinking socially and having a companion, and the subtle tyranny of institutions such as the government of the day, the law and universities – all of them lessons learned the hard way by the creature in *Frankenstein*. The novel includes several characters (in addition to the creature) who are unjustly persecuted for crimes of which they are innocent. *The Vindication* was more about the domestic sphere, the obsession men had with being competitive and making a name for themselves (like young Victor Frankenstein), and the importance of a humane careful upbringing which suits the individual concerned. 'A great proportion of the misery that wanders in hideous forms around the world', wrote Wollstonecraft, 'is allowed to rise from the negligence of parents'.

The creature has a bad enough start in life – a motherless child, a selfish father – and things get worse and worse for him from then on.

That summer, Byron, Shelley *and* Mary had also been discussing incessantly the writings of the Genevan philosopher Jean-Jacques Rousseau, and from Rousseau's *Emile, ou de l'Education* Mary probably picked up the idea that if society treats you as ugly, you will become ugly. The education of the enlightened child Emile (who is an orphan), carefully tailored to his physical and mental development – in a version of what is today called 'the psycho-genetic principle' – is precisely the education the creature is *not* offered. As he says at one point 'I was benevolent and good: misery turned me into a fiend'. He was not so much ugly to look at (although the parts did not seem to fit together properly) as ugly on the inside.

The creature gains *his* education, such as it is, by peeping through the wall of a rustic cottage, and seeing the dynamics of a happy family in action:

distance-learning is the best he can hope for, in the circumstances. He also finds some abandoned books, after which – since he is remarkably quick on the uptake – he can't stop talking about them, and trying in vain to set up seminars about their contents with his newly-acquired gift of language.

The books include *The Sorrows of Young Werther* by Goethe – the best-selling story of a romantic young man who feels misunderstood by society and ends up killing himself; Plutarch's *Parallel Lives* (or *Lives of the Noble Romans*) – which provides a crash-course in the origins of politics; and above all John Milton's epic poem *Paradise Lost* – which encourages the creature to identify both with Adam, the first man, and Satan, the fallen angel.

The importance of Milton's poem to *Frankenstein* – as a kind of parallel myth – was clearly signalled by Mary Shelley in her epigraph to the book (which she never changed from edition to edition):

> Did I request thee, Maker, from my clay
> To mould me man? Did I solicit thee
> From darkness to promote me?

In *Paradise Lost*, God provides Adam with some convincing answers: in *Frankenstein* – and this was Mary's point – there are none. Her conviction that Milton had stayed in the Villa Diodati, though wrong, was a very happy accident. Finally, among the major literary influences, as the creature chases the guilt-ridden Victor Frankenstein to the very ends of the earth, Mary made constant – and anachronistic (the story seems to be set in the early 1790s) – reference to a poem she had first heard as a small child, hiding behind the parlour sofa, recited by the poet himself: Coleridge's *The Rime of the Ancient Mariner* (1798). One stanza in particular, which she quotes in full in *Frankenstein* and which once made Percy Shelley pass out in sheer terror when he heard it, proved especially stimulating:

> Like one that, on a lonesome road,
> Doth walk in fear and dread.
> And having once turn'd round, walks on,
> And turns no more his head.
> Because he knows a frightful fiend
> doth close behind him tread.

A t the end of August, Mary, Percy and Clare (together with William and the nursemaid Elise) left Geneva for Portsmouth and for wherever home might turn out to be. Mary had continued to 'write my story', off and on, following her return from Chamonix. On 21 August, she made a point of observing that 'Shelley and I talk about my story'. She did not join Byron up at the Villa very often any more.

A Victorian photograph of 5, Abbey Churchyard, Bath (the three-storey house on the left marked 'Library and Reading Room'), where Mary Shelley stayed from autumn 1816 to spring 1817 to write much of the full-length version of Frankenstein.

By 11 September, Mary had found lodgings at 5, Abbey Churchyard, Bath, to 'settle ourselves' while Shelley sorted out his business affairs and looked for a more permanent residence around Marlow on the Thames. Number 5 was a three-storey town house next door to the recently rebuilt Grand Pump Room, in the yard facing the west door of Bath Abbey. Mary, with William and Elise, rented the rooms above William Meyler's circulating library. Today, the house at 5, Abbey Churchyard has become absorbed into the Pump Room complex, and the numbering of the houses (on the opposite side of the yard) begins at 6. There is no commemorative plaque.

Percy Shelley spent a little time in London trying to stabilise his finances, but Mary and Clare could not possibly join him – because Clare's pregnancy was by now apparent to all, and they had no wish to be cross-examined about it by members of the Godwin household. Clare took separate lodgings at 12,

New Bond Street in Bath. Shelley had a difficult time in London – dodging creditors, arguing with lawyers, disappointing William Godwin, and reading lukewarm reviews of his poems: 'why', said Mary (according to Clare) 'the world must be going mad'.

It was in Bath – from 7 October onwards – that Mary wrote of Victor Frankenstein's education at Ingolstadt (with help from Humphry Davy's lectures), and added the framing device of explorer Robert Walton's letters describing what he sees on his journey to the North Pole (with help from various accounts of voyages including Lord Anson's).

Two days after she started expanding her novel in earnest – heralding the most sustained period of work in the whole project so far – she learned that her half-sister Fanny Godwin had over-dosed on laudanum and died. By 18 October, however, she was back at her writing desk again, and by the end of the month had finished drafting 'Chap. 2 $\frac{1}{2}$' which described the effect of Professor Waldman's lectures on the impressionable young Victor.

By mid-November, she had completed what was then intended to be volume 1, which took her up to the encounter at the Mer de Glace and the beginning of the creature's autobiography.

Percy Shelley was now helping to correct her spelling and make her writing style – which he considered too 'abrupt' – more rhetorical and flowery. Many of the over-written phrases and paragraphs, for which Mary was later to be criticised, are in Percy's handwriting on the manuscript. When she wrote 'igmmatic', he added in the margin 'enigmatic, o you pretty Pecksie' ('Pecksie' was the wise robin in a children's book; on other occasions, he liked to call her 'Dormouse').

On 5 December, Mary sent him 'the 4 Chap of *Frankenstein* which is a very long one and I think you would like it': this was, presumably, the fourth chapter of volume II which, in the manuscript, is the section dealing with the creature's discovery of the De Lacy family, and piecemeal education as he observes their behaviour through the wall.

Ten days later, she learned that Harriet Westbrook Shelley had killed herself by drowning in the Serpentine. Harriet was, it transpired, heavily pregnant at the time, and Shelley wrote – cruelly and inaccurately – that:

> this poor woman ... was driven from her father's house, and descended the steps of prostitution until she lived with a groom of the name of Smith, who deserting her, she killed herself ...

Maybe writing the letter made him feel better; maybe the Godwins had been gossiping to him: it certainly bore no resemblance to the facts.

In an attempt to ensure custody of Shelley's children by Harriet, and also as a result of intense pressure from William Godwin (who apparently threatened suicide himself, as if there had not been more than enough already),

Mary and Percy were married at the end of December, in a ceremony at St Mildred's Church, Bread Street, London – with only the Godwins to witness it. Both parties were defensive about the marriage, which was still against their principles. Mary wrote to Percy 'Love me, sweet, for ever – But I not mean – I hardly know what I mean I am so much agitated', and noted in her *Journal* 'a marriage takes place on the 29th'. It in fact took place on the 30th.

By 1 January, 1817, Mary Shelley was back in Bath and two days later was again working on *Frankenstein*.

A busy ten days of writing was interrupted, on 12 January, by Clare giving birth to a baby daughter. 'C.C. Sunday Jan 12', Mary wrote somewhat sharply in her *Journal*; '4 days of idleness'. They called the child Alba. She was later to be known as 'Miss Auburn', until such time as she could be christened. In March 1818, she became Clara Allegra Byron.

A fortnight after the birth, Mary celebrated her son William's first birthday; the *Journal* reference provides a revealing contrast with the casual and cryptic 'C.C. Sunday Jan 12': 'William's birthday – How many chances have occurred – during this little year – May the ensuing one be more peaceful'.

By 10 April, she was able to write 'Correct F'.

Mary Shelley had completed volume III in February and March, and now, instead of saying 'write' each day, she began to put 'transcribe' and 'correct'. By 13 May, she had finished her transcription and the book was ready for the press. Percy Shelley copied out the final thirteen pages. On Wednesday 14 May, almost exactly eleven months after experiencing her nightmare, she wrote 'S. corrects F. write Preface – Finis'.

In between times, Mary had discovered that she was pregnant again, and moved from Bath to Albion House in the village of Great Marlow. This was (and is) a wide two-storey house facing on to West Street. The nearby river seemed like a good idea at first, but it soon began to make Percy Shelley feel ill. Today, there are three commemorative plaques on the front wall of the house – which has been subdivided. The earliest reads: 'This tablet was placed AD 1867 ... to perpetuate the record that PERCY BYSSHE SHELLEY lived and wrote in this house ... '

t was at Albion House, between the end of February and the middle of May that Mary put the finishing touches to *Frankenstein*, and from there that Percy looked for a publisher. The manuscript was turned down by two publishing houses, before it was issued in spring 1818 – by the less than fashionable Lackington, Hughes, Harding, Mavor and Jones of Finsbury Square, London – in an anonymous edition of just 500 copies. Mary Shelley made the princely sum of £28, 14 shillings on

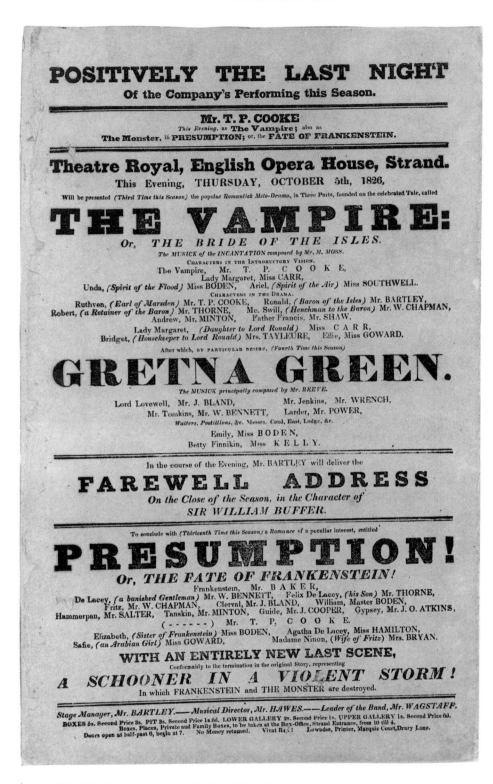

*P*laybill of 1826, advertising a double bill of The Vampire *and* Presumption! or the Fate of Frankenstein *at the English Opera House. Note how the actor Thomas Potter Cooke was billed as (- - - - - -) for his role as the Monster.*

the deal, which can't have done much for the family finances. The first edition of *Frankenstein or The Modern Prometheus*, printed in three volumes, was respectfully dedicated to her father 'William Godwin – author of *Political Justice* etc' (a late, post-marriage, decision on Mary's part) and because of this, the earliest reviews in the more conservative journals were cautious to say the very least.

The only indication the reviewers had as to authorship of *Frankenstein* was the reference to Godwin, and, in the unstable political and social atmosphere of Britain in 1818, when machines were being broken and anti-government demonstrations were mobilising in city centres, the association was thought to be dangerous. The book was *really* promoting 'the favourite passions and projects of the times', said one, and therefore to be handled with a long spoon. Another thought it was by Percy Shelley, and thus full of 'poetic imagination'; when it found out the truth, the journal added 'for a man it was excellent, but for a woman it was wonderful'. A third panned the book, saying it was a 'tissue of horrible and disgusting absurdity', containing 'passages which appal the mind and make the flesh creep'.

This panning, of course, helped ensure the book's success, and led to a more popular cut-down single volume edition – the one we know today (the third edition) – published in 1831 by Colburn and Bentley with the name Mary W. Shelley prominently displayed on the title page.

A lot of the radicalism of the first edition was excised by Mary (including explicit references to the by-now very controversial 'vitalist' controversy among scientists). Victor was given more of a conscience about his experiments and talked for the first time of his 'presumption' in challenging the Almighty, and the overall emphasis subtly shifted from William Godwin's ideas about justice to the flesh-creeping bits. A new author's introduction stressed the blood-and-thunder aspects, which went well with the specially engraved illustration. *Frankenstein* was already on its journey from novel to popular myth.

y 1831, the phrase 'Frankenstein monster' was already beginning to enter the language – meaning something monstrous, something other or something mindless. But it was in 1823, when the first theatrical version opened at the English Opera House, that the myth-making really began.

Richard Brinsley Peake's *Presumption! or the Fate of Frankenstein* opened on 28 July of that year to a demonstration outside the theatre, with placards – according to the *London Magazine* – 'professing to come from a knot of "friends of humanity" and calling on the fathers of families, etc. to set their faces against the piece'. Maybe word was getting out that the story was in some way connected with the Shelleys – and everyone 'knew' that the infamous Shelleys had engaged in group sex and/or incest at the time the story was written. Or maybe the demonstrators were worried about the 'author of Political Justice, etc'. The 'friends of humanity' need not have worried. For, the title said it all. *Frankenstein* had changed from Mary Shelley's complex fantasy into a simple-minded parable about daring to 'play God'.

The playbills had promised 'Mysterious and terrific appearance of the Demon from the Laboratory of Frankenstein ... And the FALL of an AVALANCHE', and the critic from *The Drama* was not disappointed: ' ... it is natural to suppose that the end of such an abortive creation could only be brought about by some terrible convulsion of nature'.

He loved the special effects and was perceptive about the performance of Thomas Potter Cooke as the creature: ' ... with the art of a Fuseli, he powerfully embodied the horrible, bordering on the sublime and the awful'.

Cooke was to become indelibly associated with the role over the next few years. At the Theatre de la Porte Saint-Martin in Paris, summer 1826, he played it on a record eighty successive nights in a production of *Le Monstre* at the end of which, according to *Le Journal de Paris*, there were so many dead bodies on the stage that 'it would have been difficult to do more unless one killed also the prompter and the musicians in the orchestra'. It was, seemingly, the equation Cooke = *Frankenstein* which led for the first time to confusion in the public mind between scientist and creature.

Changes to the original story which began with *Presumption* appear to have stuck fast: all surviving dramatic versions of the time include the monster crashing through a door or window, a comic servant, musical interludes, the voiceless nameless retarded monster in a blue body-stocking, and an apocalyptic ending. Some details might change (scientist and monster die in an avalanche, a Polar storm, a thunderstorm and Mount Etna), but the basic structure remained the same. And so it has continued.

The Edison Company's 1910 film kept the monster crashing through the french windows, but added an alchemical theme by having the scientist create him (on stage, unlike the theatrical versions) in a huge, bubbling pot, which somehow transformed a skeleton into an overweight human being; another addition was the ending, where the monster dissolved into a mirror – creating the impression that he had been Victor's alter ego all the time.

James Whale's 1931 Hollywood version kept the comic servant Fritz (turning him into a hunchbacked and vertically-challenged research assistant) and a grotesque, childlike, grunting monster (mimed, touchingly, by Boris Karloff), but changed Peake's line 'it lives!' into 'it's alive', added a jar containing 'Disfunctio Cerebri' or 'Abnormal Brain' and destroyed the monster

The EDISON
KINETOGRAM

VOL. 1   LONDON, APRIL 15, 1910   No. 1

SCENE FROM

FRANKENSTEIN

The Edison Company's film version of Frankenstein (1910), *based on the play seen by Mary Shelley eighty-seven years before, featured Charles Ogle as a grotesque Monster.*

at the fadeout in a burning mill. At least until the sequel *The Bride of Frankenstein* (1935), which began with Lord Byron and Percy Shelley – in a huge, over-the-top storm-drenched neo-Gothick castle next to Lake Geneva – asking Mary to tell them *another* story.

The twist, this time, was that the same actress (Elsa Lanchester) played both Mary Shelley *and* the bride of the monster (complete with fashionable Nefertari hairdo). Bride of the Monster, Bride of Frankenstein, it made no difference by then. The implication was that the dreamy young girl of the prologue had fantasised about being chased by Boris Karloff, but lost her nerve when she actually saw him. The rest is history.

Many of the changes to the original story, from 1823 to the present day, have arisen from the fact that *Frankenstein* in its original form was/is notoriously difficult to adapt. It consists of explorer Robert Walton's letters, Victor Frankenstein's reminiscences and the creature's autobiography: a novel within a novel within a novel, rather than a single linear narrative. And there are wild improbabilities and coincidences in Mary Shelley's version, such as: how does Victor create a being eight foot tall out of the body-parts of ordinary people? How does the creature become fluent in English and French, specialising in literature, in the space of less than a year? How exactly could the creature have found a cloak lying around that just happened to fit him? And so on. There is a logic to *Frankenstein*, but it is the logic of a dream. Since 1823, the popularisations of the story have managed by a process of accretion to invent another, parallel, text – which has filled in the gaps and made it 'make sense'. Or, rather, make a new sense which fits the audience's expectations.

Mary Shelley herself had no control over the adaptations of 1823 onwards. Having omitted to write *her* dramatisation, she did not own the theatrical copyright. But she did go and see Richard Brinsley Peake's *Presumption! or the Fate of Frankenstein*. On 14 August 1823, she wrote to some friends (from Paris, where she was staying for a week on her way from Genoa to London), letting them know that she had just discovered:

> … that they brought out Frankenstein at the Lyceum and vivified the
> Monster in such a manner as caused the ladies to faint away and a hubbub to
> ensue – however they diminished the horrors in the sequel, and it is having
> a run.

On the evening of 29 August, she went to the play with William Godwin and his son William, and – surprisingly – rather enjoyed herself:

> But lo and behold! I found myself famous! – Frankenstein had prodigious
> success as a drama and was about to be repeated for the 23rd night at the

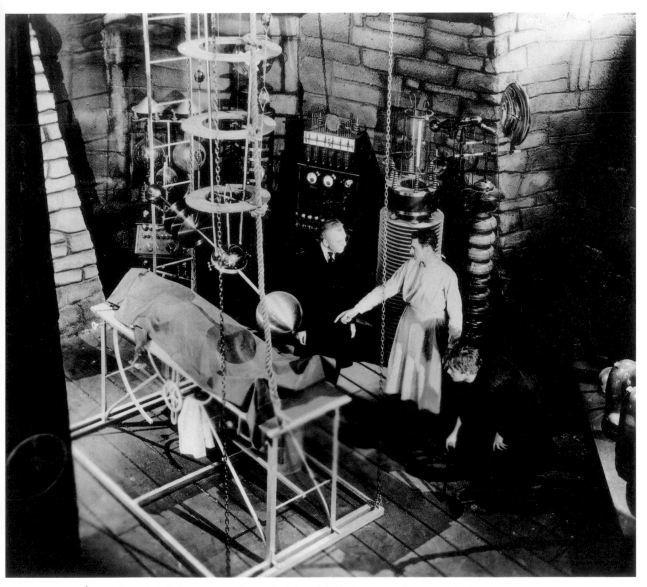

*F*rankenstein's laboratory, 1931-style: Mary Shelley's vague reference to 'the instruments of life' has become a fully equipped castle with dials, switches, a metal operating table, a lightning-arc generator and a huge battery.

English opera house … The story is not well managed – but Cooke played ————'s part extremely well – his seeking as it were for support – his trying to grasp at the sounds he heard – all indeed he does was well imagined and executed. I was much amused, and it appeared to excite a breathless eagerness in the audience …

By now, Mary evidently did not mind referring to the creature as 'the Monster', and accepting the old-fashioned morality of the piece. Her only problem appears to have been with the structure of the story. When she came to revise *Frankenstein* for the 1831 edition, she incorporated the popular – conservative/reactionary – interpretation into her own novel. The radical days of 1816-18 seemed a long time ago.

Still unsure about her literary abilities, she had written in more characteristic style to the novelist and poet Sir Walter Scott just after *Frankenstein* was first issued (to clear up a misunderstanding about the book's authorship which had appeared in Scott's friendly review):

> Mr Shelley soon after its publication took the liberty of sending you a copy, but as both he and I thought in a manner which would prevent you from supposing that he was the author we were surprised therefore to see him mentioned in the notice [in Blackwood's Edinburgh Magazine, March 1818] as the probable author – I am anxious to prevent your continuing in the mistake of supposing Mr Shelley guilty of a juvenile attempt of mine; to which – from its being written at an early age, I abstained from putting my name – and from respect to those persons from whom I bear it. I have therefore kept it concealed except from a few friends.

Mary Shelley remained convinced that *Frankenstein* was utterly unworthy of the daughter of Mary Wollstonecraft and William Godwin; unworthy of 'the daughter of two persons of distinguished literary celebrity'.

Today, however, the fame of *Frankenstein* as a literary text interpreted, variously, as a feminist allegory of birthing, or an ecological reading of mother earth, or a critique of Romantic ideology, or a response to the French Revolution, or an attack on 'masculinist science', or the origin of science fiction, or a key example of 'female Gothic', or a reaction to the rise of the industrial proletariat, or a dramatisation of the conflict between an ethic of care and an ethic of control, or ... much, much else besides – the fame of *Frankenstein* has totally eclipsed that of *An Enquiry Concerning Political Justice* and even *A Vindication of the Rights of Woman*. It lives!

Within eight years of the Geneva summer of 1816, the summer which saw the birth of *Frankenstein*, all the men who had taken part in that ghost-story session at the Villa Diodati were dead: Dr Polidori had died of brain damage (possibly a suicide); Percy Shelley had drowned when his yacht – the *Ariel* – capsized in a storm off the coast of Italy; and Byron had died, a popular hero, in the cause of the liberation of Greece.

Of Mary's five children, only one had survived infancy. Her daughter Clara, born at the beginning of September 1817, died a year later. William died, as she had always feared he would, when he was just three-and-a-half years old. Only Percy Florence Shelley, born in November 1819, still lived.

So, by the age of twenty-seven, the age when most scholars studying *Frankenstein* today are just finishing their postgraduate studies, Mary Shelley felt 'as an old woman might feel. I may not love any but the dead'.

The remainder of her life was spent struggling to earn her living as a writer, begging for an allowance from the Shelley family (who initially wanted custody of young Percy in exchange), quarrelling – one by one – with her late husband's fair-weather friends, confiding in a few close female companions, and slowly withdrawing into herself and her books.

She tried to be likeable and emotionally fulfilled – but somehow 'misfortune' always got in the way. She was a born pessimist, and her pessimism invariably came true. And so she earned the reputation of being cold and reserved. 'A cold heart', she wrote in her *Journal*, 'have I a cold heart? God knows! But at least the tears are hot'.

Mary Shelley died in London at the age of fifty-three, after a series of strokes, on 1 February 1851 – the year of the Great Exhibition, with its celebration of science, technology and Victorian notions of progress.

She was buried on a sloping patch of high ground in St Peter's Churchyard, Bournemouth, near the family home of her surviving son. Her father William Godwin and mother Mary Wollstonecraft were exhumed from St Pancras Churchyard and reburied next to her (as she had requested); a few years later, her body was joined by the heart of her husband Percy Shelley – a slice of which was buried in a small silver urn. Mary had kept it in her bedside desk, wrapped up in a piece of silk. By the mid-Victorian age, it had become fashionable to think of them as one big happy family – which, of course, they never were.

Most of the obituaries were short; all of them said that her main claim to fame was as 'the faithful and devoted wife of Percy Bysshe Shelley' – a view which continued, in the literature, until at least the middle of this century. The inscription on her gravestone reads 'Mary Wollstonecraft Shelley, Daughter of Willm and Mary Wollstonecraft Godwin, and widow of the late Percy Bysshe Shelley' – just as the nineteenth-century plaques on the places with which she was associated (Sécheron, Diodati, Albion House Marlow) mention Byron and Shelley but never Mary.

Towards the end of her life, in the mid 1840s, she had revisited the Villa Diodati, and looked up at the imposing house from the shore of Lake Geneva. 'Was I the same person who had lived there', she asked herself, 'the companion of the dead. For all were gone, even my young child had died in infancy … Storm and blight and death had destroyed all, while yet very young.'

She had no way of knowing it, but one thing had survived the storm and the blight – to take on a life of its own which its creator would scarcely recognise – the thing she called her 'hideous progeny', born in a dream.

2 *Dracula*

I was afraid to raise my eyelids, but looked out and saw perfectly under the lashes. The fair girl went on her knees, and bent over me, fairly gloating. There was a deliberate voluptuousness which was both thrilling and repulsive, and as she arched her neck she actually licked her lips like an animal, till I could see in the moonlight the moisture shining on the scarlet lips and on the red tongue as it lapped the sharp white teeth. Lower and lower went her head as the lips went below the range of my mouth and chin and seemed about to fasten on my throat ... I closed my eyes in a languorous ecstasy and waited — waited with beating heart.

But at that instant ... I was conscious of the presence of the Count, and of his being as if lapped in a storm of fury ... In a voice which, though low and almost in a whisper, seemed to cut through the air and then ring round the room as he said:-

'How dare you touch him, any of you? How dare you cast eyes on him when I had forbidden it? Back, I tell you all! This man belongs to me ... !'

BRAM STOKER

D ream-like illustration of the Count (a white-haired military commander) shinning down the walls of Castle Dracula, in the sixpenny yellow-covered paperback edition of 1901.

RACULA IS THE MOST famous vampire novel of all time, and — a hundred years after its first publication, with issues of gender and sexuality high up on the cultural agenda — more controversial than ever. It was first unleashed on a terrified British public in 1897, the year of Queen Victoria's Diamond Jubilee, the high point of the British Empire, and the year when Sigmund Freud started his researches into psychoanalysis.

In June 1897, the Anglo-Irish author Bram (Abraham) Stoker came to the end of a journey he had begun seven years before — a journey of the mind via a place he had never visited called Transylvania, the land beyond the forest. When, at the age of forty-two, he first started thinking about *Dracula*, the only full-length book he had written was a turgid tome of 248 pages entitled *The Duties of Clerks of Petty Sessions in Ireland* ('by Bram Stoker M.A., Inspector of Petty Sessions'). This book has more to do with being smothered in red tape in Dublin Castle than with being bitten by vampires in Castle Dracula.

On the surface, Bram Stoker was a pillar of late Victorian middle-class respectability. An ex-civil servant who grew up in the seaside suburb of Clontarf, Dublin, (and who kept a 'rich Irish brogue' all his life) he had been, since 1878, the business manager and front-of-house master of ceremonies at the Lyceum Theatre, off the Strand in London — a career move which led to him routinely rubbing shoulders with the artistic and political establishment.

But, not far below the glittering surface, Bram Stoker — who seemed to his friends to be the hearty, down-to-earth, practical-joker type — had something on his mind. On 8 March 1890, he wrote on a piece of scrap paper — in handwriting which he always called 'an extremely bad hand': 'young man goes out — sees girls one tries — to kiss him not on the lips but throat. Old Count interferes — rage and fury diabolical. This man belongs to me I want him'. Six days later, on 14 March, he reiterated — on Lyceum notepaper this time: 'Loneliness, the Kiss ... 'this man belongs to me'. Again and again in his notes, sometimes in a form of shorthand, he obsessively returned to the thought: 'the visitors — is it a dream — women stoop to kiss him. Terror of death. Suddenly Count turns her away — 'this man belongs to me'; 'Women kissing'; 'Belongs to Me'.

Stoker's nightmare, which, six or seven years later, was to turn into Jonathan Harker's fictional Journal entry for the night of 15 May ('I suppose I must have fallen asleep; I hope so, but I fear ... I cannot in the least believe that it was all sleep ... '), was the origin of *Dracula*.

Bram Stoker had not yet decided to incorporate the nightmare into a novel, but his first full-length piece of fiction *The Snake's Pass* — about a young Englishman's search for buried treasure in the West of Ireland — was issued as a hardback novel on the 18 November that same year, an event which may have given him the confidence to begin embellishing his nightmare. He did not yet have a title or a location; he had not decided on a cast of characters. When he *did* decide to develop the idea, he may have had a four-act play – *Styria to London, Tragedy, Discovery and Punishment* – rather than a novel in mind.

But, among the many changes that happened to *Dracula* between March 1890 and June 1897, one incident and one alone remained constant right up to publication day: the incident which Bram Stoker almost certainly dreamed during the night of 7 March 1890: a bizarre mixture of the three witches from *Macbeth* (a favourite play of Bram Stoker's employer, the actor-manager, Henry Irving), Stoker's own anxieties about his masculinity, and a voyeur's fantasy – of sex-hungry women and a power-hungry man.

Dracula was to be full of references to the plays which Irving performed at the Lyceum in the 1880s and 1890s, including a misquo-

A braham, or Bram, Stoker – *ex-civil servant from Dublin, business manager of the Lyceum Theatre from 1878 to 1905, and author of* Dracula. *He never smiled for photographs.*

tation from *Hamlet* ('My tablets, quick, my tablets!/'Tis meet that I put it down' rather than 'My tables – meet it is I set it down') which introduces Harker's waking nightmare and which Irving always insisted on including in *his* version of the tragedy: a process which Bernard Shaw called 'performing Hamlet with the part of Hamlet omitted'. But the sheer intensity of this scene, involving the brides of *Dracula*, was never to be repeated anywhere else in Stoker's writings.

Dracula began as Bram Stoker's attempt to exorcise his nightmare of kisses and a tug-of-war over his sexuality. Jonathan Harker (a surname derived from Joseph Harker, the Lyceum's in-house designer) is described in the story as a 'sweet and simple' man, one of the 'good brave men' who answer the call to arms when their way of life is threatened by an Eastern European vampire; a recently qualified solicitor from provincial England with the no-nonsense approach and writing style of a junior civil servant.

Bram Stoker himself had qualified as a barrister, and, in the month following his nightmare, was called to the Bar of the Inner Temple on 30 April 1890. When he was the same age as Harker, Stoker had written a long and

Dracula

THE STORY

Jonathan Harker, a young English solicitor's clerk, journeys to Castle Dracula in the mountains of Transylvania: he has been sent there to finalise the details of the Count's purchase of a house near Dr John Seward's lunatic asylum in Purfleet, Essex. On a night-time stroll around the castle, Harker encounters the seductive brides of Dracula and discovers to his horror that his host, too, is a vampire. He is imprisoned in the castle, while Dracula sets off for England accompanied by some wooden boxes filled with earth from the family graveyard. Eventually, the Count drifts into Whitby harbour, having gorged on the ship's crew during the long sea voyage from Varna, is seen by Mina Murray (Jonathan's fiancée) and her close friend Lucy Westenra, and meets the flirtatious Lucy in St. Mary's churchyard on the clifftop. She is slowly turned into one of the Undead, a vampire, despite the best efforts of her three suitors Arthur Holmwood, Dr Seward, and an American Quincey Morris who pump their blood into her veins under the supervision of the Dutch occult specialist and medical man Professor Van Helsing. The 'good, brave men' are joined by Jonathan, who has returned home traumatised by his ordeal.

After her death, Lucy haunts the surroundings of Hampstead Heath, resembles the Medusa, and preys on small children: she is staked through the heart in Highate Cemetery, by her lover Arthur Holmwood, now Lord Godalming – again under Van Helsing's tuition.

Now Dracula turns his attention to the more level-headed Mina, while the vampire-hunters seek and sanctify all except one of his boxes of earth (where he must rest in the hours of daylight). Renfield, a bloodthirsty patient in Seward's asylum, responds – as if by telepathy – to the comings and goings of his 'master' Dracula. After Mina has been initiated by the Count, he is pursued – in his final box – back to his Transylvanian castle, where following a hectic chase he is decapitated by Jonathan and stabbed through the heart by the dying Quincey. His brides are staked in their coffins. As Dracula crumbles into dust, Jonathan and Mina are reunited and the curse passes away. Later they return to Transylvania with their son Quincey.

candid confessional letter to his hero, the American poet Walt Whitman – whose collection *Leaves of Grass* he had defended against the 'philistines'. This letter included an assessment of himself that could easily serve as a description, in broad outline, of the hero of his novel:

> If you care to know who it is that writes this, my name is Abraham Stoker (Junior). My friends call me Bram ... I am a clerk in the service of the Crown on a small salary. I am twenty-four years old. Have been champion at our athletic sports (Trinity College, Dublin) and have won about a dozen cups ... I am six feet two inches high and twelve stone weight naked and used to be forty-one or forty-two inches round the chest. I am ugly but strong and determined and have a large bump over my eyebrows. I have a heavy jaw and a big mouth and thick lips – sensitive nostrils – a snub nose

and straight hair. I am equal in temper and cool in disposition and have a large amount of self control and am naturally secretive to the world. I take a delight in letting people I don't like – people of mean or cruel or sneaking or cowardly disposition – see the worst side of me. I have a large number of acquaintances and some five or six friends – all of which latter body care much for me. Now I have told you all I know about myself.

In a covering letter, Stoker had added that in the course of his public life he had 'felt and thought and suffered much', all of which had led him to 'truly say that from you I have had much pleasure and much consolation'. And he had concluded with the related thought:

How sweet a thing it is for a strong healthy man with a woman's eyes and a child's wishes to feel that he can speak so to a man who can be if he wishes father, and brother and wife to his soul. I don't think you will laugh, Walt Whitman …

So the young Bram Stoker – like Jonathan Harker – was seeking a 'father and brother and wife to his soul', and when finally he met Walt Whitman (during a tour of the USA which he had masterminded for the Lyceum company), the poet said of him 'I think the man Stoker repeats, fulfils, the boy'. The big difference was that by then, Stoker had found another hero – and a far less open-minded one – in the person of Henry Irving. The same Henry Irving who denounced *Salomé* by Stoker's friend and fellow Trinity alumnus Oscar Wilde in front of the Lord Chamberlain, and who was subsequently to be praised in the press for helping to save England from 'the cult of Oscar Wilde'.

The Stoker who defended *Leaves of Grass* seems to have changed quite a bit, since joining the management of the Lyceum Theatre. In the meantime, Bram Stoker had also been reading a fair number of horror stories and *grand guignol* plays, which provided him with just the metaphors he needed.

he folkloric vampire, more often than not a ruddy-faced agricultural labourer from Eastern Europe – complete with bellowing voice, wide-open mouth, three-day growth of beard and serious breath problem – a figure who was just as likely to attack sheep and cows as his own relatives, had been much discussed and debated in the salons of the philosophers and glitterati of eighteenth-century Paris and London. Most of them had concluded that this 'primitive superstition' (subscribed to by *them* not *us*) was really about the spread of contagious diseases, the natural growth of hair and nails after death, and the funerary customs of pre-literate societies: but, in explaining away the series of vampire epidemics which were said to have happened in Eastern Europe and Greece, Voltaire and the Encyclopedists made the vampire visible for the first time among the chattering classes, and launched him (and it was usually him) into the literary bloodstream.

The *literary* vampire – more often than not a fashionably pallid aristocrat, complete with seductive voice, pouting lips, and mean, moody and magnificent personality – was born in prose at the Villa Diodati some seventy-five years before Bram Stoker had his nightmare. His birth was part of the same ghost-story session that had prompted Mary Godwin to write *Frankenstein*. After Mary had told *her* story, Lord Byron began a tale about a blue-blooded aristocrat of an ancient family called Darvell who accompanies a young man on a trip to Turkey and dies in a graveyard there – having promised to return from the dead a month later:

> As he sat [in a Turkish burial ground], evidently becoming more feeble, a stork, with a snake in her beak, perched upon a tombstone near us; and, without devouring her prey, appeared to be steadfastly regarding us. I know not what impelled me to drive it away, but the attempt was useless; she made a few circles in the air, and returned exactly to the same spot. Darvell pointed to it, and smiled – he spoke – I know not whether to himself or to me – but the words were only, 'Tis well!'
>
> 'What is well? What do you mean?'
>
> 'No matter; you must bring me here this evening, and exactly where that bird is now perched. You know the rest of my injunctions'.
>
> He then proceeded to give me several directions as to the manner in which his death might be best concealed. After these were finished, he exclaimed,
>
> 'You perceive that bird?'
>
> 'Certainly'.
>
> 'And the serpent writhing in her beak?'…
>
> He smiled in a ghastly manner, and said faintly, 'It is not yet time!' As he spoke, the stork flew away …

And there the story ended.

But, three years later, in April 1819, the story was resurrected back in London by twenty-three-year-old Dr John Polidori, Byron's ex-physician, who had re-written and expanded it during 'two or three idle mornings' to while away the time in summer 1816 while Byron and Shelley were otherwise engaged. He had done this, without permission, under the title *The Vampyre*, but was not responsible for *publishing* the tale.

In Polidori's version, poetic Darvell turned into villainous Lord Ruthven – a satire on Lord Byron himself as mad, bad and dangerous to know. (Lady Caroline Lamb, one of Byron's more flamboyant ex-girlfriends, had published her novel *Glenarvon* in May 1816, in which she revenged herself on her arro-

Print of George Gordon, Lord Byron, disembarking with his valet after a sail on Lake Geneva: in The Vampyre, *Byron was to turn into the villainous Lord Ruthven.*

gant, if stylish, lover through the satanic character of Clarence de Ruthven, Lord Glenarvon.) So, with his 'dead grey eye' and 'the deadly hue of his face', Polidori's revamped vampire returned from Turkey to bite his way through London society during the season, and the story became an instant best-seller partly because everyone thought it was by Byron himself! The story began:

> It happened that in the midst of the dissipations attendant upon a London winter there appeared at the various parties of the leaders of the ton a noble-man, more remarkable for his singularities than his rank. He gazed upon

the mirth around him, as if he could not participate therein. Apparently, the light laughter of the fair only attracted his attention, that he might by a look quell it, and throw fear into those breasts where thoughtlessness reigned. Those who felt this sensation of awe, could not explain whence it arose: some attributed it to the dead grey eye, which, fixing upon the object's face, did not seem to penetrate ... His peculiarities caused him to be invited to every house ...

And the story ended – not with a snake in a stork's beak, but with the marriage of Lord Ruthven and the narrator's sister, a marriage which ends in tears because the narrator, bound by oath, is unable to tell anyone about Ruthven's guilty secret: 'when they arrived, it was too late. Lord Ruthven had disappeared, and Aubrey's sister had glutted the thirst of a VAMPYRE!'

Some editions even bore the initials 'L.B.' on the title page, though most were anonymous, and Goethe thought it was 'the English poet's finest work'.

In fact, it was entirely written by Polidori, and very loosely based on an original idea by his employer. Polidori had left the manuscript behind in Geneva and thought no more about it. But when an enterprising publisher (the same house as published *Glenarvon*) got hold of and issued *The Vampyre* – complete with a new introduction about the Noble Lord who 'never went to sleep without a pair of pistols and a dagger by his side' – Polidori started petitioning for an author's fee. He did not like the attribution to Byron, and, if the story *was* to be

*P*ortrait by F.G. Gainsford of the handsome, highly-strung Dr John Polidori who wrote the first fully-fledged vampire story in English literature over 'two or three idle mornings' in summer 1816.

published, he understandably wanted some credit for it. Eventually, he was paid £30 in retrospect for his pains.

Even after the question of authorship had been cleared up, publishers of Byron's works were reluctant to let *The Vampyre* slip away: in Paris, there were so many complaints by subscribers when the story was dropped from the second edition of Byron's *Works* ('we did not wish to speculate with the name of the English Lord') that a corrected and revised version of Polidori's tale was reinstated in the third edition in 1820 ('we have decided to give way to the pressure of numerous subscribers by resuscitating *The Vampyre*').

It was ironic, said one literary critic of the day, that it took 'an absurd story, not even by him' finally to establish the reputation of Lord Byron on the continent of Europe. Byron, meanwhile, was furious – 'I have besides a personal dislike to Vampires', he wrote, 'from the little acquaintance I have with them' – and urged the publisher John Murray to issue his *Fragment of a Story* (appended to his poem *Mazeppa*) as quickly as possible, in self-defence. 'Damn the Vampyre – what do I know of Vampyres?'

Polidori was disgraced, and died two years later – at the age of twenty-five – of brain damage, following a carriage accident. Byron, among others, immediately put it around that the doctor had committed suicide.

For the first thirty years of its literary life, from 1820 to round about 1850, the vampire was to be indelibly associated with the public image of Lord Byron. This association tended seriously to limit the possibilities of character development within the *genre*, but it did help to reinforce the malodorous reputation of the British aristocracy on the continent. Charles Robert Maturin began his Gothick novel *Melmoth the Wanderer* with an old Spanish crone screaming 'No English … Mother of God protect us … Avaunt Satan', which would suggest that Byron wannabes wandering around Europe had a similar reputation to today's football hooligans.

The aristocratic vampire had been launched with the finest credentials.

y February 1820, Polidori's *The Vampyre* had been expanded into a two-volume novel – the first full-length vampire novel in literature – with Cyprien Bérard's *Lord Ruthwen ou les Vampires*, published in Paris and dedicated to Lord Byron, which chronicled the adventures of '*Ce Don Juan vampirique*' (or, as a contemporary critic put it '*ce Lovelace des tombeaux*') on a bloody grand tour around Venice, Florence, Naples, Modena, the Tyrol, Poland, Moravia, Athens, Benares and Baghdad.

Each of these stop-overs gave the wicked Milord an opportunity to return from the dead to debauch a blushing bride, before moving on to the next, and the novel finished with the threat 'We could perhaps publish Lord Ruthven's *History of My First Life*, if we are encouraged to do so by some success with this publication'.

Before they had the chance, the romantic and royalist writer Charles Nodier (who had been accused – the word he would have chosen – of the authorship of *Lord Ruthwen ou les Vampires*) retaliated with his three-act

Engraving of Lord Ruthven (right) – complete with kilt, tam o-shanter and breastplate – and his victim Lady Margaret (left), from the published version of J. R. Planché's The Vampire or the Bride of the Isles.

melodrama *Le Vampire* – set in '*une grotte basaltique*' at Staffa in Scotland, with incidental music by Alexandre Piccini and main characters called Lord Rutwen and Sir Aubray.

The new twists to the story (apart from the Scottish location) were that Aubray does not *know* that Rutwen is a vampire although the audience does, which turns the climactic wedding sequence into much more of a cliff-hanger; and an angel of marriage was added, to remind the paying customers of the sanctity of that institution even in the most trying circumstances.

Alexandre Dumas (who was himself later to contribute to the craze with a five-act dramatised version of *Le Vampire*) went to see the play at the Théâtre de la Porte-Saint-Martin – by which time no less than *three* rival productions were running simultaneously in Paris, including a farce called *Les trois vampires ou la clair de la lune*, in which a M. Gobetout (a Byron fanatic) thinks that the lovers of his two daughters and their maid must be vampires because of the way they loiter in the garden, with intent. The one-liner which stopped the show every night was, apparently, 'vampires … they come to us from England … a nice present from them to us I must say'.

By 9 August 1820, an English adaptation of Nodier's *Le Vampire*, by James Robinson Planché, was ready for the stage of the English Opera House (later the Lyceum). Once again, as Planché was to recall, it was set in 'the Basaltic Caverns of Staffa':

> The scene was laid, with the usual recklessness of French dramatists, in Scotland, where the superstition never existed. I vainly endeavoured to induce the manager to let me change it to some place in the East of Europe. He had set his heart on Scotch music and dresses – the latter, by the way, were in stock – laughed to my scruples, assured me that the public would neither know nor care – and in those days they certainly did not – and therefore there was nothing left for me but to do my best with it …

The Vampire or the Bride of the Isles: a romantic melodrama bears a certain family resemblance to Polidori's tale *and* the play which Dumas saw in Paris, but certain embellishments had evidently taken place. Lord Ruthven made his first appearance in a kilt, an outrageous tam o'shanter and a breastplate. Why he should have been dressed in a tartan outfit which in those days was thought to be more suitable for gardeners or estate-workers was never explained. And what the *real* Lord Ruthven thought of all this has not been recorded. His family – at least according to books of folklore – had been associated in some way with witchcraft in the eighteenth century, and the image had evidently stuck.

The prologue now concluded with Ariel, the spirit of the air (in 'white muslin dress, with spangles, sky-blue robe, rings, tiara and silver wand') and Unda, the spirit of the flood (in 'white satin dress, trimmed with shells, with blue satin robe, hair in long ringlets, tiara and wand') performing magical ceremonies as the vampire rises from a tomb, then sinks as the scene closes.

'Phantom, from thy tomb so drear,

At our bidding swift arise;

Let thy vampire-corpse appear

To this sleeping maiden's eyes …'

Thunder.

CHORUS, WITHOUT: Appear! appear! appear!

The vampire rises from the tomb, and springs towards Margaret.

VAM: Margaret!

ARIEL: Foul spirit, retire!

VAM: She is mine!

ARIEL: The hour is not yet come.

UNDA: Down, thou foul spirit; – extermination awaits thee:

Down, I say

Music – The vampire, shuddering, sinks and the scene closes.

This special effect – the first of many in the afterlife of *The Vampire* – represents perhaps the most important contribution of Planché's production to popular culture. For, the vampire disappeared in a puff of smoke through 'a vampire trap consisting of two or more flaps, through which the sprite can disappear almost instantly, where he falls into a blanket fixed to the under surface of the stage'. This trap-door is still known in theatrical circles as 'the vampire trap', and was first invented for *The Vampire or The Bride of the Isles*.

But the special effect did not impress everyone. In 1826, a holidaying German princeling drifted into the English Opera House, searching for something typical of the region. By then, in an attempt to breathe life into dying tissue, the management had combined *The Vampire* with his fellow monster from June 1816 in an horrific double-bill (another first). The princeling later recalled with surprise:

> There was no opera, however. Instead we had terrible melodramas. First *Frankenstein*, where a human being is made by magic, without female help – a manufacture that answers very ill; and then *The Vampire*, after the well-known tale falsely attributed to Lord Byron … The acting was, indeed, admirable throughout, but the pieces so stupid and monstrous that it was impossible to sit out the performance.

He would, presumably, have been better pleased with Planché's follow-up to *The Vampire* which had originally premièred in Leipzig on 28 March 1828. The libretto for this, 'founded on the original French melodrama', by Wilhelm August Wohlbrück, was accompanied by the music of his brother-in-law Heinrich August Marschner.

Planché's version opened to great success at the Lyceum (as by then it was called) in the summer of 1829. Planché remembered:

> I was engaged to write the English libretto and consequently laid the scene of action in Hungary, where the superstition exists to this day, substituted for a Scotch chieftain a Wallachian Boyard, and in many other respects improved upon my earlier version.

And so, in the wake of popular Byronism, several pieces of the vampire mosaic were added to Polidori's *Vampyre* – by a process of product differentiation, almost. These included multiple seductions; a happy ending where the sanctity of marriage is upheld; the villainous aristocrat who debauches peasant girls (rather than travelling companions or *débutantes*); the special effects; and the vampire as 'a Wallachian Boyard' who is at home with a chorus dressed in 'the national dress of the Magyars and the Wallachians'.

The *Vampyre* graph reached its peak in 1846-7, with the serial publication of *Varney, the Vampire or The Feast of Blood* by the Scots penny-a-liner and ex-civil engineer James Malcolm Rymer (also known as Errym and Merry and author of *Ada the Betrayed* among many other works). This marathon penny-dreadful consisting of 868 double-column pages re-told Polidori's twenty-page tale in increasingly lurid detail, over and over again: Sir Francis Varney of Ratford Hall Yorkshire attempts to seduce the innocent heroine; the local villagers realise that Varney is a vampire (in disguise) and organise a mass counter-attack; then there is a wedding scene, where Sir Francis is denounced in the nick of time and chased out of the area. Eventually, in a scene that was lifted straight from the melodramatisation of *Frankenstein*, the vampire – exhausted by his unsuccessful endeavours and disillusioned with an unsympathetic world – leaps into Mount Vesuvius, never to be heard of again. Well, not quite *never* …

Rymer, who wrote 'with a detachment that borders on the camp', managed

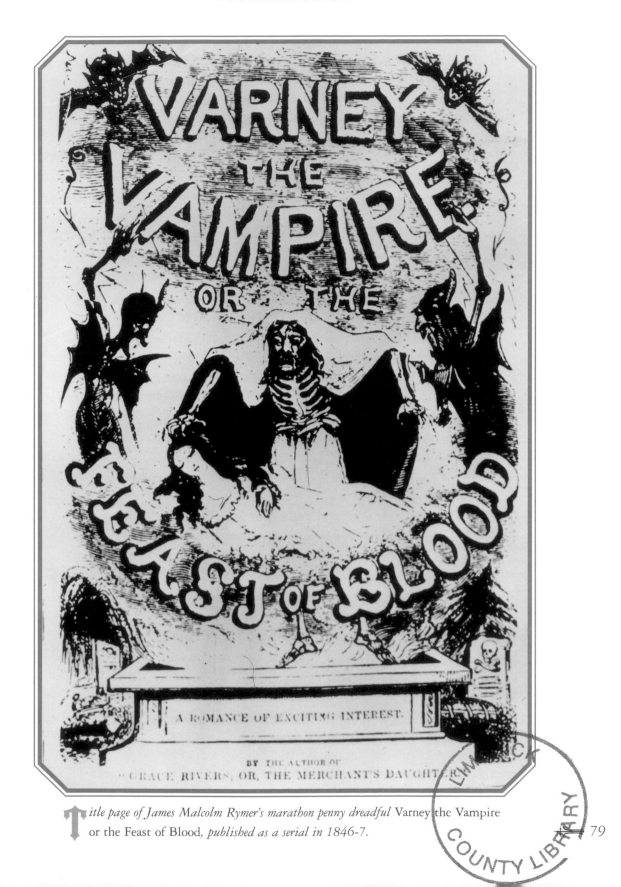

Title page of James Malcolm Rymer's marathon penny dreadful Varney the Vampire
or the Feast of Blood, *published as a serial in 1846-7.*

to invent some new variations on the theme which were to have quite an impact on the development of the *genus vampiricus*.

One sub-plot concerns a Hungarian vampire count; there is a running gag about a double-act of two old salts (Admiral Bell and Able-Seaman Jack Pringle) who provide the obligatory folk wisdom; a whole series of scenes is set in and around country churchyards, crypts, charnel houses and undertakers' parlours – the detail of which was evidently based on close observation of Victorian funerary customs; Sir Francis Varney (unlike Polidori's version and its many derivatives) is an *unpredictable* villain. His vampirism is more of an addiction than a 'hiss the villain'-style characteristic. A long way away from the Byronic aristocrat, who effortlessly circulates among 'the leaders of the *ton*', Sir Francis starts life as a scruffy, shambling, misunderstood Restoration decadent and things get worse for him from then on. The Bannerworth family (his main victims) are embarrassed to be seen near him, even when his addiction to blood has been repressed; and he is 'killed' so often that the interest in his demise eventually becomes a purely technological – how will it be done this time?

You can almost tell from Rymer's prose that he was being paid a penny for every line by his employers Lloyd's printing house. But there's a terrible beauty about it as well:

> … she could not scream – she could not move. 'Help – help! – help!' was all she could say. But, also, that look of terror that sat upon her face, it was dreadful – a look to haunt the memory for a lifetime – a look to obtrude itself upon the happiest moments, and turn them to bitterness.
>
> The figure turns half round, and the light falls upon the face. It is perfectly white – perfectly bloodless. The eyes look like polished tin; the lips are drawn back and the principal feature next to those dreadful eyes is the teeth – the fearful-looking teeth – projecting like those of some wild animal, hideously, glaringly white, and fang-like. It approaches the bed with a strange, gliding movement. It clashes together the long nails that literally appear to hang from the finger ends. No sound comes from its lips. Is she going mad – that young and beautiful girl exposed to so much terror? She has drawn up all her limbs; she cannot even now say help. The power of articulation is gone …

The 'initiation' of the heroine ('her eyes are fascinated [by] the glance of a serpent') is new, as is the folkloric touch of the vampire's protruding fangs 'like those of some wild animal'. Sir Francis seems to combine the traditional vampire of folklore with his Byronic descendent. And the *incongruity* of an Eastern European folk-myth in an English rural setting is stressed throughout the story. Later on, Rymer adds a vigil at midnight by the tomb of a suspected vampiress, the vampire shape-shifting into a wolf, the arrival of a deserted ship and a chase to the vampire's resting-place – all ideas which found their way, half a century later, into *Dracula*. (Bram Stoker, in fact, was born the same year that *Varney the Vampire* leapt to his doom). And the hapless Bannerworths use a methodical scientific approach to coping with the vampire which pre-figures the methods of Professor Van Helsing: Victorian scientific positivism encounters the forces of the unknown; the icons of religion are not quite enough.

T he Byronic vampire was one of the first examples of the concerns of 'high culture' being transmitted – through the new media – into the culture of the increasingly crowded inner cities. And while the Byronic vampire was stalking the variety shows and the comics, various French writers – such as Prosper Mérimée, Théophile Gautier and, later, Charles Baudelaire – more obsessed than their British counterparts with the female of the species, were busy transforming the vampire from melodramatic villain into a more personalised kind of sexy predator.

Gautier's Clarimonde (from *La Morte Amoureuse*, 1836) has 'sea-green eyes and teeth of purest Orient pearl', with which she easily manages to efface even 'the divine portrait of the Madonna' in the mind of a young country priest, and turn him – through his dreams – from man of God into 'a dissolute, supercilious young lord'.

Baudelaire's 'woman with the strawberry mouth' – who 'squirms like a snake upon the coals/kneading her breasts against the iron of the corset' – equally easily seduces the poet, until he awakens to the 'clear reality' of her appearance ('an old leather bottle with sticky sides and full of pus'). But before the awakening, he certainly has a night to remember – 'she sucked the pith from my bones, and, drooping, I turned towards her to give her the kiss of love'.

Although the female of the vampire species made a few tentative appearances during the Byronic phase, she only came into her own during 1860-90, a period of fascination (among male authors) with the exotic, the aesthetic and the decadent. It was also the period of the bourgeois century when, as historian Peter Gay has put it, 'man's fear of women ... became a prominent theme in popular novels and medical treatises', and when it had increasingly become a commonplace to 'deny women native erotic desires' as a way of safeguarding 'man's sexual adequacy'. So if women *did* reveal 'native erotic desires', they tended to be turned into demons or vampires; or tended to be protected from their own desires by 'misplaced chivalry [and] a timid clinging to tradition'. The art critic Walter Pater even saw a hint of the toothsome in the best-known portrait of a woman in Western art, the *Mona Lisa*:

> She is older than the rocks among which she sits; like the vampire, she has
> been dead many times, and learned the secrets of the grave; and has been a
> diver in deep seas, and keeps her fallen day about her ...

Which presumably explained that enigmatic smile.

Perhaps the finest of the *belles dames sans merci* in this period was contained in the dreamy short story *Carmilla* (1872) by Dublin writer Sheridan Le Fanu. This told of the rich and strange lesbian relationship between the Styrian Countess Carmilla Karnstein and the young female narrator – a vampiric relationship which eventually destroys both of them. 'Think me not cruel', says the seductive Countess, 'because I obey the irresistible law of my strength and weakness ... In the rapture of my enormous humiliation, I live in your warm life, and you shall die – die, sweetly die – into mine. I cannot help it ... '

This undoubtedly had an influence on Stoker's *Dracula* – not just thematically, but biographically as well. (*Dracula* was originally to be set in Styria; Lucy and the brides of the Count court their prey in ways which owe much to Le Fanu's listless *femme fatale* – and the supine reaction of their victim 'if I lie still and half close my eyes, I will not really be guilty' – is similar, too.)

Both Le Fanu and Stoker came from a similar Anglo-Irish, Protestant background – the cultural and administrative élite of Dublin society. Abraham Stoker, father of Bram, worked as a third-class clerk in the Chief Secretary's office at Dublin Castle at the same time as William Richard Le Fanu – Sheridan's brother – was a Commissioner of Public Works. Thomas Phillip Le Fanu, son of William Richard, became a first-class clerk in the Chief Secretary's office at the same time that Bram Stoker was working in the next-door Petty Sessions office. Stoker's first published works appeared in the *Dublin Evening Mail*, of which Sheridan Le Fanu had been proprietor and co-editor; and *Carmilla* was first published in a Trinity College magazine, at the same time that Stoker was beginning to produce short supernatural stories as well as acting as Auditor of the T.C.D. Historical Society.

Perhaps, as has been suggested above, it was Bram Stoker's feeling of being strangled by red tape at the gingerbread castle of the viceroy which gave him a peculiar sense of affinity with the victims of Count Dracula.

But by March 1890, when Stoker had his nightmare, he had impetuously moved on from Dublin Castle to the Lyceum Theatre – giving up his chance of a pension, much to the distress of his mother who called him 'manager to a strolling player'.

The same year that he left Dublin (1878), he had also married Florence Balcombe – an 'exquisitely pretty' girl who was his neighbour – and Oscar Wilde's sweetheart, on and off, for the previous three years. At the end of the first year of their marriage, she had given birth to their only child, Noel Thornley Stoker. In the decade of *Dracula*, she would be depicted as a fragile, Pre-Raphaelite beauty in a profile pencil sketch by Edward Burne-Jones, and as a cool, knowing society hostess – reclining on a dead animal, probably a fox – by the young Dublin portraitist Walter Frederick Osborne.

In retrospect, those visual images have been interpreted to mean that she was a cold, remote sort of person who – according to her grand-daughter Ann – was: 'cursed by her great beauty and the need to maintain it … she was very anti-sex. After having my father in her early twenties [she was 20 when she married Bram in Dublin], I think she was quite put off'. If this is true, she may indeed have coloured her husband's – and thus Jonathan Harker's – fantasies about predatory females. But she was also described by one of Stoker's Lyceum colleagues as 'a charming woman and brim full of Irish wit and impulsiveness', which is about as far from a *femme fatale* as you can get. There simply is not enough evidence to be sure, except between the lines of Bram Stoker's published stories – a dangerous source, to say the least.

Anyway, according to the *Whitby Gazette*, 'Mr, Mrs and Master Bram Stoker from London' – that is, Bram, Florence and eleven-year-old Noel – arrived in Whitby on the northeast coast of Yorkshire for their annual summer holidays, around 8 August 1890. They stayed at no.6, Royal Crescent, a house facing the sea set back from the town's West Cliff (proprietor: Mrs Veasy) in a bedroom on the third floor with a sitting room below.

The *Whitby Gazette* – which studiously recorded the comings and goings of out-of-towners, very publicly, on its inside page – repeated the information a week later on 15 August. Also staying at no.6 at the same time were three ladies from Hertford – the Misses Isabel and Marjory Smith, accompanied by their chaperon Miss Stokes – who may well have been the originals for Mina Murray, Lucy Westenra and Mrs Westenra in the novel which Bram Stoker was just beginning to plan.

In fact, Bram Stoker seems to have arrived in Whitby at the end of July and spent at least a week there by himself.

t was at Whitby that Stoker's nightmare began the lengthy process of turning into *Dracula*. His conversations with local fishermen and coastguards, his researches in the Whitby Museum, Subscription Library and Warm Bathing Establishment on the Quay (now Pier Road), and the notes and drawings he made while he sat in the churchyard of the parish church of St Mary – 199 steps known as 'the Church Stairs' above the east side of the harbour – were to become Chapters VI to VIII of the novel which cover the period 24 July to 19 August. Stoker's handwritten and typewritten accounts of his experiences at Whitby have survived, and they provide a unique insight into both his writing methods and the way his imagination worked.

On 30 July, he chatted with three old fishermen on the East Cliff who told him about a whaling ship – the *Esk* – which had recently foundered at sunset: 'Master (Dunbar) would go on – said "Hell or Whitby tonight" and men prayed him to slacken sail. He knocked them down one by one as they came to implore him'. These fishermen also discussed with Stoker the local legends of the bells which could be heard ringing out at sea whenever there was a wreck, and of the ghost of the White Lady, the first abbess St Hilda, who haunted Whitby Abbey – but dismissed them with the words 'these things is all wore out'.

On 11 August, after he had been joined by the family, he sat on the so-called 'suicide's seat' near the edge of the cliff in St Mary's Churchyard and observed – with a few flourishes – that the weather was not exactly suitable for buckets and spades:

Grey day – sun high over Kettleness – all grey – green grey – grey every rock – sand points jutting out all grey – grey clouds tinged with sunburst, grey sea tumbling in over flats. With roar muffled in sea, mist drifting … lost in grey mist – all vastness. Clouds piled up and a 'brool' over the sea – like a presage – dark figures on beach here and there. Men like trees walking – fishing boats, going and coming through mist.

But at least this 'grey day' gave him the opportunity to pass the time with the Coast Guard, one William Petherick, who told Stoker of various wrecks he had seen, including a Russian schooner of 120 tons from the Black Sea which had run into Tate Hill Pier with all sails up on the stormy afternoon of 24 October 1885. 'The Russian vessel was light', he noted. 'Ballasted with silver sand'.

Another grey day, or perhaps a whole series of them, gave Stoker the opportunity to list, with the meticulous detail of a careful administrator, the inscriptions on 'Tombstones. Whitby Churchyard on Cliff (note MM means Master Mariner)' – eighty-seven of them in all. They included, just beyond the path next to the south transept and still *just* readable:

SWALES

In memory of Thomas Swales who died July 5th 1786 aged 91 years
also Ann his wife who died 6th February 1795 aged 100 years.

Our heavy loades and days are past.

We hope our Souls in Heaven will dwell at last.

And, between the southeast walk and the church gates – an inscription which has been fortunately protected from the wind and salt by a dense area of gravestones:

TULLEY

Sacred to the Memory of Samuel Tulley Master Mariner who perished with
all the crew of the *King George* of Whitby on their passage from New York,
January 2nd 1782 aged 33. Also Alice Tulley wife of the above who died
May 2nd 1843 aged 92 years ...

On 13 August, at 6.30 p.m., Bram Stoker made an ink sketch of the view
from the cliff down to Whitby harbour, and along the mouth of the River
Esk. He also visited the Museum and Subscription Library (which by lucky
chance held the extensive book collection of the Literary and Philosophical
Society), where he paid the 'special subscription rate for visitors' and took
notes on a *Glossary of words used in the neighbourhood of Whitby* by F.K. Robinson, a local chemist. Robinson's dictionary began with an essay on the
folklore of the region (including funerary customs), which presumably
fascinated Stoker since the words he proceeded to jot down included
'bad lad = devil ... bier-bank = churchyard path ... fool-talk = nonsense ...
Rowantree = mountain ash (keep off witches) ... wuff = wolf ... yabblins =
possibly ... yeth foist = smell of damp earth'. And 'barguests or boh-ghosts':

> Terrifying apparitions, taking shape human or animal ... Some say barguest
> signifies Castle-spectre (most ancestral buildings having their haunting
> inhabitant) ... According to the popular version, the barguest, whether dog
> or demon, glares with large eyes, 'like burning coals' ... the barguest is a
> harbinger of death to those who happen to hear its shrieks in the night.

He did some further research on the shipwreck of five years earlier which
the Coast Guard had told him about: it transpired that the vessel was called
the *Dmitry* – out of Narva, Russia, with a Captain Säkki at the helm and a
crew of seven hands – that she had been first sighted off Whitby about
2 p.m., in a force 8 gale 'with a cargo of silver sand from the mouth of the
Danube', and that she had been blown into the sands of the harbour – minus
her masts – 'by fine chance avoiding the rocks'.

Stoker pieced this story together from the log of the Coast Guard Station
Detail of wrecks at Whitby (which he noted on a sheet of O.H.M.S. paper), a
back-number of the *Whitby Gazette* (31/10/85), and Mr Petherick's eye-
witness account. He may also have seen Frank Meadow Sutcliffe's photograph
of the *Dmitry* beached on Tate Hill Sands – surrounded by a group of
onlookers and sailors, with her rigging laid out on the beach in front of her.
Certainly – with the opening of his second shop, on the West Cliff, 'for sale of
studies of Fisher Folk and Views' – Sutcliffe was very much in the local news
during the Stoker family holiday.

Because it specialised in historical and topographical books, the Library
also contained – at class-mark 0.1097, which Stoker dutifully recorded – *An
Account of the Principalities of Wallachia and Moldavia: with various political*

observations relating to them by one William Wilkinson, Esq., Late British Consul Resident at Bukarest. Page 19, which was annotated *verbatim*, included an esoteric little piece of information:

> DRACULA in the Wallachian language means Devil. The Wallachians were, at that time, as they are at present, used to give this as a surname to any person who rendered himself conspicuous either by courage, and actions, or cunning.

Bram Stoker carefully copied Wilkinson's description of the campaigns of the Voivode DRACULA across the Danube against the Turks in the late fifteenth century. He also copied details of the road-system and means of transportation in the Carpathian Mountains; the ornate carriages – or *calèches* – used by the now impoverished Boyars (who claimed, apparently, that 'none in Europe can boast of more genuine nobility'); and the traditional costumes worn by the Wallachian and Moldavian locals. He evidently did not realise at the time that this book – with its unprepossessing title and dull text – would eventually become Count Dracula's birth certificate. (It is, in fact, the one and only explicit reference to the historical Dracula, Vlad the Impaler, in all of Stoker's extensive research papers.)

Finally, shortly before he left Whitby, Bram Stoker observed on the evening of 18 August – again, from the churchyard on the cliff-top – that the band on the pier was playing Last Waltzes, while a Salvation Army band was simultaneously playing in a street off the Quay: 'neither hearing each other. We hearing both' (which suggests that – on this occasion at least – he was accompanied by his family). According to the *Whitby Gazette* the repertoire of the band on the pier also included the evergreen *Come Back to Erin* and Tennyson's *Come into the Garden Maud/For the black-bat night has flown.*

ack home at 17, St Leonard's Terrace, Chelsea, Bram Stoker made a few embellishments to his Whitby notes. What if the captain of the schooner were to be buried in St Mary's Churchyard? Stoker must have known that the cemetery had been closed twenty years earlier, but it made for a dramatic detail. On 15 October 1890, he added another fictional detail to the *Dmitry* incident: 'Big dog jumped off … and ran over pier – up kilnyard and church steps and into churchyard. Local dog found ripped open and graves torn up'. And he later toyed with the idea – subsequently rejected – of having the vampire make Lucy fall into a sleep-walking trance by means of a magic brooch which he has left – and which she has found – buried in the sands at Whitby. Rather like the whistle found on the beach in M.R. James's ghost-story *Oh, Whistle and I'll Come to You My Lad* (1904).

*P*hotograph by Frank Meadow Sutcliffe of the Russian schooner Dmitry, *out of Narva,* *which was beached on Whitby's Tate Hill sands one stormy afternoon in October 1885:* *this was the original of the Russian ship* Demeter, *out of Varna, which brings the Count to* *England in Bram Stoker's* Dracula.

Apart from these embellishments, the notes he took on the spot at Whitby were to find their way – almost word for word, regardless of character – into the finished novel. It seems clear that, following his nightmare, he was by summer 1890 *looking for* material (the words he chose from the glossary, his fascination with the churchyard, the folklore, the book on *Wallachia*, the shipwreck incident), which could turn into a horror story, but he was not quite sure as yet how to use it. The story of the *Dmitry* could, for example, have found its way into any one of Stoker's mysteries of the sea – a *genre* he evidently enjoyed writing, perhaps because he so often wrote on holiday – and, in fact, some of his Whitby reminiscences did become a short story – *The Red Stockade – A Story Told by the Old Coastguard*, published in America (though not in Britain) in October 1894.

o, the arrival of Dracula in England arose from a chance remark by a Coast Guard. The vampire's name – Stoker's early notes refer to the villain as the more downbeat 'County Wampyr' – came from a book he happened to discover in the Subscription Library. The setting for Dracula's arrival – and Lucy's seduction – arose from the place he had chosen for his summer holiday in 1890. The shaping device – the nightmare – was already there. The rest seems to have been added as he went along.

Stoker's discussion with the three old fishermen on the East Cliff about local legends, his notes on the gravestone inscriptions and his reading of the *Glossary* were to be turned in the novel into the 'dialect' conversations with the old salt of 'nearly a hundred' Mr Swales: Swales, too, reckons that the legends 'be all wore out', refers to several of the real-life tomb inscriptions and liberally – if somewhat incredibly – peppers his comments with words and phrases such as 'bad lad', 'bier-bank', 'fool-talk', 'yabblins' and of course 'boh-ghosts an' barguests an' bogles an' all anent them'. The schooner *Dmitry* became the *Demeter* with its ballast of silver sand and cargo of 'wooden boxes filled with mould', while Stoker's research sources became the log of *Demeter*, extracts from Mina Murray's journal, and a cutting from the *Dailygraph* for 8 August:

> The wind suddenly shifted to the north-east, and the remnant of the sea-fog melted in the blast; and then, mirabile dictu, between the piers, leaping from wave to wave as it rushed at headlong speed, swept the strange schooner before the blast, with all sail set, and gained the safety of the harbour. The searchlight followed her, and a shudder ran through all who saw her, for lashed to the helm was a corpse ...

The vessel, adds the local correspondent – allowing himself a romantic touch from the *Ancient Mariner* – had seemed out to sea 'as idle as a painted ship up on a painted ocean'.

Bram Stoker's preferred research base – the 'suicide's seat' in the church-yard – became the location for the first sighting of the Count on British soil. For, as Mina Murray writes on 11 August:

> ... there, on our favourite seat, the silver light of the moon struck a half-reclining figure, snowy white [Lucy Westenra]. The coming of the cloud was too quick for me to see much, for shadow shut down on light almost immediately; but it seemed to me as though something dark stood behind the seat where the white figure shone, and bent over it. What it was, whether man or beast, I could not tell ... I called in fright, 'Lucy! Lucy!' and something raised a head, and from where I was I could see a white face and red, gleaming eyes.

From the same vantage-point, Mina also notes that:

The band on the pier is playing a harsh waltz in good time and further
along the quay there is a Salvation Army meeting in a back street. Neither
of the bands hears the other, but up here I hear and see them both.

Her description of the atmosphere of impending gloom surrounding
Whitby, on 6 August, almost exactly matches her creator's:

To-day is a grey day, and the sun as I write is hidden in thick clouds, high
over Kettleness. Everything is grey – except the green grass, which seems
like emerald amongst it: grey earthy rock; grey clouds, tinged with the sunburst at the far edge, hung over the grey sea, into which the sand-points
stretch like grey fingers … The horizon is lost in a grey mist. All is vastness; the clouds are piled up like giant rocks, and there is a 'brool' over the
sea that sounds like some presage of doom. Dark figures are on the beach
here and there, sometimes half shrouded in the mist, and seem 'men like
trees walking'. The fishing boats are racing for home, and rise and dip in the
ground swell as they sweep into the harbour, bending to the scuppers. Here
comes old Mr Swales.

Incidentally, Stoker's reference to 'men like trees walking', written in
August 1890 and published some seven years later, is not – as might be
expected – a reference to Birnam Wood moving to Dunsinane in the last Act
of *Macbeth*, but a quotation from the Gospel of St Mark, 8: 'and he looked up,
and said, I see men as trees, walking'. A rather different kind of miracle.

But Bram Stoker was certainly thinking theatrical thoughts, as he pieced
his story together. Some time after he returned from Whitby, he wrote a
checklist of 'characteristics of County Wampyr' (the name DRACULA had
not yet sunk in) – on Lyceum Theatre notepaper – which makes the creature
seem as if he would have been very much at home at a Lyceum première:

• loves creating evil thoughts in others, and banishing good ones – thus
destroying their will;

• can see in the dark, and can even get through the thickest of London fogs
by instinct;

• is insensible to the beauties of music;

• painters can't make a likeness of him – however hard the artist tries, the
subject always ends up looking like someone else;

• equally, it is impossible to 'Codak' him – the resulting print always makes
him appear 'black or like skeleton corpse';

• and there are no looking glasses in the Count's house – because he has no
reflection and casts no shadow; the lights in his house must therefore be
specially arranged 'to give no shadow'.

In this checklist, the vampire seems to belong to the world of Aubrey
Beardsley's *Yellow Book* – in 1897, *Dracula* was to be published in a fashionable yellow cover – and to have more to do with Oscar Wilde than Eastern

European folklore. Stoker's *fin de siècle* vampire cannot appreciate good music, just *loves* to create evil thoughts for the hell of it, cannot possibly have his portrait painted – or his studio photograph taken – and cannot *stand* looking in a mirror. He seems to bear a close family resemblance to *The Picture of Dorian Gray* (published 1891), with its society aesthete who has a passion for the latest *risqué* French yellow-backed novels.

B y 1897, however, all the characteristics listed by Stoker – except the looking-glass one – would be jettisoned. Perhaps out of deference to his employer's known prejudices – and in the wake of Oscar Wilde's trial of 1895, with subsequent hue and cry – Stoker decided to repress the *aesthetic* side of his demon's personality. As, indeed, he had repressed his own. But, still: 'This man belongs to me … '

To put it mildly, the relationship between Irving and his 'acting manager' was one of superstar and devoted fan. Stoker had first seen the up-and-coming Irving in action – at the Theatre Royal, Dublin – when he was nineteen:

> What I saw, to my amazement and delight, was a patrician figure as real as the person of one's dreams, and endowed with the same poetic grace … A man of quality who stood out from his surroundings on the stage as a being from another social world. A figure full of dash and fine irony, and whose ridicule seemed to bite …

It was Irving, Stoker wrote, who sowed the seeds of his lifelong love for the theatre – he became a volunteer theatre critic for the *Dublin Mail* at almost the same time – and, he further implied, who fed his adolescent fantasies about 'a patrician figure as real as the person of one's dreams'.

They met in Dublin one December Sunday evening some nine years later – round about the time when Stoker was promoted to Inspector of Petty Sessions at the Castle. Stoker honoured Irving's version of *Hamlet* with no less than one preview and two gushing reviews ('My tablets, quick, my tablets!/'Tis meet that I put it down').

Irving enjoyed flattery – rather too much, if his critics are to be believed – and repaid the young civil servant and part-time drama critic with a stirring rendition (in white tie and tails) of Thomas Hood's barn-storming poem of 1829 *The Dream of Eugene Aram*. The result – calculated or not (Irving was actively on the hunt for staff to run his proposed new Lyceum company) – was quite extraordinary:

> 'Oh God!', intoned Irving with eyes as inflexible as Fate,
> 'that horrid, horrid dream
> Besets me now awake
> Again – again with dizzy brain

Book I.
Story in London
England

Chap 1 — The lawyers letters &c
" 2 — (visit) Munich
" 3 — the journey — wolves — the flowers
4 & 4 — Arrival the Castle
5 — Loneliness the Kiss "this man belongs to me"
5 —
" 6 — old Chapel carrying earth. Sortes Virgiliana (notes in letters)
7 — The warehouse of London estate
or servants diary. fly patient. Lunol down

Book II
Tragedy

Chap 1 — The auctioneer Whitby — argument — mesmerism things
" 2 — The Doctor Whitby. the storm. ship arrives
" 3 — the lawyers Clerk Whitby. they walk in sleep. Lucy
" 4 — a flight of time London — mina's wedding
" 5 — a medical impasse a flight of terror (wolf rising) Madville visit asylum
" 6 — The Tragedy A medical impasse Lucy dies
" 7 — The vow Opening vault. The vow

Book III
Discovery

Chap 1 — the suspicion — Harker's diary
" 2 — Enquiries — the dinner. the Vampire
" 3 — D Mina content Dracula Trans for t Transylvania
" 4 — On the track Texan in Transylvania
" 5 — Strange Clues — Count's house searched bloodstained box
" 6 — a test of Sanity (?)
" 7 — Conviction Harker sees the Count

Book IV
Punishment

Chap 1 — A Dinner of Thirteen
" 2 — a Vigilante Committee
" 3 — Disappearance
" 4 — a choice of dwellings
" 5 — Closing the net (removing earth
" 6 — Back to Styria Transylvania
" 7 — a Tourists Tale

Quincey the Texan   (one killed by wolf (wolf?)

28   7 nova
     156 lett

Bram Stoker's working notes for Dracula, discovered in the Rosenbach Library, Philadelphia, some twenty years ago: this contents page includes several incidents which would be dropped from the finished book; note how the word 'Styria' becomes 'Transylvania'.

The human life I take
And my red right hand grows raging hot
Like Cranmer's at the stake'.

At the end of the performance, Irving fell into a chair, exhausted. Bram Stoker was silent for a few seconds, then burst into an uncharacteristic fit of hysterics: 'I was no hysterical subject,' he was to recollect in tranquillity. 'I was no green youth; no weak individual, yielding to a superior emotional force. I was as men go a strong man … I was a very strong man … When, therefore, after his recitation I became hysterical, it was distinctly a surprise to my friends; for myself surprise had no part in my then state of mind …'

Irving, having recovered himself, rushed into his hotel bedroom and came out with a signed photograph: 'My Dear Friend Stoker. God Bless You! God Bless You! Henry Irving. Dublin, December 3 1876'. If it was a ploy, it was a good one. The following year, Stoker spent his summer holiday visiting Irving at the Lyceum Theatre. In November, he wrote 'London in view!' in his diary. And from 1878 to 1905, he became his hero's 'faithful, loyal and devoted servitor' at the Lyceum Theatre. One critic has concluded, bluntly, from all this:

> The Svengali-like Irving was mannered to the point of grotesquerie; his intensely self-obsessed performance, on stage and off, moved his adoring assistant Bram Stoker to create the lordly vampire Dracula.

The reality was probably a little more subtle. Stoker's job as business manager, general administrator and what we would today call 'public relations officer' certainly involved intense devotion to duty. It was a job which began at breakfast time and usually ended late in the evening – with a short break mid-afternoon to go home to St Leonard's Terrace. And, according to Bram Stoker's *Personal Reminiscences of Henry Irving* (1906), just pandering to the actor-manager's gigantic ego was, by the 1890s, a full-time occupation in itself. 'Here Bram, Bram I say', Irving would shout, whenever he was in difficulties, which was often.

Sometimes, after the evening show, Irving, Stoker and the stage-manager Harry Loveday would have a midnight supper in the 'Beefsteak Room' behind the stage, which, with typical flamboyance, Irving had had decked out as a Gothick parlour (complete with its own chef) for the purposes of making contacts. Here, under a John Singer Sargent portrait of actress Ellen Terry as Lady Macbeth, and over a chop or two, they discussed future plans and adapted the texts of plays to the actor's inimitable talents. They would often be joined by artists and public figures of the day – lists of whom, compiled with all the enthusiasm of a confirmed scalphunter, appear in volume one of the *Personal Reminiscences* (to be cut out of the popular edition of 1907).

On one such occasion, on 30 April 1890 – just seven weeks after Stoker's nightmare – they were joined by Hall Caine, the popular novelist from the Isle of Man and a friend of the Stokers, and Arminius (Armin or Herman) Vambery, a distinguished Orientalist from the University of Budapest.

Later on, Vambery was to make a fleeting appearance in *Dracula* as a world authority on vampires (which, sadly, he was not: Stoker probably enjoyed his exotic name). Many of the subjects for discussion did, however, concern the supernatural – the Flying Dutchman, the Demon Lover, Mephistopheles in *Faust*. The trouble was that Irving had already played them all in one form or another. As Hall Caine later recalled, 'the truth is, great actor that Irving was, the dominating element in his personality was for many years a hampering difficulty': the parts just had to be big, with a large slice of ham.

According to Stoker, the roles they discussed tended to be 'too young – too rough …[or] too tall': several reasons why 'the conversation tended towards weird subjects'. And it may be that, at one stage, the character of Dracula was considered as a possible custom-made vehicle for Irving. The vocal tricks of the vampire Count, and some of his physical mannerisms (such as holding women at arm's length and shouting at them) would seem to resemble Irving's performances during his twilight years at the Lyceum. Homage? Or revenge? Perhaps an element of both. To judge by *Reminiscences*, Stoker both worshipped and feared his master.

iven the demands of his job with Irving, Bram Stoker had to do most of his writing – as the letter-heads of his notes for *Dracula* attest – in hotel bedrooms while on tour, in railway trains, and during occasional lulls in the proceedings at the Lyceum. And, of course, during his annual summer holiday.

In August 1893, he visited – alone this time – the Buchan coastline of northeast Scotland, probably to pick up some visual ideas and local colour for a spectacular new Irving production of *Macbeth*. He seldom used his holidays for relaxation, and it was not uncommon for Irving to summon him back to the Strand to sort out some crisis or other before the holidays were over.

Basing himself at Peterhead, Bram Stoker walked south along the coast and stumbled upon the little-known fishing village and harbour of Port Erroll (population 200, of whom most of the men were herring fishers), situated between Peterhead and Aberdeen. As he was later to write:

> When first I saw the place I fell in love with it. Had it been possible, I should have spent my summer there in a house of my own, but the want of any place in which to live forbade such an opportunity. So I stayed in the little hotel, the Kilmarnock Arms. The next year I came again, and the next and the next.

op-hatted Henry Irving, followed – a couple of steps behind – by his 'faithful, loyal and devoted servitor' Bram Stoker, outside the stage door of the Lyceum.

The one small hotel in the village had been built in 1887, and the proprietors had proudly adopted the coat of arms of Lord Kilmarnock – the father of the 15th Earl of Erroll, who had been beheaded for his part in the 1745 Jacobite uprising. In summer 1894, Stoker brought Florence and Noel with him, and wrote in the hotel's *Visitor's Book* (now lost) 'Second visit – delighted with everything and everybody and hope to come again'. Mrs Cruickshank, who delivered the post in Port Erroll in the mid 1890s, recalled in 1976 at the age of ninety-six that Stoker: '… was a big, cheery, handsome Irishman and his wife was the most beautiful woman I ever set eyes on … Mr Stoker told me that he got all his ideas for his stories when he was holidaying in Cruden Bay [as it was known, from 1924 onwards], walking the sands to Whinnyfold [a village three miles south of Port Erroll, along the beach] or scrambling over the rocks north to the Castle and the Buller'.

George Hay, who lived in Whinnyfold when Bram Stoker rented a little whitewashed cottage there in the late 1890s (now called *The Crookit Lum*, because its chimney lists slightly towards the sea) recalled also in 1976 how: 'the tall, bearded Irishman, his cloak flying in the wind, stamped about on the hard sand, prodding it with a heavy stick, waving his arms and shouting at the great rollers as they thundered up the beach, and altogether behaving in such an outlandish way that my second cousin Eliza, who worked at the Kilmarnock Arms, was afraid to walk home across the sands to Whinnyfold, and took the long way round'.

In much the same way as he did with Whitby, Bram Stoker certainly incorporated his observations of Port Erroll into his fiction – notably, into *The Watter's Mou* (published in January 1895); the short story *Crooken Sands* (December 1894); and *The Mystery of the Sea*, written in 1901 from the cottage at Whinnyfold; all of which lamented the gradual commercialisation of the region.

I t is evident from Bram Stoker's working notes for *Dracula* that he was still researching his novel as late as 1896. Among his papers, there are memos dated 1895 and 1896, a press cutting of February 1896 and some notes on the medical symptoms of head wounds and brain damage ('mem: the Professor is speaking of Dracula's brain growth') arising from a conversation with Bram's successful elder brother 'Sir William Thornley Stoker Bart, President of the Royal College of Surgeons Ireland'. William was knighted in 1895, at the same time as Henry Irving (the first-ever theatrical knight) so these notes must post-date the early summer of that year. They relate to the sections of the novel set in a private lunatic asylum recorded 'in phonograph' by Dr Seward (= Siward in *Macbeth*?). The dates and days of the week featured throughout *Dracula* show that it was set in the year 1893, the year Stoker first discovered Cruden Bay.

Although there are no surviving notes in the *Dracula* files which specifically relate to Port Erroll (why should there be, when Whitby had supplied so much material?), it is more than likely that between 1893 and 1897 Bram Stoker spent part of his holidays there planning and drafting his novel.

According to biographer Harry Ludlam, Stoker spent hours passing the time with 'the coastguard in the little lookout on the cliff'. We know from his other novels that he chatted with fisherfolk about local customs – such as the funerary custom of preventing the deceased from passing his or her own home, in case this might subsequently lead to a haunting, by taking a different route to the cemetery. No doubt, he also researched the local dialect. The heroine of *The Watter's Mou*, Maggie McWhirter, is, for example, much given to saying things like 'Oh Willy, Willy! dinna turn frae me this nicht! My heart is sae fu' o' trouble that I am nigh mad! I dinna ken what to dae'. And then there's the castle.

Slains Castle – the 'new' Slains Castle – home of the Hay family Earls of

Erroll, had been built to replace an older one, situated nearby, which had been blown to pieces in 1594 on the order of King James VI (following a disastrous rebellion, involving the 9th Earl supported by King Philip of Spain). Begun in 1597, the granite castle – perched on the edge of a sheer cliff just to the north of the bay – had been extensively altered in 1664 and reworked, in 1836-7, as a huge country house in the style of Scots-baronial-meets-Jacobean-manor, with the turreted tower attached. Dr Johnson had stayed there in 1773, and reckoned that the building in its remote sea-swept setting was 'the noblest Castle'. Boswell had found it 'disagreeable'.

By 1893 when Bram Stoker first came to Port Erroll, the 20th Earl was in residence and the edifice – which seemed to grow out of the sheer granite rocks, even though it was by now a domestic dwelling – must have been quite something.

Today, Slains Castle is a ruin, with just the basic granite structure, part of the tower, a stone spiral staircase and an arched entrance remaining. It looks even more sinister now, as a ruin, than it did a hundred years ago, when, in *The Watter's Mou*, Stoker imagined 'the happy faces of those clustered round the comforting light' in the Castle.

But he may well have had Slains in mind as he thought and wrote about his alter-ego Jonathan Harker's arrival at another Castle perched on a rock in the land beyond the forest:

> [I was] in the courtyard of a vast ruined castle, from whose tall black windows came no ray of light, and whose broken battlements showed a jagged line against the moonlit sky … In the gloom the courtyard looked of considerable size, and as several dark ways led from it under great round arches, it perhaps seemed bigger than it really is … I stood close to a great door, old and studded with large iron nails, and set in a projecting doorway of massive stone. I could see even in the dim light that the stone was massively carved, but that the carving had been much worn by time and weather … At the end of [the passageway, the Count] threw open a heavy door, and I rejoiced to see within a well-lit room in which a table was spread for supper, and on whose mighty hearth a great fire of logs, freshly replenished, flamed and flared.

Harker's first thought is 'was this a customary incident in the life of a solicitor's clerk … ?', but he is soon reassured that the interior of the castle is more welcoming than its vast, remote silhouette. Maybe the carving over the arched door *in fact* said 'Built 1664 by Gilbert XI Earl of Erroll, Chief Constable of Scotland, and rebuilt 1836 and 1837 in the reign of William IV by William George XVII Earl of Erroll, Great Constable and Knight Marischal of Scotland', as it did when Bram Stoker first clambered over the rocks and saw the arched door of Slains Castle. Local legend in Cruden Bay still has it

*S*lains Castle, perched on the cliffs north of Cruden Bay on the Buchan coastline of *northeast Scotland, which Bram Stoker first visited in 1893 – the year in which the* novel Dracula *is set.*

that Sir Henry Irving's acting manager was invited into the Castle, by the Earl and Countess of Erroll, and that he, too, rejoiced to see that a table was spread for supper and the great fire was blazing.

It was, however, back in Bloomsbury, in the circular reading room of the British Museum, that Bram Stoker found much of the detailed reference material which would flesh out his holiday reading. And this material concerned not Whitby or Port Erroll, but Transylvania.

On the very first page of *Dracula*, he wrote:

> … having had some time at my disposal when in London, I had visited the British Museum, and made search among the books and maps in the library regarding Transylvania; it had struck me that some foreknowledge of the country could hardly fail to have some importance …

Originally, he had intended to set his novel in Styria – part of Austria and the location of *Carmilla* – but reading fashionably romantic travellers' tales and collections of folklore about eastern Europe, written by retired British officials (such as William Wilkinson, late consul of Bukarest) persuaded him to change his mind and push the location further east. Among the books he read at this time was *The Land Beyond the Forest* by Emily Gerard, the wife of a serving officer in the Austro-Hungarian cavalry, who argued that 'Transylvania might well be termed the land of superstition': 'For', she went on, 'nowhere else does this curious crooked plant of delusion flourish as persistently and in such bewildering variety. It would almost seem as though the whole species of demons, pixies, witches, and hobgoblins, driven from the rest of Europe by the wand of Science, had taken refuge within this mountain rampart ... '

She has much to say, too, about the diabolical *Scholomance*, where occult practices may be learned; and about 'the vampire, or *nosferatu*, in whom every Roumenian peasant believes as firmly as he does in heaven and hell'. In general, her theme is the relationship between folk tales (or superstitions, as she calls them) and the daily routines of rural life – the changing seasons of the earth, the fear of the wolf, old-style funerary customs, the purifying power of garlic.

'I read', notes Jonathan Harker on 3 May, 'that every known superstition in the world is gathered into the horseshoe of the Carpathians, as if it were the centre of some sort of imaginative whirlpool ...'

Another book, *Transylvania: its products and its people* by Charles Boner provided Stoker with much detail on the history and geography of the Carpathian Mountains (the town of Bistritz, Borgo's Prund or the Borgo Pass, the state of the roads and so on) and had excellent pull-out maps:

> To the east of Bistritz lies Borgó Prund ... here is the so-called 'Mittel Land', a ridge of low hills rising in the vale between the higher mountains. Even now their bold forms and gentle slopes were most attractive; and in summer, when the woods on the upland are in full leaf, and the pastures green ... the scene must be most lovely.

'There was everywhere a bewildering mass of fruit blossom', notes Jonathan Harker on St George's Eve, 'and as we drove by I could see the green grass under the trees spangled with fallen petals. In and out amongst these green hills of what they call here the "Mittel Land" ran the road ... the driver was evidently bent on losing no time in reaching Borgo Prund. I was told that this road is in summertime excellent ... '

In yet another, *Round About the Carpathians*, Andrew Crosse, a 'fellow of the Chemical Society' describes in hearty style how he travelled round the wild Carpathians – armed only with a bowie knife, a revolver and a double-barrelled shotgun – and managed to bump into an old school friend from Westminster in the process. Some of Harker's nicer phrases (such as 'the vast Carpathian horseshoe') came from here, as did the recipe for *paprika handl*:

> In all parts of the country where travellers are possible, the invariable reply to a demand for something to eat is the query, 'would the gentleman like

paprika handl?' and he had better like it, for his chances are small of getting anything else. While I was seeing after my horse, the woman of the inn caught a miserable chicken, which I am sure could have had nothing to regret in this life; and in a marvellously short time the bird was stewed in red pepper, and called paprika handl.

'I had for dinner', records Jonathan Harker, 'or rather supper, a chicken done up some way with red pepper, which was very good but thirsty (*Mem*, get recipe for Mina). I asked the waiter, and he said it was called *paprika handl*, and that, as a national dish, I should be able to get it anywhere along the Carpathians'.

On the track of the Crescent: *Erratic notes from the Piraeus to Pesth* by Major E.C. Johnson – who had served on the Nepalese frontier and in Ireland as well (to judge by his many comparisons between Wallachian peasants and 'our friend Paddy') told Stoker of the effects of the aforementioned *paprika* ('my throat next morning was a "caution" … '); gave him some of the vocabulary with which to describe the castle ('its frowning battlements and grim old towers'); and some excellent local detail:

> A large cross, with a coarsely carved figure of our Saviour, was a prominent object by the roadside, and to it all the Wallachs paid the greatest reverence … In front of us, as far as the eye could reach, was an interminable stretch of forest, right up to the base of the mountain range, brilliant in numberless shades of green, blue, and brown, and melting into a dusky purple as it became more stunted, and was lost in the haze surrounding the rocky crags. These towered range above range till they were crowned by the mighty 'Isten-Szék' (God's Seat), the abode of eternal snow.

Bram Stoker noted 'many crosses by roadside' and 'torture tower-narrow windows', and Jonathan Harker wrote:

> Right and left of us [the mountains] towered, with the afternoon sun falling full upon them and bringing out all the glorious colours of this beautiful range, deep blue and purple in the shadows of the peaks, green and brown where grass and rock mingled … One of my companions touched my arm as we swept round the face of a hill and opened up the lofty, snow-covered peak of a mountain, which seemed, as we wound on our serpentine way, to be right before us:- 'Look! Isten Szék – God's seat!' – and he crossed himself reverently … By the roadside were many crosses, and as we swept by, my companions all crossed themselves.

The Book of Were-Wolves by the Rev. Sabine Baring-Gould – the Rector of a remote Dartmoor parish who wrote the hymn 'Onward Christian Soldiers' as well as over a hundred books about topography and folklore – was full of fact and fiction about the behaviour of wolves and were-wolves (the ones who are hairy on the *inside*).

And these animals were to play an important part in *Dracula* – from the wolves of the Carpathians with their 'wild howling', to the immense dog which leaps ashore from the *Demeter* at Whitby, to the Norwegian grey wolf named Bersicker in London Zoo.

'Listen to them – the children of the night. What music they make!' says the Count.

Bram Stoker's music of the wolves came from Baring-Gould's chapter on 'folk-lore relating to were-wolves'.

So, putting Stoker's research notes in the British Museum side by side with his published text, it seems clear that he was writing the 'Carpathians' section of the novel – Jonathan Harker's uninterrupted *Journal* from 3 May to 30 June, Chapters I-IV, the best-known section of *Dracula* – at exactly the same time as he was reading his sources.

Phrases and thoughts from his reading-matter which he did not bother to copy down were nevertheless transposed – virtually unaltered – into the *Journal*. And the attitudes contained in the travel books certainly chimed with Stoker's own: gypsies and colourful locals are to be distrusted on principle; they touchingly tug at their forelocks whenever a member of the nobility rides by; they look handsome or pretty from a distance, but not 'when you get near them'; their 'picturesque attire' is unusual but 'very clumsy' by Western standards; the perceptions of a British Colonial official are much more reliable than those of people who 'on the stage ... would be set down at once as some old Oriental band of brigands': anything emanating from the East is probably against the British interest. And so on.

As Stoker doubtless realized, such books were fashionable in the 1890s precisely *because* the rural East of Europe was 'beyond the wand of science', and thus an exotic and attractive antidote to the Victorian inner city.

espite the resemblances between novel and sources – in *Dracula*, the local colour serves a different purpose. It is there to provide a suitable setting for a vampire mystery, and belongs to a hallowed tradition in vampire *literature* which goes back to the 1820s. The opening section of the novel lacks the immediacy of the Whitby section which follows it, but more than makes up for this in atmosphere and detail. The detail came from the travel books and from Baedeker's *Southern Germany and Austria (including Hungary and Transylvania)*: hotels, train timetables, town guides, places of interest. The atmosphere was of a Transylvania of the mind, a place where wolves howl, villagers cross themselves in the foothills of the castle, garlic flowers hang from doors, and the dark forest is full of surprises.

In truth, Bram Stoker's Transylvania is more like the Black Forest – or Brothers Grimm Land – than the real thing, but that is not the point.

Take his account of Vlad Dracula, Vlad IV who was also called 'Tepes' or 'the Impaler' because of the nasty things he did (with blunted wooden poles – which hurt more) to rival Wallachian boyars and Turkish prisoners. Vlad was *voivode* of Wallachia in 1448, from 1456 to 1462 and in 1476. Stoker had read a bit about him in Wilkinson's *Wallachia and Moldavia* (and his notes on the book suggest that he had confused Vlad senior with his second son Vlad the Impaler). He probably looked at a pamphlet printed in 1491 in Bamberg, which featured a woodcut portrait of Vlad on the cover, and which the British Museum had acquired earlier in the nineteenth century. I say 'looked at' because apart from the woodcut and the cover-sheet, the printing (in old German) would have been extremely difficult for him to decipher.

Much has been made of Bram Stoker and Vlad Dracula and, today, an entire tourist industry in Romania is based on the association. And yet, Stoker's Dracula is a Count who has a home in Transylvania and a castle near the Borgo Pass. Vlad was a *voivode* or prince, his home was in Wallachia and his castle in Poenari near Curtea des Arges, nowhere near the Transylvania-Bukovina border.

Basically, Bram Stoker needed a Gothick villain, and they tended to be 'Counts'. They tended, too, to be members of a shabby genteel aristocracy and for some reason often Hungarian as well. He needed a powerful name and with *Dracula* he certainly got one (even if 'Dracula' should really have been pre-fixed with another proper name: Vlad Dracula means 'Vlad, son of the dragon' or 'son of the devil'). He needed a fairytale setting, and the set of travel books about a land of 'witches and hobgoblins' delivered the goods. He needed a genealogy for his vampire Count which went back as far as Attila the Hun and read in one of his sources that the 'Szekelys' claimed kinship with Attila – so Count Dracula became a proud member of the race. He needed a physical description of Vlad, and the woodcut on the front of the British Museum pamphlet was as good as: aquiline face, thin nose, arched nostrils; massive eyebrows, heavy moustache; a general effect of extraordinary pallor. A military commander rather than a lounge-lizard.

Bram Stoker's use of the historical character Vlad Tepes was like his use of all his research materials on the land beyond the forest: a Transylvania of the mind, where a fifteenth-century princeling turned into a vampire. While he was preparing *Dracula*, Stoker never went further east than Whitby.

Since his 'Carpathian' notes are undated, we cannot know for sure whether

Woodcut of Vlad Dracula, voivode of Wallachia in the mid-fifteenth century, in a pamphlet printed in 1491 in Bamberg: this pamphlet was in the British Museum when Bram Stoker researched there.

he wrote them before or during the Cruden Bay period. He was tinkering with the order of events, in the 'Carpathian' section of the novel, until at least 1892. The likeliest scenario is that, following his nightmare, he wrote up the 'Whitby' section first, then parts of the 'Carpathian' section – and prepared the 'Dr Seward' and 'London' sections during the years he was visiting Cruden Bay. We know that he did not write the novel in sequence and that he left gaps when he felt a section required further research.

For, in the story, after Count Dracula has arrived in England aboard the *Demeter*, and moved from Whitby in the north to Carfax and London in the south, his contagion begins to spread. Lucy Westenra, friend of the heroine Mina Harker (née Murray), is bitten, dies and rises again from her 'lordly death-house where the air is fresh' in Highgate Cemetery, to terrorise small children on nearby Hampstead Heath. She was beautiful in life, we are told, but has a more terrible beauty about her – the beauty of the Medusa – in death.

When preparing this latter part of his novel, Bram Stoker was inspired by a real-life story he had heard about the Pre-Raphaelite poet Dante Gabriel Rossetti. Rossetti, whom Stoker knew – through the Lyceum, and as a sometime neighbour when he lived at 27 Cheyne Walk, Chelsea – and who was in fact a nephew of Dr John Polidori, had buried a little book of love poems in the coffin of his late wife Elizabeth Siddal, in the Rossetti family tomb at Highgate Cemetery. Seven-and-a-half years later, Dante Gabriel Rossetti changed his mind and decided he wanted to *publish* the poems after all, so he got Home Office permission to have the body exhumed.

One night, a fire was built by the family graveside in Highgate, the coffin was raised – and opened – and Rossetti extricated the book from the red-golden hair in which he had tied it. Elizabeth Eleanor Siddal was described as perfectly preserved, and still beautiful with a kind of spectral halo about her, on coming to light – for just a moment or two, that is. 'When the book was lifted', wrote the novelist Hall Caine in his *Recollections of Dante Gabriel Rossetti* (1882), 'there came away some of the beautiful golden hair in which

Rossetti had entwined it'. It has to be said that this spectral halo was, for Rossetti as for other romantic poets of late Victorian times, often a substitute for taking their wives or girlfriends seriously as women in *this* life.

Stoker perhaps heard the story from Hall Caine, or perhaps from Rossetti himself. Whatever the source, in his hands it turned into something completely different – a way of disposing of Lucy Westenra, after she had died and turned into a sexy, full-blooded vampire. Lucy has become a creature of erotic desire, and she must be put back in her box.

Dr John Seward writes on 27 September:

> She was, if possible, more radiantly beautiful than ever; and I could not believe that she was dead. The lips were red, nay redder than before; and on the cheeks was a delicate bloom ... 'Are you convinced now?' said the Professor ... and in a way that made me shudder, pulled back the dead lips and showed the white teeth. 'See', he went on, 'see, they are even sharper than before. With this and this' – and he touched one of the canine teeth and that below it – 'the little children can be bitten' ...

And the following night, Dr Seward continues:

> Another [the Hon. Arthur Holmwood, Lord Godalming, who was in love with Lucy] took the stake and the hammer, and when once his mind was set on action his hands never trembled nor even quivered. Van Helsing opened his missal and began to read ... Arthur placed the point over the heart, and as I looked I could see its dint in the white flesh. Then he struck with all his might. The Thing in the coffin writhed; and a hideous, blood-curdling screech came from the opened red lips ... But Arthur never faltered. ... There in the coffin lay no longer the foul Thing that we had so dreaded and grown to hate ... but Lucy as we had seen her in her life, with her face of unequalled sweetness and purity.

Although Stoker evidently intended his crusading company of 'good brave men', led by Lord Arthur, to be heroes, today they seem more like villains – the destroyers of Lucy's sexual desires.

Part of the power of the cemetery scene lies in the detail. For example, the moment when Professor Van Helsing touches 'one of the canine teeth and that below it', shows that Stoker had thought about what vampires actually *did* when they sank their teeth into their victims – something which had confused most authors of vampire stories.

In horror literature – and the countless films based on it – the vampire tends to attack his or her victims with upper canine teeth, and leaves two telltale marks in the neck through which the vampire drinks. But if he or she did that, the vampire would probably have got his upper set stuck in wound-holes – and, following withdrawal of the teeth, would have left two puncture marks very wide apart. However, in folklore – and in Bram Stoker's *Dracula* –

the vampire uses the *upper and lower* canines on one side of the mouth – to tear at the victim, like a rodent or a wolf – catching a fold of skin in between. Hence two puncture marks which are close together – like those in Lucy's neck in Whitby, and in her victims' necks on Hampstead Heath. Here, the vampire does not use the incisors – the teeth which slice – but the canines – the teeth which tear. The Byronic vampire may have belonged to the upper set, but that was no excuse for getting his dentistry wrong!

Having turned all his research notes and drafts into a novel – which itself takes the form of a series of letters, diary and journal entries, press cuttings etc., matching the novel's process of creation and describing the bizarre events from the points of view of all the main characters except the Count himself – Bram Stoker decided at the very last minute to change its title from *The Undead* or *The Dead Undead* to *Dracula*. Confusingly, however, Stoker's contract with the publishers Archibald Constable and Co – which was signed on 20 May 1897, long after the book had been typeset – still refers to the novel as *The Undead*. At least *The Undead* was better than *Count Wampyr*. But *Dracula* was far, far more effective than both.

Stoker seems to have tinkered with his typewritten text right up to the last minute. It is cut into pieces and glued together in what was to become the final sequence of events. The opening chapter of the novel, which described in some detail Jonathan Harker's stop-over in Munich on the way to Transylvania, was excised from the printer's copy. According to Florence Stoker, this was done because of 'the length of the book', but it may also have had something to do with its resemblance to Le Fanu's *Carmilla*. The pagination of the typewritten text shows that Bram Stoker may have excised a lot more from the opening: presumably, the exchange of solicitors' letters setting up Dracula's house purchase in England which appears in the notes of 1890-3. In April 1914 (two years after Bram's death), the Munich chapter was published by Florence, in a different form, as the short story *Dracula's Guest*.

Also, the American character Quincey Morris was originally to have been bitten by a werewolf, on his visit to the Carpathian Mountains, but Stoker changed his mind. And, according to a Californian antiquarian bookseller's prospectus announcing the discovery of the original typescript printer's copy of *Dracula* in 1984, the ending of the book was also radically changed. Originally, it was to have been even more apocalyptic, with the complete destruction of Castle Dracula in a volcanic eruption.

'The castle of Dracula now stood out against the red sun', writes Mina Harker on 6 November in the published version, 'and every stone of its broken battlements was articulated against the light of the setting sun'. Stoker's typescript continued:

> As we looked there came a terrible convulsion of the earth so that we seemed to rock to and fro and fell to our knees. At the same moment, with a roar that seemed to shake the very heavens, the whole castle and the rock and even the hill on which it stood seemed to rise into the air and scatter in fragments while a mighty cloud of black and yellow smoke, volume on volume, in rolling grandeur, was shot upwards with inconceivable rapidity. Then there was a stillness in nature as the echoes of that thunderous report seemed to come as with the hollow boom of a thunder-clap – the long rever-berating roll which seems as though the floors of heaven shook. Then, down in a mighty ruin falling whence they rose came the fragments that had been tossed skyward in the cataclysm …

With the deletion of this passage – and of Quincey Morris's wound – Stoker seems to have been making any future sequel to *Dracula* much more difficult for himself. Stoker was not, it seems, tempted by the prospect. Once was enough. Or perhaps he deleted the 'volcano' passage simply because it was so badly written.

Also at the last minute, Bram Stoker added his address to the *Preface* – '18 St Leonard's Terrace, Chelsea, London SW' where he had recently moved from next door at no. 17 (though this address was never printed), and added the dedication 'to my dear friend Hommy-Beg'. Hommy-Beg was a Manx-Gaelic term of endearment meaning 'little Tommy', and it was used by the grand-mother of Thomas Henry Hall Caine (actually 'an Thommy beag') of her nov-elist grandson.

Hall Caine had, as we have seen, taken part in the Beefsteak Room discus-sions about parts for Henry Irving, had written about Rossetti and Elizabeth Siddal, and was a friend of the Stokers. He may even – it has been speculated – have helped Stoker in the drafting of the novel, although the manuscript does not seem to show any evidence of this. The only other handwriting on the setting copy is of a surgeon, maybe Sir William Thornley Stoker – who offered advice about blood transfusions and post-mortems.

*D*racula was published in June 1897, price 6 shillings, in a print-run of 3000 copies. Three years later, in 1901, it was reissued in a slightly abridged form as a sixpenny yellow-covered paperback – with the only illustration Stoker ever had the chance to approve himself on the jacket. This shows a white-haired military commander in a bat-like cloak and over-sized bare feet, shinning down the stone walls of Castle Dracula, while a moustached Jonathan Harker observes in horror from a barred upper window. Bram Stoker's widowed mother Charlotte wrote from Ireland immediately after the first publication:

> My dear it is splendid, a thousand miles beyond anything you have written before, and I feel certain will place you very high in the writers of the day … No book since Mrs Shelley's *Frankenstein* or indeed any other at all has come near yours in originality or terror – Poe is nowhere. I have read much but I have never met a book like it at all. In its terrible excitement it should make a widespread reputation and much money for you.

The published reviews were less convinced: *The Athenæum*, for instance, which had in the past panned both *The Watter's Mou* and *The Shoulder of Shasta* (the romantic tale of a mountain man called Grizzly Dick, set around Mount Shasta in northern California) for their lack of credible characters and general staginess, reckoned that *Dracula* was 'wanting in the constructive art as well as in the higher literary sense'. Others were more kind after a fashion ('the very weirdest of weird tales' – *Punch*; 'we read nearly the whole with rapt attention' – *The Bookman*; '*Dracula* is … appalling in its gloomy fascination' – *Daily Mail*).

But the critical response was a long way away from the 'widespread reputation' which Charlotte Stoker had predicted. Most reviewers found the book distasteful, but not nearly as distasteful as the works of Oscar Wilde, the plays of Henrik Ibsen and the illustrations of Aubrey Beardsley.

As to the question of money, although *Dracula* went through eight English editions in Stoker's lifetime, he never made much from it.

In one thing, however, Charlotte Stoker was absolutely right: it *was* a thousand miles beyond anything her son had ever written; or indeed was to write. He cobbled together seven more novels, and three volumes of non-fiction, but nothing he did rose above the mediocre. As a critic has written, 'When such a man, just once, is thoroughly afraid, the charade stops and what you get is *Dracula*'.

A hundred years later, the critical context has changed beyond all recognition: successive waves of Freudian, Marxist, Feminist and Postmodernist critics have all had a go at Dracula – especially in the last twenty years – and it is more discussed now that ever it was in Bram Stoker's lifetime. Freudians have interpreted the text as a parable of repressed sexual desires and the dilution of the sexual drive. Maurice Richardson called it: ' … a kind of incestuous, necrophilous, oral-anal-sadistic all-in wrestling match. And this is what gives the story its force'.

Others have related it to the Oedipus Complex – Dracula as big daddy – to a defence of traditional family values against the discontents of modern civilisation, and to a yearning to break every taboo you can think of.

One of the reasons why *Dracula* has remained so popular with adolescents, it has been argued, is that it is about sex from the neck up. 'Sex', as literary scholar James Twitchell has written, 'without genitalia, sex without confusion, sex without responsibility, sex without guilt, sex without love – better yet, sex without mention'.

Marxist critics have seen *Dracula* as an allegory of colonialism (the East tries to get its own back on the West), or the Victorians harnessing the forces of nature against the forces of supernature, and – most plausibly – as a cosmic racial conflict between representatives of modern Anglo-Saxon stock and the representative of the 1400-year-old line of Attila the Hun.

Feminist views have ranged from the dismissive ('a narrative destined to become the twentieth century's basic commonplace book of the anti-feminine obsession' – Bram Dijkstra; 'the women are transformed into ... great foul parasites ... [who] begin to learn sex in dying' – Andrea Dworkin) to the intrigued (the thesis that the book is about the *empowerment* of the female). Certainly, with the rise of gender politics, *Dracula* has become – if one may put it this way – a seminal text, especially on American campuses.

Bram Stoker himself would have been amazed at all this analysis. He would have considered the subjects of sex and sexuality as among the great unmentionables. By September 1908, when he published an article on *The Censorship of Fiction*, he was convinced that:

> ... it is through the corruption of individuals that the harm is done. A close analysis will show that the only emotions which in the long run harm are those arising from sex impulses, and when we have realized this we have put a finger on the actual point of danger ... That restraint in some form is necessary is shown by the history of the last few years with regard to works of fiction ... We should at least try to prevent for the future such filthy and dangerous output.

His novel *Lady Athlyne*, about the obsession of American girl Joy Ogilvie for the heroic British Earl of Athlyne, was published in the same year as *The Censorship of Fiction*, and it contains his most considered statement on what he called 'the problem of sex' – a 'problem' which had surfaced with a vengeance in his nightmare of 1890. In *Lady Athlyne*, he summarises a recently published study of *Sex and Character* by Otto Weininger:

> All men and all women, according to him, have in themselves the cells of both sexes; and the accredited masculinity or femininity of the individual is determined by the multiplication and development of those cells. Thus the ideal man is entirely or almost entirely masculine, and the ideal woman is entirely or almost entirely feminine. Each individual must have a preponderance, be it ever so little, of the cells of its own sex; and the attraction of each individual to the other sex depends upon its place in the scale between the highest and the lowest grade of sex. The most masculine man draws the

most feminine woman, and vice versa; and so down the scale till close to the border line is the great mass of persons who, having only development of a few of the qualities of sex, are easily satisfied to mate with any one …

Stoker thought of himself as outwardly 'almost entirely masculine' ('accredited' as such) but inwardly more 'feminine' (in Weininger's terms, sentimental with a tendency to dependence). He had been drawn to Florence Balcombe, regarded by many as a 'most feminine woman'. He had anxieties about his own masculinity, and some observers were surprised at the marriage.

Dracula cut through these confusions by setting a group of 'ideal men' the project of reminding 'ideal women' of their essential femininity. In real life, Stoker found the answer to these confusions in the latest theory of 'the cells'.

He would not have been amused by more recent commentaries. The complete absence of humour from his books was often noted by contemporary critics, and of the extant photographs of Bram Stoker, not one of them shows him even trying to smile. If the character of Count Dracula himself is anything to go by, we may assume Stoker believed that too much indulgence leads to hairy palms, a pale complexion and very bloodshot eyes. It is likely, from the evidence, that he saw the book as an adventure story (a form of 1890s techno-fiction, involving traveller's typewriters, phonographs and blood-transfusions) about a gang of fine upstanding chaps who defend their women-folk, and do not care much for Eastern Europeans who want to ensnare Brits in their evil empire.

But that does not *begin* to explain why the story has remained so popular…

The one person Bram Stoker *did* want to impress, was his employer Henry Irving. And he had his chance when a reading of the novel was staged at the Lyceum Theatre to protect theatrical copyright, at 10 o'clock in the morning of 18 May 1897 – just before the novel reached the bookshops. This lasted nearly five hours, consisted of five multi-scene Acts (forty-seven scenes in all, with twenty-three changes of scene), had two special programmes printed, and featured a Mr Jones as Dracula and Ellen Terry's daughter Edith as Mina Harker. Posters were put outside the theatre just half an hour before the show, and the admission was an exorbitant one guinea: evidently, this was a show to which the public was *not* expected to come.

The title-page of the programme made no mention of Bram Stoker as the author – 'Dracula or The Un-Dead. First Time' – but the back-page, a reprint of the usual Lyceum information, asked of the public 'should there by any cause of complaint, to refer at once to the Acting Manager'. Since the audience consisted, according to Harry Ludlam, entirely of friends of the cast –

and of Bram Stoker – members of the Lyceum staff and cleaners, and the Stokers' cook Maria Mitchell, there were not likely to be any complaints. Except that Sir Henry Irving ('Sole Lessee and Manager') was there as well.

After the semi-dramatised reading, Bram Stoker asked Irving what he thought of it. 'Dreadful!' was the reply, and it was uttered in a very loud voice so that everyone could hear. Presumably this was intended as a joke – the reading most likely *was* dreadful – but one wonders if Stoker took it as one.

That the copyright needed protecting was amply shown when in spring 1922 Bram's sixty-four-year-old widow Florence – who by then lived in William Street, Knightsbridge, and was struggling to make ends meet – tried to extract some form of payment from the German company Prana Film for the first film version of *Dracula* called *Nosferatu – eine symphonie des grauens*, directed by the young Friedrich Wilhelm Murnau. They had made their adaptation of the book – with a few changes of name, but without asking anyone's permission. (This was not, in fact, the first *Dracula* film: there had been a version made in Hungary in 1920; but this film (now lost) would appear to have been about Prince Vlad rather than the Count himself.) Prana proceeded to go into liquidation, so three years later Florence decided that the most she could hope for was the removal of the film from circulation. This she succeeded in achieving and a German court ruled that all positive and negative copies of the film *Nosferatu* be destroyed. But then, a print surfaced in London and ... so on: a tiresome business, which dragged on until April 1929.

It is clear from Florence Stoker's persistence that she was aware of the commercial value of *Dracula* – alone among her late husband's works – and that, once the story had entered the public bloodstream, there was no stopping its circulation. The transformation of Bram Stoker's military commander into a red-eyed lounge lizard in evening dress had begun. No longer a repulsive creature of folklore, he was to become – through successive stage and screen adaptations – utterly irresistible to all the women characters (and, it was doubtless hoped, the paying customers as well). When the first Hollywood version of *Dracula* opened at the Roxy Theatre in New York, on Valentine's Day 1931, it was billed as 'good to the last gasp!'.

ram Stoker died on 20 April 1912, at the age of sixty-four, shortly after completing yet another article about Henry Irving. Stoker had been the one who closed the old man's eyelids when he died in 1905, and as a result of the shock suffered a minor stroke which damaged *his* sight for the rest of his life. 'And now', he wrote, 'this *silence* ... !' He might also have added, this loss of a regular income.

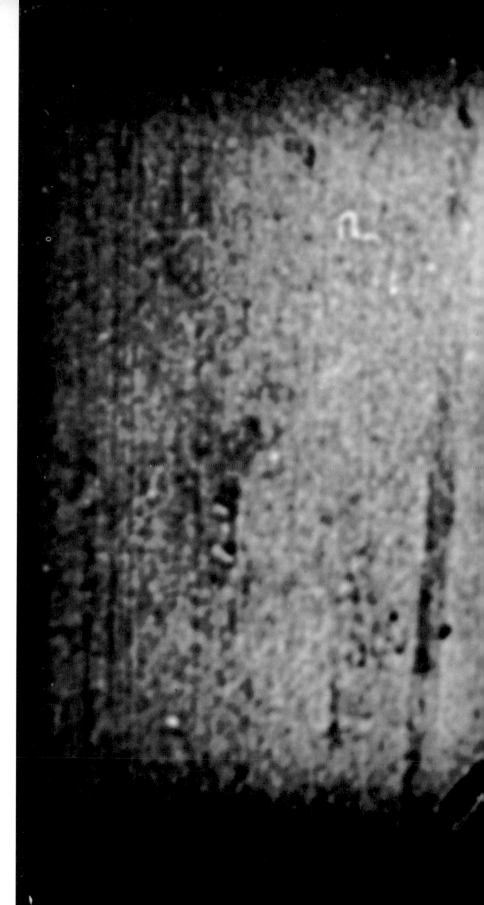

Count Orlok climbs the stairs to Ellen Hutter's bedroom – and reveals that he does have a shadow – in F.W. Murnau's illegal film version of Dracula called Nosferatu (1922).

From then on, he had to keep his family by writing: eight full-length books and seventeen articles in six years. One of the articles he ground out at this time was about the Harland and Wolff shipbuilding yard in Belfast.

He died just five days after the *Titanic* went down. Very few papers — except *The Times* and *Telegraph* — noted his death. Most of *The Times*' obituary was about his long-standing partnership with Henry Irving, but there was brief mention of the 'particularly lurid and creepy kind of fiction' he insisted on writing in his spare time. He was cremated at Golders Green, and his nondescript marble urn was placed in the East Columbarium: Bram Stoker Born 8th Nov 1847 Died 20th April 1912. A small group of mourners was present, including Hall Caine who wrote on the day of the funeral in the *Daily Telegraph* (under the headline *Bram Stoker — the story of a great friendship*):

> The big, breathless, impetuous hurricane of a man who was Bram Stoker had no love of the limelight ... In one thing our poor Bram, who had many limitations, was truly great. He was indeed the genius of friendship. I speak as perhaps the oldest of his surviving associates, outside the immediate circle of his family, when I say that never in any other man have I seen such capacity for devotion to a friend. Much has been said of his relations to Henry Irving, but I wonder how many were really aware of the whole depth and significance of that association. Bram seemed to give up his life to it ... in the strongest love that man may feel for man ... I cannot truly say that this deeper side of the man ever expressed itself in his writings. He took no vain view of his efforts as an author. Frankly, he wrote his books to sell ...

Which makes it all the more sad that Bram Stoker left just £4,700. But he left something else as well — even if his wife never benefitted from it. He left a story which laid down the ground-rules for countless sequels, adaptations, and parodies — the ground-rules for a whole industry in the twentieth century. No-one can write a vampire story — or, it could be argued, a mass-market horror story of *any* description — without acknowledging the sheer power of *Dracula* — for better or for worse.

Today, we can confront the dark themes of Stoker's novel head-on, in ways he could not even imagine: repression, contagion, defilement, dependency, sexual initiation ... But we still seem to prefer the metaphor of the vampire, the fairy-tale version. So *Dracula* has taken on a life of its own, and flown away from the literary world altogether. The Count has been so successful, that he simply will not lie down. If the obituaries were being written today, they would mention nothing BUT *Dracula*.

Christopher Lee satisfies his thirst for blood in the Hammer Films version of Dracula *(also known as* Horror of Dracula), *directed by Terence Fisher in 1958.*

3

Dr Jekyll and Mr Hyde

I had long been trying to ... find a body, a vehicle, for that strong sense of man's double being, which must at times come in upon and overwhelm the mind of every thinking creature ... For two days I went about racking my brains for a plot of any sort; and on the second night I dreamed the scene at the window, and a scene afterwards split in two, in which Hyde, pursued for some crime, took the powder and underwent the change in the presence of his pursuers. All the rest was made awake, and consciously, although I think I can trace in much of it the manner of my Brownies. The meaning of the tale is therefore mine ... Mine, too, is the setting, mine the characters. All that was given me was the matter of three scenes, and the central idea of a voluntary change becoming involuntary.

ROBERT LOUIS STEVENSON

The nightmarish shadow of Hyde haunts Dr Jekyll in his laboratory: an illustration, based on the German Expressionist film The Cabinet of Dr Caligari, by S.G. Hulme Beaman (1930).

T THE BEGINNING of 1886, a story was published which redrew the map of horror: instead of demons and devils *outside*, it dealt explicitly with demons and devils *inside*, and in the process added a new phrase – a Jekyll and Hyde personality – to the English language. It was priced at one shilling ('shilling shockers' being the stand-alone equivalent of serial 'penny dreadfuls'), was 141 pages long, was called *Strange Case of Dr Jekyll and Mr Hyde* (later editions would change this to *The Strange Case ...*), and it brought commercial success to the thirty-five year old writer Robert Louis Stevenson for the first time.

In its fawn-coloured paper cover, the book *looked* downmarket, but the contents were far from the usual straightforward fare. With two personal memoirs, a newspaper-style report and a third-party narrative based on hearsay – all describing the same series of events – the narrative was mosaic rather than linear. Nevertheless, by September 39 000 copies had been sold in Britain alone and, by the end of the century (according to Stevenson's first biographer), at least a quarter of a million copies of authorised and pirate editions had been sold in America.

The theme of 'man's double being' (as Stevenson himself put it) had reached the highstreet like a juggernaut. It was a theme with which writers had become obsessed by the 1880s – as they grappled with a consciousness of themselves as artists and as people, and reflected on late Victorian 'dualities', such as public/private, inner/outer, masculine/feminine and the beast in man.

Stevenson's friend, the writer and critic Andrew Lang, who had read the book in manuscript form, immediately related it to this literary tradition of 'doubles' and 'mirrors' by drawing parallels with Edgar Allan Poe's short stories *William Wilson* and *The Tell-tale Heart*, and Théophile Gautier's *Le Chevalier Double*. He could have chosen much more obvious examples, such as – earlier in the century – Mary Shelley's *Frankenstein*, the *Tales of Hoffman* or nearer to home (since it was set in Calvinist Scotland) James Hogg's *Confessions of a Justified Sinner*, or even Dostoevsky's *Crime and Punishment* which Stevenson had read in French translation, and reckoned to be 'the greatest book I have read easily in ten years'. But Lang preferred to compare *Dr Jekyll* with Poe and Gautier:

> This little shilling work is like Poe with the addition of a moral sense ...
> Mr Stevenson's idea, his secret (but a very open one) is that of the double
> personality in every man. The mere conception is familiar enough ... yet
> his originality of treatment remains none the less striking and astonishing.
> The double personality does not in this romance take the form of a
> personified conscience, the doppel/ganger of the sinner ... We would
> welcome a spectre, a ghoul, or even a vampire gladly, rather than meet
> Mr Edward Hyde.

So Stevenson had gone beyond diabolical possession, 'the double', and the re-establishment of normality at the end of the story, and had created a physical embodiment of the heart of darkness (with a 'terrible power of growth and increase') which takes the reader from normality towards a world of chaos and disintegration. A *truly* frightening prospect, and a challenge to Victorian complacency.

Robert Louis Stevenson's reply to Lang's perceptive comments early in December 1885 was:

'Yes, I knew *William Wilson*; but now I hear for the first time (and with chagrin) of the Chevalier Double. Who in hell was he? I hope he didn't shoot over my preserves. My point is the identity with difficulty preserved; I thought it was quite original: a fresh start ... '

At first, the critics appear to have been suspicious of *Dr Jekyll*. It was packaged as a popular paperback (one critic called it 'a shilling shocker for the railway bookstalls', difficult to take seriously as 'literary art'), and thus resembled countless other examples of the cheap sub-literature of horror and bodice-ripping which were pouring off the new high-speed presses. At the time – in senior common rooms, journal articles and letters to the newspapers – there was much wringing of hands about the parlous state of popular taste and the creeping dangers of 'sensationalism'. The new mass culture could become, it was thought, like a 'contagion' if arbiters of cultural values did not take a stand.

*E*ngraving of Robert Louis Stevenson at work in *Bournemouth (1886-7), from a photograph taken by his stepson Lloyd Osbourne.*

Stevenson himself tended to be prickly on the subject of his little book – especially if he was writing about it to authors or critics he admired. He called *Dr Jekyll* his 'gothic gnome ... but the gnome is interesting I think', 'an ignoble shillingsworth', 'a penny (12 penny) dreadful; it is dam dreadful', 'a fine bogey tale' and 'the fault of the Brownies' ('the Brownies' were what he called his nocturnal dream-spirits, or rather his unconscious mind), and attributed it to 'financial fluctuations', a cure for 'bankruptcy [which was] at my heels' or one of those works 'rattled off ... for coins'.

Strange Case of Dr Jekyll and Mr Hyde

THE STORY

Dr Henry Jekyll, Fellow of the Royal Society, is a respected physician and chemist. Gabriel Utterson (his lawyer) and Dr Hastie Lanyon (his schoolfriend and colleague) are concerned about the direction his scientific research is taking him, and about his close association with the sinister and brutish Mr Edward Hyde. Utterson and his cousin Richard Enfield witness Hyde knocking over an eight-year-old girl, near the dingy back entrance to Jekyll's house. Dr Jekyll has given his lawyer a Will in which he has left a quarter-of-a-million pounds to Hyde. Although Utterson fears that this document hides some 'disgrace' (such as blackmail) he agrees with Jekyll that, come what may, he will see it honoured. Then, in a foggy street not far from the river, Hyde clubs to death the elderly Sir Danvers Carew, M.P., who is on his way to post a letter to Utterson. The police search Hyde's rooms in Soho, and find a half-burnt cheque-book there. Utterson notes how Hyde's handwriting closely resembles Jekyll's. But Hyde disappears, and Dr Jekyll devotes himself to charitable work and religion.

Some weeks later Dr Lanyon – who is dying of shock – gives Utterson a sealed document to be opened only after Jekyll's death, but refuses to discuss its contents. Then Utterson and Enfield catch sight of Dr Jekyll, at the window of his handsome town-house, suddenly turning away from them in distress. Utterson breaks into Jekyll's laboratory, and finds that Hyde has poisoned himself; he also finds religious books 'annotated with blasphemies'. But Jekyll is nowhere to be found. *Dr Lanyon's Narrative* tells of how, at Jekyll's request, he once broke into the laboratory, stole some white powders and a phial of blood-red liquid and gave them to the fugitive Mr Hyde – who then proceeded to transform himself into Dr Jekyll. *Henry Jekyll's Full Statement* confesses the double life he has led, his researches into separating his personality into good and evil, and the gradual ascendancy of evil Mr Hyde over hypocritical Dr Jekyll. One day the transformation becomes involuntary, and Jekyll is unable to reverse it because he has run out of the original batch of the powders. 'The brute that slept within me' is now in control.

He very much wanted to be taken seriously as a literary artist, complete with bohemian lifestyle – even though he had been living, since the beginning of April 1885, in a suburban villa in Bournemouth which he called Skerryvore – and had picked up on the widespread distaste among the metropolitan élite for what Matthew Arnold had recently called 'a cheap literature, hideous and ignoble of aspect … which seems designed for people with a low standard of life'.

At the beginning of January 1886, three days before the publication of *Dr Jekyll and Mr Hyde*, Stevenson expressed his anxieties about 'popularity' to the writer and critic Edmund Gosse:

> You aim high, and you take longer over your work; and it will not be so
> successful as if you had aimed low and rushed it. What the public likes is

work (of any kind) a little loosely executed; so long as it is a little wordy, a little slack, a little dim and knotless, the dear public likes it … I do not write for the public; I do write for money, a nobler deity; and most of all for myself, not perhaps any more noble but both more intelligent and nearer home. Let us tell each other sad stories of the bestiality of the beast whom we feed … there must be something wrong in me, or I would not be popular.

The point was that he was determined to be a *professional* writer – no longer dependent on an allowance from his ageing and ailing father: by his mid-thirties, he ought surely to be able to stand on his own two feet. Whatever the well-mannered metropolitan writers on private incomes might say, the bills still had to be paid. So 'I do write for money'. Yet, he wanted to command respect in *their* world too.

By the end of January 1886, an anonymous review in *The Times* had helped to make the book respectable reading. The critic in *The Times* reckoned:

> Nothing Mr Stevenson has written as yet has so strongly impressed us with the versatility of his very original genius as this sparsely-printed little shilling volume. From the business point of view we can only marvel in these practical days at the lavish waste of admirable material, and what strikes us as a disproportionate expenditure on brain-power, in relation to the tangible results. Of two things, one, either the story was a flash of intuitive psychological research, dashed off in a burst of inspiration; or else it is the product of the most elaborate forethought, fitting together all the parts of an intricate and inscrutable puzzle. The proof is, that every *connoisseur* who reads the story once, must certainly read it twice.

Stevenson's 'sensational' story of a respectable character 'steadily and inevitably succumbing to the influence of besetting weaknesses' was likely, in short, to appeal both to general readers of shilling volumes *and* to the 'most cultivated minds' and the 'most competent critics'. The people who read it once *and* the connoisseurs who read it twice.

The point about not being able to tell this book by its cover, was echoed in the *Academy* magazine. The review was written by James Noble, who was shortly to publish his study of *Morality in English Fiction* – a subject on which he had strong views:

> [Dr Jekyll] is not an orthodox three-volume novel; it is not even a one-volume novel of the ordinary type; it is simply a paper-covered shilling story, belonging, so far as external appearance goes, to a class of literature familiarity with which has bred in the minds of most readers a certain measure of contempt. Appearances, it has once or twice been remarked, are deceitful; and in this case they are very deceitful indeed, for, in spite of the paper cover and the popular price, Mr Stevenson's story distances so unmis-

takably its three-volume and one-volume competitors that its only fitting place is the place of honour.

The review then went on to say that, although *Dr Jekyll* might *look* like a shudder-novel, it was in fact 'a parable' of the struggle between good and evil – an interpretation which was soon to be endorsed by numerous churchmen and their house journals. On 6 February, *Punch* joined in the sermonising:

CHAPTER THE LAST – The Wind-up.

... I, Dr Trekyl (i.e. Treacle to rhyme with Jekyll) found one day that I had a great deal of sugar in my composition. By using powdered acidulated drops I discovered that I could change myself into somebody else. It was very sweet! So I divided myself into two, and thought of a number of things. I thought how pleasant it would be to have no conscience, and be a regular bad one, or, as the vulgar call it, bad'un. I swallowed the acidulated drops, and in a moment I became a little odd creature, Mr Hidanseek, with an acquired taste for trampling out children's brains, and hacking to death (with an umbrella) midnight Baronets who had lost their way. I had a grand time of it! It was all the grander, because I found that by substituting sugar for the drops I could again become the famous doctor ...

Punch had been in the vanguard of the attack on 'sensationalism': but, so long as *Dr Jekyll and Mr Hyde* was a parable – about the war between sugary-sweet Dr Treacle and the man with no conscience Mr Hidanseek – then the book was quite acceptable.

One of Stevenson's early biographers J.A. Stuart, writing in the early 1920s, described this process of diffusion. The most enthusiastic critics, he wrote, were keen to point out that *Dr Jekyll* 'offers both art and ethics in a remarkable union'; that although 'a good many people might miss it ... a noble moral underlies the marvellous tale'. From that moment on:

... it was caught up and proclaimed with quite apostolic fervour. A Canon of the English Church, reading his *Times* over the matutinal bacon and eggs, noticed what was said of the book, became interested, procured a copy, read it; and, seizing so rare an opportunity, made it a text for a sermon to the elect in St Paul's Cathedral. Other canons, vicars, and Nonconformist divines, following a distinguished lead, expounded the parable from scores of pulpits all over the land ... There is no more effective advertisement for a story than a series of sermons ... It was first-rate business. From the pulpit *Jekyll & Hyde* passed triumphantly to the boudoir, the drawing room, and the dinner-table. Society took it up ... Elderly ladies of severely mid-Victorian minds shook their hands with a 'My dear, it is dreadful' ... and at any rate it served as a convenient topic for small-talk, like Dr Darwin's apes or Mr Gladstone's Irish policy. When a book is thus selected for honour it 'booms' and *Jekyll & Hyde* was soon booming ...

A review of *Dr Jekyll*, headed *Secret Sin*, appeared three months after publication in *Rock* – the journal of the Unified Church of England and Ireland.

> [The book] is an allegory based on the two-fold nature of man, a truth taught us by the Apostle PAUL in Romans vii., 'I find then a law that, when I would do good, evil is present with me'. We have for some time wanted to review this little book, but we have refrained from so doing till the season of Lent had come, as the whole question of temptation is so much more appropriately considered at this period of the Christian year …

In fact, *Dr Jekyll and Mr Hyde* was not about the war between good and evil at all. As Stevenson was, privately, at pains to point out, the strange case happened 'because [Jekyll] was a hypocrite … the Hypocrite let out the beast of Hyde': Hyde was in Jekyll just as Jekyll was in Hyde; the tragedy was that Jekyll was not prepared to accept the fact and so tried to win 'the perennial war among my members' [a reference to James 4:1: ' … your lusts that war in your members'] by separating these two sides of his personality. Jekyll writes:

> If each could but be housed in separate identities, life would be relieved of all that was unbearable; the unjust might go his way, delivered from the aspirations and remorse of his more upright twin; and the just could walk steadfastly and securely on his upward path, doing the good things in which he found his pleasure, and no longer exposed to disgrace and penitence by the hands of this extraneous evil. It was the curse of mankind that these incongruous faggots were thus bound together … How, then, were they dissociated?

In other words, the doctor recognises (in high Victorian style) 'the thorough and primitive duality of man', but draws the conclusion from this that he ought to work towards 'the *separation* of these elements'. His hypothesis is that 'man is not truly one, but truly two': what he has, in fact, unwittingly discovered is that the two men are really one man. Furthermore, he has discovered that human beings may have *more* than 'two natures' – may have multiple personalities.

Where Hyde is concerned, he is *not* 'a regular bad'un' to start with, and he never goes around 'trampling out children's brains' (whatever *Punch* might claim). His behaviour worsens the more Jekyll fails to 'own' him, until in the end – after a long period of repression – he forces his way out; 'my devil had long been caged and he came out roaring'. If only Jekyll had been able to say – as Prospero says of Caliban in *The Tempest* – 'this thing of darkness I acknowledge mine', Mr Hyde would have had no reason to emerge. Those who catch sight of Mr Hyde experience a diffuse sense of unease, which they subsequently find difficult to put into words: 'I never saw a man I so disliked, and yet I scarce know why … '

He *is not* a bogey-man, but the aura he projects 'somehow' bears witness to his origins – particularly if the witness is the kind of individual who normally represses the 'unjust' side of *his* personality and pretends to be better adjusted than he really is.

So, the version of *Dr Jekyll and Mr Hyde* which was preached from countless pulpits in the mid-to-late 1880s was not the book which Stevenson wrote – just as the phrase 'a Jekyll and Hyde personality', describing as it did (and does) a psychopath who hears voices, belongs to a different *Strange Case*. The 'shilling-shocker' people could enjoy it as a thriller; the literati (or most of them) and churchmen could enjoy it as a 'parable' or 'allegory' – a parable which was in the end, they thought, *optimistic*. Where *Dr Jekyll and Mr Hyde* is concerned, these two reading publics have been going in separate directions ever since.

By February 1886, the story was out of its author's hands and thoroughly launched into the public domain. When summarising the plot, most published reviews concentrated on the straightforward single-point-of-view chapter called *Henry Jekyll's full statement of the case* (the last fifth of the text). They ignored the perspectives of his fellow bachelors Mr Gabriel Utterson the lawyer ('cold, scanty and embarrassed in discourse; backward in sentiment … and yet somehow lovable'), Utterson's relation Mr Richard Enfield ('a well-known man about town') and Henry Jekyll's friend Dr Hastie Lanyon (whose heartiness and geniality were 'somewhat theatrical to the eye', and whose cocooned world falls to pieces when he realizes what his schoolfriend and colleague has been up to). As Henry James noted, the one thing these chaps all have in common (apart from their social class) is that they live and work 'without the aid of women'.

These perspectives, subtle variations on the theme of 'the Hypocrite', extended Stevenson's purpose well beyond Dr Jekyll's laboratory experiment and provided important glimpses of Mr Hyde before the autobiographical version of the man himself. They also added to the strangeness, the mystery, by delaying, until just before the *dénouement*, the revelation that Jekyll and Hyde are the same person. It is difficult to imagine now, but readers in 1886 did not *know* that yet.

Stevenson was no more able to control the *reception* of his book – and the range of permissible interpretations – than he could control how the central character's name was to be pronounced. He was keen that it should be pronounced Jeekyl – partly because that was the way educated people said it, partly so that Hyde and Jekyll could rhyme with Hyde and Seek. Or, come to that, Jekyll with Treacle. In the first theatrical version, the actor Richard Mansfield pronounced it *Jeck*yll – and so it has remained ever since.

But Stevenson's story – which we all *think* we have read – was a great deal richer than the establishment reviews at the time, or the blood-and-thunder

"DAILY MAIL" SIXPENNY NOVELS

DR JEKYLL & MR HYDE WITH OTHER FABLES

Robert Louis Stevenson

Cover illustration by Edmund J. Sullivan for a popular paperback edition (1897) of Dr Jekyll and Mr Hyde: *the murderous Hyde has become a 'man about town'.*

versions on stage or film since then, have allowed. It dramatised tensions within Robert Louis Stevenson himself: tensions which ran along the border-line between reality and dreams, public life and private life, bourgeois and bohemian, sedentary and active – and even between the alleyways or *closes* of the Old Town of Edinburgh, and the well-planned open spaces of the New; above all, perhaps, between the child and the adult.

There are dangers in too readily accepting Victorian notions of 'duality' and the Biblical 'perennial war among the members', but that is clearly how Stevenson interpreted his own behaviour, and sometimes his own art.

Strange Case of Dr Jekyll and Mr Hyde begins with the nightmares which Robert Louis Stevenson experienced as a child. Nightmares, he told a reporter from the *New York Herald* in September 1887, had afflicted him all his life. Sometimes they made him 'cry out aloud'. But, in adult life he had learned to control them. He would be thinking about a story *before* he went to sleep, and then allow his unconscious mind to take over:

> I am never deceived by them. Even when fast asleep I know that it is I who am inventing, and when I cry out it is with gratification to know that the story is so good. So soon as I awake, and it always awakens me when I get on a good thing, I set to work and put it together. For instance, all I dreamed about Dr Jekyll was that one man was being pressed into a cabinet, when he swallowed a drug and changed into another being.

This 'cabinet' triggered another memory, of 'the room in which I slept when a child in Edinburgh [where] there was a cabinet – and a very pretty piece of work it was too – from the hands of the original Deacon Brodie'.

The association between the two was to be taken up – more or less – by Mrs Fanny Stevenson, in her introduction to *Dr Jekyll and Mr Hyde* (published in the 1920s):

> In the room in Edinburgh occupied by my husband as a child, was a book-case and a chest of drawers made by the notorious Deacon Brodie – the respectable artisan by day, a burglar by night. [His nurse] to whom my husband dedicated his *Child's Garden of Verses*, wove, with her vivid Scottish imagination, many romances about these prosaic articles of furniture to amuse her nursling. Years afterwards my husband was deeply impressed by a paper he read in a French scientific journal on sub-consciousness. This article, combined with his memories of Deacon Brodie, gave the germ of the idea that afterwards … in a hectic fever following a haemorrhage of the lungs, culminated in the dream of Jekyll and Hyde.

The room in question was on the top floor of 17 Heriot Row – a tidy and solid south-facing terrace of four-storey houses, built in the early nineteenth century in the heart of Edinburgh's New Town. Robert Louis Balfour Stevenson had been born on 13 November 1850 lower down the city at the more dingy 8 Howard Place, a Georgian row of squat, two-storey houses just to the north of Canonmills. But when he was two, his family had moved across the road to a less cramped house in Inverleith Terrace. In 1857 they moved again, to the higher ground and better neighbourhood of Heriot Row, to the house which, because of his reminiscences, is always associated with Stevenson.

In the mid-eighteenth century, the New Town (the first 'New Town' in Britain) had been carefully planned and laid out on a grid system of wide streets, squares and crescents. As it developed over the ensuing sixty years, it made that part of Edinburgh seem more like a central European city, such as Prague, than London.

Stevenson's bedroom overlooked a gas street-light and the Queen Street Gardens, and the room contained *that* wardrobe (rather than 'a bookcase and a chest of drawers') constructed by 'the notorious Deacon Brodie'. As a child, 'Louis' (as he came to be called – still pronounced 'Lewis') had many fantasies about the things that went bump in the shadowlands of Brodie's cabinet, a cabinet which 'creaked eerily in the night'.

His father Thomas belonged to a family of engineers and inventors who had built most of the deep-sea lighthouses on the dangerous coasts of Scotland ('whenever I smell salt water', Louis wrote, 'I know I am not far from one of the works of my ancestors'). His mother Margaret Isabella Balfour came from a family of lawyers and ministers of the Church ('and I believe them related to many of the so-called good families of Scotland'). So Louis, their only child, was raised within the strict mid-Victorian rules of Edinburgh's professional class where the word 'respectable' was the highest possible praise.

But he was a sickly, breathless child, who always seemed undernourished and who suffered from bronchitis, gastric fever, digestive problems, pneumonia and what he called 'nervous excitability'. He may also have had a thyroid condition, which would account for his distended bone structure (his parents did not share his fragile build). Because he was sickly, he spent most of his early life up in the bedroom of 17 Heriot Row – and, later with the benefit of hindsight, added – 'full of fear, nightmare, insomnia, painful days and interminable nights'.

Since his father Thomas was often away on business, as a consultant engineer to the Northern Lighthouse Board, and his mother Margaret was a permanent invalid at this time (suffering from weak lungs exacerbated by stress), and often confined to her room, Louis' closest relationship was with his full-time nurse Alison Cunningham or 'Cummy' – a fisherman's daughter and fundamentalist Christian from Fife.

Cummy filled his impressionable mind with stories of hell-fire and damnation, and read religious tracts and the entire Bible to him over and over again – trying to convince him that 'there are but two camps in the world – one of the perfectly pious and respectable, one of the perfectly profane, mundane and vicious; one mostly on its knees and singing hymns, the other on the high road to the gallows and the bottomless pit'. She helped him learn the words of hymns, wove improving stories around the furniture of the room, and encouraged him to play with his 'penny plain and twopence coloured' pasteboard theatre – provided the dramas had a moral ending.

Cummy, in other words, put the fear of God into her surrogate child – even in his play. Fiction, as he later observed, is to the grown man as play is to the child.

At night, by his own account in *Memoirs of Himself* (1879-80), when Cummy was asleep, he would lie awake for hours weeping for Jesus, terrified to close his eyes lest he went to hell. Not surprisingly, when he *did* manage to close his eyes, he often had nightmares which then stayed with him, indelibly, for the rest of his life. Once he woke up from 'a dream of Hell, clinging to the horizontal bar of the bed, with my knees and chin together, my soul shaken, my body convulsed with agony'.

Drawing up a balance-sheet of his childhood experiences, some twenty years after they happened, Stevenson concluded that Cummy was devoted, patient and tender, but she was also superstitious and sometimes thoughtless about the 'religious pattern' she pumped into his little head. There was a danger, he said, of over-dramatising the memories which had stuck. But, even bearing that in mind:

> On the whole I have not much joy in remembering those early years. I was as much an egotist as I have ever been; I had a feverish desire for consideration … I was sentimental, snivelling, goody, morbidly religious … I have touched already on the cruelty of bringing a child among the awful shadows of man's life; but it must not be forgotten, it is also unwise, and a good way to defeat the educator's purpose. The idea of sin, attached to particular actions absolutely, far from repelling, soon exerts an attraction on young minds … I can never again take so much interest in anything, as I took, in childhood, in doing for its own sake what I believed to be sinful. And generally, the principal effect of this false, common doctrine of sin, is to put a point on lust.

Specific examples of the sinful thoughts which he recalled were: asking Cummy 'why has God got a hell?', denying the very existence of God (as a 'dire experiment' to see what would happen) and worrying about the spiritual welfare of his parents who liked to play cards in the drawing-room.

He was encouraged to think these things – out of sheer devilment – because of the absolute, undifferentiated notion of sin which had been drummed into him. In some of his dreams, the idea of sin became strangely attractive. In *Dr Jekyll and Mr Hyde*, the person who finds it most difficult to adjust to the very *thought* of Mr Hyde is called Dr Hastie Lanyon: Hastie was the maiden name of nurse Alison Cunningham's mother.

Stevenson grew up in a city which, as he noted, was 'half a capital, half a country town; the whole city leads a double existence'. On the other side of the great divide, beyond the Castle Cliffs, was the 'old black city, which was for all the world like a rabbit-warren, not only by the number of its indwellers, but the complication of its passages and holes'.

In his *Edinburgh; Picturesque Notes* (published in 1879), he described – in the florid literary style of his early essays – the grim and sooty Old Town, with its *closes* (or narrow alley-ways) and *lands* (or tall tenements), as if from the outside looking in. It was like watching an old derelict fall down and die. A late medieval quarter in a modern city (and thus, to some, 'picturesque'), which nostalgic writers of 'the correct literary sentiment' preferred to the open spaces and clean air of the New. But it was too easy 'to be a conservator of the discomforts of others'. In fact, the Old Town was an over-crowded hellhole and a vivid symbol of 'ostentatious ... social inequality'.

Number 17, Heriot Row in the heart of Edinburgh's New Town – where Robert Louis Stevenson lived from the age of six until he left home.

The skull beneath the skin, he wrote, was laid bare on a Sunday morning, when one of the tall *lands* in the High Street – which had 'grown rotten to the core' – imploded with a hideous roar and tumbled to the ground. The private lives of thirty families were suddenly on view – 'here a kettle on the hob ... there a cheap picture of the Queen pasted over the chimney' – cut off from their history. To be old was *not* the same thing as to be picturesque. But if the Old Town was decaying and insanitary (the 'liver' of the city), the New Town ran the risk of being commonplace and 'short-sighted':

The architect was essentially a town bird, and he laid out the modern city with a view to street scenery, and to street scenery alone. The country did not enter into his plan; he had never lifted his eyes to the hills. If he had so chosen, every street upon the northern slope might have been a noble terrace and commanded an extensive and beautiful view. But the space has been too closely built; many of the houses front the wrong way …

But, that said, 'what slices of sunlight, what breaths of clean air, have been let in!', and it was a form of literary snobbery to suggest otherwise. The contrast between the two was like the two entrances to Henry Jekyll's establishment: the patrician front door which 'wore a great air of wealth and comfort', and the dingy back entrance 'by the old dissecting-room door' which was 'equipped with neither bell nor knocker'. The crumbling, grimy tenements around the Old Mint at Cowgate, and the crisp neo-Georgian buildings on the north side of George Street (a street as wide as a Paris *boulevard*), were captured in the photographs of Thomas Vernon Begbie, mostly taken in the late 1850s from his base in Leith Street.

For Stevenson in his teenage years, the contrast was epitomised by the legends surrounding William Brodie (1741-1788), a respectable and respected deacon of a guild of craftsmen and town councillor by day, leader of a gang of Old Town burglars by night.

Brodie had been arrested in 1788, following a robbery at the Excise Office in Canongate. He claimed as usual that he was in a more respectable part of the city at the time, but his alibi did not stand up in court. He was hanged in front of a crowd of 10 000 people, on a gallows of his own design.

During Stevenson's youth, Brodie's 'dark lamp' and bunch of twenty-five skeleton keys were on display at the Museum of the Society of Antiquaries. Today, there is still a pub on the High Street which has a two-faced sign: on one side, daytime Brodie; on the other, night-time Brodie; the keys are in the Lady Stairs Museum.

When he was fourteen years old, Louis wrote what he later called 'a sort of hugger-mugger melodrama' about the Deacon for all seasons, which was 'fished out' in autumn 1878 to become a four-act play *Deacon Brodie, or, The Double Life* (written with his friend and associate William Ernest Henley). In its early drafts, said Stevenson, this play was based on 'an idea that bad-heartedness was strength', that Brodie was a 'man of men'. As performed in the mid-1880s (at London's Prince's Theatre), its most popular moment came when Brodie first revealed his guilty secret to the audience:

BRODIE: Now for one of the Deacon's headaches! Rogues all, rogues all! *(Goes to the cupboard and proceeds to change his coat)* On with the new coat and into the new life! Down with the Deacon and up with the robber! *(Changing neck-band and ruffles)*. Eh God! how still the house is! There's something in hypocrisy after all. If we were as good as we seem, what would the world be? The city has its vizard on, and we – at night we are our naked selves … My father and Mary – Well! The day for them, the night for me; the grimy cynical night that makes all cats grey, and all honesties of one complexion. Shall a man not have half a life of his own – not eight hours out of twenty-four?

There is a similar moment in *Strange Case of Dr Jekyll and Mr Hyde*: the disguise, the sheer excitement of leading a double life, the thought that the villain can be *true to himself* (away from domestic pressures) in his nocturnal persona. This occurs when Henry Jekyll is describing the feeling of euphoria which follows his first successful experiment.

It is possible that, at one stage, the story of Jekyll and Hyde was to have been closer to *Deacon Brodie*: an adventure story involving a disguise (Hyde as a 'new coat'), the excitement of undetected crime (down with the Doctor and up with the robber), and a schoolboyish glee at shedding all adult responsibilities. There are occasional traces of such a story in the published version, but they are only traces. *Dr Jekyll and Mr Hyde* goes much deeper.

A t the age of seventeen, Robert Louis Stevenson registered at Edinburgh University to study engineering under Professor Fleeming Jenkin. Mrs Jenkin remembered him at that time as 'a slender, brown, long-haired lad with great dark eyes, a brilliant smile, and a gentle, deprecating bend of the head'. He wore an arty 'Velvet Coat', played practical jokes with his cousin Bob, drank with his student friends in the Rutherford Arms, Drummond Street (still there), spent time with – and wrote about – prostitutes, and enjoyed talking ten-to-the dozen at dinner parties in a 'recklessly brilliant' way about the poet Robert Fergusson (a contemporary of Robert Burns) who drank himself into an early grave.

It was to become trendy in the 1920s to write of Stevenson at this time as if *he* drifted into a wild double life, like a student version of Henry Jekyll: Presbyterian days/debauched nights; religion/freethinking; New Town girls/Old Town harlots; and so on.

A legend then evolved (for which there is no documentary evidence) that he fell in love with a prostitute from the Highlands called Kate Drummond, and intended to marry her until his father forbad it – after which he was to be more discreet about his liaisons, playing 'the Hypocrite'.

There is no doubt that Stevenson did spend a lot of time in the Old Town underworld: he wrote of his sympathy for the plight of prostitutes, many of whom he judged to be more honest individuals than their clients; he found them kind and refreshingly free of cant. And he developed a scornful attitude towards 'nice concrete comfortable things'. But the 'double life' idea may be a

case of making the life too closely match the art. Beneath his cavalier attitude to his university course, and self-consciously bohemian image, he was actually working hard:

> All through my boyhood and youth, I was known and pointed out for the pattern of an idler; and yet I was always busy on my own private end, which was to learn to write. I kept always two books in my pocket, one to read, the other to write in. As I walked, my mind was busy fitting what I saw with appropriate words …

And he was thinking hard. In January 1873, he had a serious row with his father about his religious and moral convictions:

> 'My father put me one or two questions as to beliefs', he immediately confessed to a friend, 'which I candidly answered. I really hate all lying so much now – a new-found honesty that has somehow come out of my late illness [the result of another damp Edinburgh winter] – that I could not so much

mages of Edinburgh's sooty Old Town, with its narrow alley-ways (or closes*) and crumbling tenement buildings (or* lands*), and of the clean New Town, with its wide streets, squares and crescents laid out on a grid system: local photographer Thomas Begbie recorded both, in the mid-nineteenth century, from his base in Leith Street.*

as hesitate at the time, but if I had foreseen the real Hell of everything since, I think I should have lied as I have done so often before. ... They don't see either that my game is not the light-hearted scoffer, that I am not (as they call me) a careless infidel. I believe as much as they do, only generally in the inverse ratio ... '

That Stevenson should have been so concerned about the hypocrisy which was expected of him – apparently, his Presbyterian father would have *preferred* him to lie, in the interests of family peace – shows how far, in a crude sense, he was from being a 'Jekyll and Hyde' character. The real shocks arising from the confrontation (apart from his father's fury and his mother's hysterics) were that he was still – at the age of twenty-two – not being taken seriously enough, and there was still parental pressure to 'live my whole life as one falsehood'. In reaction against his hellfire upbringing, Stevenson had become a very uncompromising character indeed.

uring his time as an undergraduate, Robert Louis Stevenson kept having what he called a strange 'dream adventure', in which he would spend his days working in a surgical theatre 'his heart in his mouth, his teeth on edge, seeing monstrous malformities and the abhorred dexterity of surgeons', and his nights climbing a never-ending staircase somewhere in the Old Town, in wet clothes, watching a parade of down-and-outs descending the stairs past him. When at last he reached the top, it was time to go back to the surgical theatre – with its 'monstrosities and operations' – again.

The dream, which happened in sequence, seems to have been about the kind of ambition which was expected of him, his guilt at being such a relatively privileged young man, and the horror of those malformed bodies (which perhaps reminded him a little of his own). It was also about the pervasive medical atmosphere of the University of Edinburgh, which was evidently getting to him. We know he spent time, after hours, with his fellow students in the Medical Faculty. Eventually, this dream came to leave 'a great black blot upon his memory, long enough to send him, trembling for his reason, to the doors of a certain doctor – whereupon, with a simple draught, he was restored to the common lot of man'. This draught, a compound of opium, helped him to sleep more soundly. Much later he would locate Dr Jekyll's laboratory in 'an old dissection-room'.

But, although he dreamed about anatomy classes, he was supposed to be studying engineering – a subject he found deeply boring (despite its romantic associations with the achievements of his ancestors). He made this boredom clear to most of his lecturers, by interrupting them or just not turning up. When he plucked up the courage to tell his father that he was not cut out to be a civil engineer, they compromised on law but that did not interest him much either. He was called to the Scottish bar in 1875, and had his photograph taken in a wig, but he was only going through the motions.

As he wrote in his essay on *A College Magazine*, it was not that he was lazy or feckless: he was reading avidly, seeking 'models' against which to judge his own development as an author, learning how to condemn his own derivative performances. While he taught himself his craft, he was – predictably – drawn to the legends of Edinburgh, especially 'ugly actions, in ugly places [which] have the true romantic quality and become an undying property of their scene':

> In the low dens and high-flying garrets of Edinburgh, people may go back upon dark passages in the town's adventures, and chill their marrow with writer's tales about the fire.

Legends such as that of Deacon Brodie, whose story 'is kept piously fresh'; and of the Ulstermen William Burke and William Hare, who in the 1820s had supplied sixteen fresh corpses for payment to the extramural teacher Dr Robert Knox, for use in his anatomy classes. Others preferred to rob graves for this purpose, and were known as 'resurrection men', but Burke and Hare took a short cut by suffocating their victims and thus producing the freshest corpses in the business. After Burke was publicly hanged (on 28 January 1829), his body was dissected by the Professor of Anatomy at the University – and his skeleton donated to the permanent collection.

It can still be seen in the Anatomy Museum there, together with his death-mask and a small wallet made out of his skin.

When Stevenson was an undergraduate, people still 'hushed their voices over Burke and Hare; over drugs and violated graves, and the resurrection-men smothering their victims with their knees'. And one or two of the Edinburgh cemeteries he visited (such as St Cuthbert's, in the shadow of the castle) still had stone watchtowers – built before the passage of the Anatomy Act of 1832 – to protect the graves. The graveyard next to Colinton manse, where Stevenson had played as a child with his cousins on his mother's side and listened intently at the wall for 'the voices of the dead', still possessed a heavy metal coffin-cover which in the 1820s would have been placed over a recently buried coffin to protect it (for the first few weeks) from the unwelcome attentions of the resurrection-men.

When at last he became a professional writer, he adapted this legend into the short story *The Body Snatcher* – in which it was the competitive and ambitious *doctor* who was ultimately the guilty party. The story, originally entitled *The Body-Snatchers*, was published in the *Pall Mall Gazette Christmas 'Extra'* of 1884. It had been partly drafted three years before (June-July 1881, in Pitlochry), but Stevenson had put it aside 'in a justifiable disgust, the tale being horrid'. He later dusted it up because the *Gazette* had promised its readers 'a vivid GHOST STORY, and when ghosts are walking Mr Stevenson is at his weirdest'. The author hoped it would prove 'blood curdling enough' for the purpose: 'it ought to chill the blood of a grenadier', he wrote a month before publication. But the promotional hype embarrassed him – not least when sandwich boards, advertising the product with a lurid illustration, were seized by the police for being too 'sensational'.

y the time *The Body Snatcher* was published, Robert Louis Stevenson had been living in Bournemouth – in hotel, boarding house, and rented accommodation – for five months, with his wife of four-and-a-half years Fanny Vandegrift (later Van de Grift) Osbourne. He had left the 'inclement city' of Edinburgh in summer 1873, with mixed feelings: he would not miss the climate (which seemed to be killing him) or the obsession with the trappings of respectability (which encouraged him to lie 'as I have done so often before'); he would miss very much the sense of romance and tradition which the city gave him (and about which he always felt strongest when he was somewhere else).

His collection of essays *Edinburgh; Picturesque Notes* was too critical to be welcomed by the more dour city dignitaries and burghers, and there are still some Scottish commentators who have not forgiven him for what he wrote. Since then, he had travelled – and written roughish guides to his travels – in France, England and America (back-packing was evidently good for him), had become an admired essayist in fashionable literary periodicals, and had met Fanny who was about eleven years his senior.

Fanny originated from Indianapolis on the rugged urban frontier, and had been married to Sam Osbourne for nearly twenty years. In 1878, she went back to California (from France, where she had met Louis), and Stevenson soon followed her there – a journey during which he experienced terrible health problems, and genuine poverty. Following Fanny's divorce from her husband, the couple were married on 19 May 1880, and arrived in England three months later – with her twelve-year-old son Lloyd Osbourne in tow. Stevenson's most productive period – when he was also at his most unwell – was about to begin.

The seaside town of Bournemouth boasted more hotels than any other town in the land – after London. The building of a main-line railway link had recently boosted its population tenfold from 1700 to 17 000 people and its pier – for those who wanted to walk out into the sea without getting their feet wet – had just opened. As a metropolitan critic who visited Robert Louis Stevenson there in 1887 wrote of the town, it had become 'a colony of health hunters' – attracted by the sea air and the scent of gorse and heather – and 'a home of British invalidism and British Philistinism'.

The Stevensons moved there in summer 1884, partly because Lloyd was at boarding school in the neighbourhood, and partly because some (though not all) of Louis' doctors judged that a seaside environment in the south of England might be good for his lungs. As it happened, they were wrong: between 1884 and 1887, Robert Louis Stevenson was permanently ill, not just with the usual colds, sciatica and flu, but with serious haemorrhaging and congestion as well.

It was almost a fulltime job for Fanny to protect this chronic invalid from visitors, with their conversations and their germs, and to create an environ-ment in which he could get on with his writing.

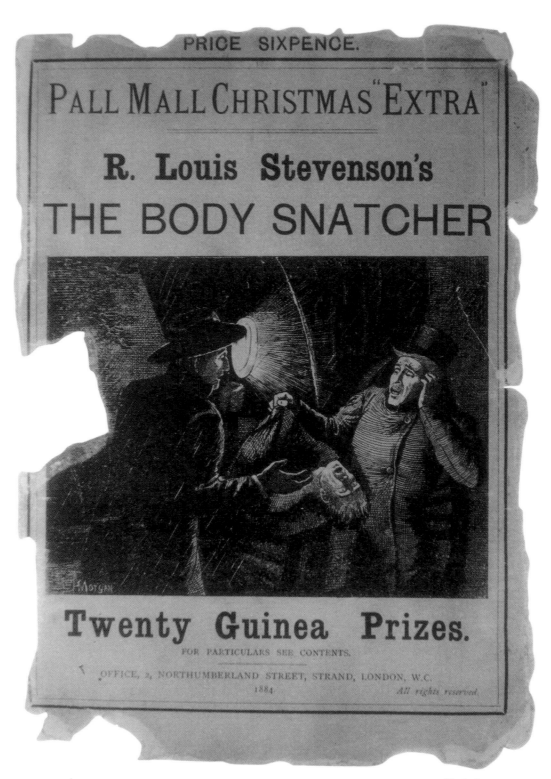

PRICE SIXPENCE.

PALL MALL CHRISTMAS "EXTRA"

R. Louis Stevenson's
THE BODY SNATCHER

Twenty Guinea Prizes.
FOR PARTICULARS SEE CONTENTS.

OFFICE, 2, NORTHUMBERLAND STREET, STRAND, LONDON, W.C.
1884   *All rights reserved.*

Original blood-curdling illustration of Stevenson's The Body Snatcher, *published as a Christmas story in 1884: sandwich boards featuring this picture were seized by the police for being too 'sensational'.*

When the 'Bluidy Jack' (as he called his congestion of the lungs) was at its worst, he was forced to communicate domestic messages by writing on a small board. But, despite all this, he usually managed about six hours' productive work a day – writing up to 3000 words of story.

The *Child's Garden of Verses* was published, and both *Dr Jekyll and Mr Hyde* and *Kidnapped* (as well numerous shorter stories, critical essays and poems) were written in the Bournemouth period. A combination of no distractions; confinement to bed and an almost permanent state of misery and depression actually helped him focus on various tasks in hand. And, not surprisingly, 'blackened' his already 'dreary view of life'.

In some ways, the contrast between the 'home of British invalidism and British Philistinism' and the bohemian artist who happened to find himself living there could scarcely be more extreme.

There was the sneaking suspicion in his mind that the place, and the affluent people who were drawn to him there, were turning Robert Louis Stevenson into a dreaded *bourgeois*. 'The social revolution', he wrote to critic William Archer, 'will probably cast me back upon my dung heap'; he was sure, he added, that he would 'go to hell (if there be such an excellent institution) for the luxury in which he lives'.

Fanny did not see it that way at all. She enjoyed being fêted by members of the aristocracy and she appreciated a settled existence at last. But it made Louis feel, to use his stepson's words, 'a prisoner'.

arly in 1885, in middle-class western Bournemouth, Thomas Stevenson bought Fanny a house on Alum Chine – one of the creeks which lead steeply down to the sea through the chalk cliffs on the outskirts of Westbourne. It was a belated wedding present for his daughter-in-law (whom he liked), and a way of ensuring that Louis would stay put for the foreseeable future. He gave Fanny £500 to furnish it.

Today, only the layout of the foundations remains, traced in Portland stone, and a vague idea of what the acre of garden (Fanny's 'special charge and delight') must have looked like, because the house was flattened by an incendiary bomb on 16 November 1940 during a Second World War air-raid.

The entrance to the house, according to the stone layout, fronts on to the main road, but, according to photographs taken in Stevenson's time, it was to the more secluded right-hand side of the building. The best views, over the garden, were to the south and away from the road. It was a modern two-storey villa in yellow brick, with a slate roof and ivy growing up the wall, called *Sea View* – which it had from the top floor facing away from the road.

Louis, Fanny and Lloyd – together with their French maid/nurse Valentine

Roch and a parlour maid Mary Anne – moved in at Easter 1885. They changed the name of the villa from *Sea View* to *Skerryvore* – after the most famous Scottish lighthouse designed and built by Uncle Alan Stevenson. The Stevensons lived in this villa for two-and-a-half years, and were visited there by one of the neighbours – Clive Holland – who recorded his memories in the early 1950s:

> I went one afternoon, and was shown into a little room in the opening into the hall, which had a door looking on to the staircase: a little room that I understood had been made as a supplementary study for him, to save him the constant going up stairs to the library – which was on the first floor, lined with books. I waited a quarter of an hour or so, and Mrs Stevenson came down and said 'Louis is rather tired this afternoon. He is resting. But he won't be long before he comes down, because he didn't want to disappoint you'. I was sitting quietly there and

The Bournemouth villa where the Stevensons lived from 1885 to 1887: they changed its name from Sea View *to* Skerryvore *(after a famous lighthouse designed and built by Louis' uncle).*

> thinking, when I heard a rustling and I looked through the door to the staircase, and saw Mrs Stevenson descending with Robert Louis in her arms, carried just as she would have a baby, with his dark hair falling over her arm. She brought him into the little room and put him down on the sofa and then she said 'You will … you must not talk very long' and went away. In about ten minutes or a quarter of an hour she came back – we talked of books in her absence – and she said 'You must not talk any more'. And – er – Louis got up and I noticed what I thought a rather rebellious cast in his smile! And he took her arm, after shaking hands with me, and went upstairs.

Louis' weight was about seven stone at this time, and falling: Fanny was not a tall woman (everyone was struck by her 'shortness') but she must have been strong both physically and mentally. Her protection of Louis ('You will … you must not talk very long') and his rebellious reaction were noted by other visitors. Stevenson's old friends tended to see this as over-protection,

Double portrait of Louis and Fanny Stevenson, painted at Skerryvore in Bournemouth, summer 1885, by John Singer Sargent, who described it as 'a caged animal lecturing about the foreign specimen in the corner'.

as Fanny trying to muscle in on his act, or as an attempt to separate Louis from his early carefree life. Others, such as another neighbour – Adelaide Boodle who first met the Stevensons when they had just moved into the villa – saw Fanny's possessiveness as essential to Louis' well-being, and indeed to his art.

She also reckoned that Fanny's role in Stevenson's life had been seriously under-valued by biographers and critics, and wrote her gushing book *RLS and his Sine Qua Non* (1926) partly to redress the balance.

The best-known visual image of the Stevenson marriage was made in summer 1885, when the American painter John Singer Sargent produced a double-portrait – his second attempt at capturing Louis at work. When Fanny was introduced to Sargent, at Skerryvore, she told him that she was of course in the shadow of her husband's greatness – just a little help-mate – and in the portrait she appears on the right-hand side, in the background, cut off by the frame, sitting on a large armchair bequeathed from Heriot Row and dressed in an Indian sari with her bare feet poking out of it. Louis is pacing up and down, on the left-hand side of the picture, tugging at his moustache and wearing his trademark velvet jacket.

Evidently, Sargent had taken Fanny literally – too literally, for her taste: she never cared for the picture. In February 1886, she referred to the double-portrait as 'Sargent's picture of Louis', and did her own ink sketch of it: in this, Louis is a stick man, and she is an indecipherable black blob. It was, she said, 'too peculiar to be satisfactory'. Sargent said the picture was of a 'caged animal lecturing about the foreign specimen in the corner'. Maybe Fanny talked about Sargent's painting to Miss Boodle, who subsequently wrote:

> Most people, naturally enough, and doing only as she would have had them
> do, have placed RLS in the foreground, sketching her in, as Mr Sargent did,
> like a kind of lurking shadow … But how different the picture would have
> been could he himself have painted it! … How dependent he was (almost
> like a child in this) upon her good opinion!

Others were less sensitive: they wrote of Fanny's determination to steer Louis towards money-making projects, of her own literary ambitions, and of her tendency to develop illnesses herself when too much attention was being paid to Louis. The truth probably lies in the middle.

After passing the model lighthouse in the porch of Skerryvore, visitors – such as Clive Holland or Adelaide Boodle, Henry James or the critic William Archer – would walk through a wood-panelled entrance hall into the dining room or 'blue room' (named after the blue china) to the right. This room had William Morris-style wallpaper (Fanny favoured the Arts and Crafts style, and according to Adelaide Booth her 'skill in all sorts of handicraft was far above average'), Sheraton furniture, an engraving of J.M.W. Turner's painting *The Bell Rock Lighthouse* over the fireplace, prints of the conventional portraits of Percy Shelley and Mary Wollstonecraft, an ornate Venetian mirror given to them by Henry James and beneath it a small armoury of buccaneering weapons nailed to the wall – donated by fans of *Treasure Island*. Or visitors would be ushered into the drawing room (the 'supplementary study') to the right, where – if he was well enough – Louis would spend a little time with them, smoking like a chimney (he had taken it up again, with a vengeance). This was his favourite room, where if he was not bed-ridden, he would work: it was 'stamped much more thoroughly with the Stevensonian individuality'.

The room was sparsely furnished: wicker-work chairs, a long couch made up of wooden boxes covered with yellow silk cushions, and an oak cabinet beside the door with a plaster group by Rodin (whom he had defended in print against stick-in-the-mud Royal Academicians) on top of it on. On the wall was the double-portrait, painted in the same room, by Sargent.

Between Mr and Mrs Stevenson, Sargent's portrait depicted (as Louis put it) 'an open door showing my palatial entrance hall and part of my respected staircase'. At the top of the respected staircase was a small library lined with books and Louis' bedroom – with its south-facing 'sea view' – where he spent most of his time, surrounded by bottles of medicine bought at the local chemist's and with a small writing board lying on his counterpane. It was in this bedroom that he wrote most of *Strange Case of Dr Jekyll and Mr Hyde*, after a particularly unpleasant three-day attack of fever and haemorrhaging.

R obert Louis Stevenson had for some time been thinking about characters who lead double lives, and who appear morally correct on the surface but whose inner thoughts lead them towards immorality. Earlier in 1885, he had written the short story *Markheim*, about an unrepentant murderer who meets a figure resembling the devil, a figure 'like himself'. Ever since he started working on *Deacon Brodie*, his fiction – and his life – had been riddled with 'dualisms'. So when he had his nightmare in September 1885, he had – as he recalled – 'long been trying to write a story on this subject, to find … a vehicle'. The dream was an example of his conscious mind thinking of a story and his unconscious mind taking over from there.

According to Fanny, her husband had been 'deeply impressed by a paper he had read in a French scientific journal on sub-consciousness [which] gave the germ of the idea'. But there were, in fact, various strands of contemporary scientific research which could have stimulated *Dr Jekyll and Mr Hyde*.

Where Dr Jekyll's experiment was concerned, there were the very recent discoveries in germ theory and immunisation, which had created the impression in the popular press that 'the doctors' could do almost anything. The early 1880s had produced important advances in the understanding of tuberculosis and diphtheria, and it is likely that Stevenson was aware both of the researches and the resulting debate. He was also writing at a time when psychology was still thought to be a matter for 'the doctors'.

Where 'the beast in man' was concerned, Darwin's *The Origin of the Species* (1859) had apparently established that human beings were descended from the beasts – so 'animal passions' could be as natural as the human variety: Mr

Hyde was simply several steps down the evolutionary ladder; 'ape-like' to Jekyll, 'troglodytic' to Utterson, and known to all as 'the beast Hyde'.

Where 'man's double being' was concerned, there were the researches of the French neurologist Charcot and his colleague Pierre Janet into the relationship between hypnosis, hysteria and aspects of 'consciousness' (rather than the 'unconscious', at this stage) which had somehow detached themselves from the normally functioning mind. Hypnosis, it was thought, was a way of reaching hysteria, which was itself attempting to colonise the whole of the patient's mind; so what *seemed* to be 'the mind' was in fact the product of at least two warring sensations, sensations which could be isolated and described through hypnotism.

In 1885, the year of *Dr Jekyll*, the young Sigmund Freud observed Charcot giving a public display of hypnotism in Paris. But the concept of 'sub-consciousness' (as mentioned by Fanny in the 1920s) was a thing of the future, when psychoanalysis ceased to be a purely descriptive discipline.

Where 'the perennial war among my members' was concerned, *Dr Jekyll and Mr Hyde* – which is presented as a 'case-study' or a 'casebook' – was published in precisely the same year as Krafft Ebing's *Psychopathia Sexualis*, an attempt to describe the conflict between 'animal instincts' and 'morality' through a series of bizarre case-studies of sexual perversion.

As successive editions of the *Psychopathia* were published, the author simply added more and more anecdotes (with the perversions written in Latin, on the highly questionable assumption that classical scholars were incorruptible): the earliest contributions to the new 'science' of sexology seem to have been entirely concerned with describing pathological manifestations, 'perversions', and criminal activities such as 'lust murder', which were then contrasted with the norm. The animal was in there somewhere, but it was in everyone's interests to keep it caged up. Sometimes it fed on men who thought they could get by 'without the aid of women' – men like all the characters in Stevenson's story.

At some level, *Dr Jekyll and Mr Hyde* clearly belongs in Krafft Ebing's case-book: but perhaps the strangest aspect of it (given the context in which it was written) is the complete absence of sex, explicit sex, from the story. Mr Hyde does *not* behave like one of Krafft Ebing's perverts: he tramples a little girl, and beats a distinguished Member of Parliament to death after bumping into him. Several critics noted that, given the power of the narrative, Hyde's behaviour seemed somehow 'inadequate'.

When questioned about this, Stevenson was far from consistent. The writer John Addington Symonds, himself a homosexual unable to come out and shortly to co-author *Studies in the Psychology of Sex*, wrote to Stevenson on 3 March 1886. *Dr Jekyll,* he reckoned, was 'as a piece of literary work … the finest you have ever done'. But: 'It makes me wonder whether a man has the right so to scrutinise "the abysmal deeps of personality". It is indeed a dreadful book, [and] it has left such a painful impression on my heart that I do not know how I am ever to turn to it again'.

To which Stevenson immediately replied: '*Jekyll* is a dreadful thing, I own; but the only thing I feel dreadful about is that damned old business of the war in the members. This time it came out; I hope it will stay in, in future'.

So *Dr Jekyll and Mr Hyde was* partly about sex – and all those references in the story to closed doors, locked cabinets and secret rooms were to do with hoping 'it will stay in, in future'. The subject of sex was unmentioned, but it was there.

To a reviewer who had drawn attention to a 'confusion of ethics' in *Dr Jekyll*, Stevenson responded that the criticism was 'all too true'. He was fascinated by ethical problems, but 'baffled' by their deeper significance: 'It is, as you say, where I fall, and fall most consciously. I have the old Scotch Presbyterian preoccupation about these problems; itself morbid; I have alongside of that a second, perhaps more – possibly less – morbid element – the dazzled incapacity to choose, of an age of transition'.

And to a drama critic who had judged the story, in its stage adaptation, to be 'ugly' and Mr Hyde to be 'a mere voluptuary', Stevenson thundered back in a letter marked 'Private', mid-November 1887: '[Hyde] was not, Great Gods! a mere voluptuary ... The harm was in Jekyll, because he was a hypocrite – not because he was fond of women; he says so himself; but people are so filled full of folly and inverted lust, that they can think of nothing but sexuality. The Hypocrite let out the beast Hyde – who is no more sexual than another, but who is the essence of cruelty and malice, and selfishness and cowardice; and these are the diabolic in man – not this great wish to have a woman, that they make such a cry about ... '

So *Dr Jekyll and Mr Hyde* was, according to its author, about 'that damned old business of the war in the members', 'the old Scotch Presbyterian preoccupation' with ethics and sin, the difficulty in understanding what lay at the root of ethical dilemmas during 'an age of transition' – and at the same time it was *not* about 'the sexual field' at all but about hypocrisy and the thin veneer of civilisation (as much a social as an ethical problem). Or perhaps it was not the *author's* role to say 'what was meant' at all: perhaps that was up to the commentators.

Stevenson admitted that he was confused about which 'category' Mr Hyde should be filed under. He could not have read the *Psychopathia Sexualis* before writing his book, although as Krafft Ebing points out in his introduction questions about 'the pathology of sexual life' were very much in the air in the mid-1880s. *Dr Jekyll and Mr Hyde* works very hard to deny any necessary connection between 'the sexual field' and 'the essence of cruelty and malice' (which operated at a different level of ethics). But as the book entered the public bloodstream – *after* the publication of the *Psychopathia* – many readers and playgoers were in no doubt that, whatever the author might say, it was *really* about sex.

tevenson's nightmare – which followed, according to Andrew Lang, 'a copious supper of bread and jam' – distilled his thoughts about 'man's double being', and his impressions of the latest medical and psychological researches, into two clear visual images: 'the scene at the window, and a scene afterwards split in two, in which Hyde, pursued for some crime, took the powder and underwent the change in the presence of his pursuers … ' The first of these scenes involves Messrs Utterson and Lanyon catching sight of Dr Jekyll as he sits ('taking the air with an infinite sadness of mien') by an open window. Mirrors and portraits had often been used in nineteenth-century literature, to express the theme of the *doppel-ganger*. This time it was to be a window, which reveals 'a voluntary change becoming involuntary'.

'I would ask you and Mr Enfield up, but the place is really not fit'.

'Why then', said the lawyer good-naturedly, 'the best thing we can do is to stay down here, and speak with you from where we are'.

'That is just what I was about to venture to propose', returned the doctor, with a smile. But the words were hardly uttered, before the smile was struck out of his face and succeeded by an expression of such abject terror and despair, as froze the very blood of the two gentlemen below …

The second, which is part of *Dr Lanyon's Narrative*, involves Lanyon meeting the fugitive Mr Hyde in his consulting-room at Cavendish Square, and giving him a dose of the all-important 'powders' (plus a phial 'about half-full of a blood-red liquor') which he has collected from Dr Jekyll's secret wooden cabinet:

He put the glass to his lips, and drank at one gulp. A cry followed; he reeled, staggered, clutched at the table and held on … and as I looked, there came, I thought, a change – he seemed to swell – his face became suddenly black, and the features seemed to melt and alter – and the next moment I had sprung to my feet and leaped back against the wall, my arm raised to shield me from that prodigy, my mind submerged in terror.

This scene is revisited by Dr Jekyll in his *Full Statement* (hence 'split in two'): Hyde never, in the published story, undergoes the change in full view of his pursuers – just Dr Lanyon, whose mind collapses as a result.

The process of turning these fragmentary images into *Strange Case of Dr*

Jekyll and Mr Hyde – between the end of September and the end of October 1885 – have become almost as famous as the book itself. The first full account was published in 1901 (some seven years after Stevenson's death) at the beginning of volume two of Graham Balfour's *The Life of Robert Louis Stevenson*. Balfour was Stevenson's second cousin, and had corresponded with the surviving witnesses Fanny Stevenson and Lloyd Osbourne when compiling his version of events:

> ... so vivid was the impression [of his dream] that he wrote the story off at a red heat, just as it had presented itself to him in his sleep.
>
> 'In the small hours one morning', says Mrs Stevenson, 'I was awakened by cries of horror from Louis. Thinking he had a nightmare, I awakened him. He said angrily: "Why did you wake me? I was dreaming a fine bogey tale". I had awakened him at the first transformation scene'.
>
> Mr Osbourne writes:
>
> '... [there was never] such a literary feat before as the writing of Dr Jekyll ... Louis came downstairs in a fever; read nearly half the book aloud; and then, while we were still gasping he was away again, and busy writing. I doubt if the first draft took so long as three days.'
>
> He had lately had a haemorrhage, and was strictly forbidden all discussion or excitement. No doubt the reading aloud was contrary to the doctor's orders; at any rate Mrs Stevenson, according to the custom then in force, wrote her detailed criticism of the story as it then stood, pointing out her chief objection – that it was really an allegory, whereas he had treated it purely as if it were a story. In the first draft Jekyll's nature was bad all through, and the Hyde change was worked only for the sake of a disguise. She gave the paper to her husband and left the room. After a while his bell rang; on her return she found him sitting up in bed (the clinical thermometer in his mouth), pointing with a long denunciatory finger to a pile of ashes. He had burned the entire draft. Having realised that he had taken the wrong point of view, that the tale was an allegory and not another 'Markheim', he at once destroyed his manuscript ...
>
> It was written again in three days ('I drive on with Jekyll: bankruptcy at my heels'); but the fear of losing the story altogether prevented much further criticism. The powder was condemned as too material an agency, but this he could not eliminate, because in the dream it had made so strong an impression upon him.
>
> 'The mere physical feat', Mr Osbourne continues, 'was tremendous; and instead of harming him, it roused and cheered him inexpressibly'.

Fanny Stevenson's version of the same story was first published in 1924 – some thirty years after Stevenson's death – as her introductory *Note* to the collected edition of *Dr Jekyll and Mr Hyde*:

For the first time in his life [my husband's] sleep now became restless and broken. 'The Brownies' busied themselves during all hours of the night, tormenting him with phantom problems on the chess-board, or more often reviving some almost forgotten train of thought. During an enforced cessation from dramatic collaboration [with W E Henley] the *Strange Case of Dr Jekyll and Mr Hyde* was thus inspired. My husband's cries of horror caused me to rouse him, much to his indignation. 'I was dreaming a fine bogey tale,' he said reproachfully, following with a rapid sketch of Jekyll and Hyde up to the transformation scene, where I had awakened him.

At daybreak he was working with feverish activity on the new book. In three days the first draft, containing thirty thousand words, was finished, only to be entirely destroyed and immediately re-written from another point of view, – that of the allegory, which was palpable and had yet been missed, probably from haste, and the compelling influence of the dream. In another three days the book, except for a few minor corrections, was ready for the press. The amount of work this involved was appalling ... He was suffering from continual haemorrhages, and was hardly allowed to speak, his conversation usually being carried on by means of a slate and pencil.

And Lloyd Osbourne's fuller version was published in his *Intimate Portrait of RLS* (also 1924), as part of the chapter *Stevenson at Thirty-Seven*. It differs slightly from his mother's, and contains much more padding. Apparently, Stevenson came down from his bedroom to lunch one day in 'a very preoccupied frame of mind', gulped down his meal, and said he was 'working with extraordinary success on a new story that had come to him in a dream'. He was not, under any circumstances, to be interrupted:

For three days a sort of hush descended on 'Skerryvore'; we all went about, servants and everybody, in tiptoeing silence; passing Stevenson's door I would see him sitting up in bed, filling page after page, and apparently never pausing for a moment. At the end of three days the mysterious task was finished, and he read aloud to my mother and myself the first draft of *Strange Case of Dr Jekyll and Mr Hyde*.

I listened to it spellbound ... [but my mother's] praise was constrained; the words seemed to come with difficulty; and then all at once she broke out with criticism. He had missed the point, she said; had missed the allegory; had made it merely a story – a magnificent bit of sensationalism – when it should have been a masterpiece. Stevenson was beside himself with anger. [Later, my mother and I] heard Louis descending the stairs, and we both quailed as he burst in as though to continue the argument even more violently than before. But all he said was: 'You are right! I have absolutely missed the allegory, which, after all, is the whole point of it – the very essence of it'. And with that, as though enjoying my mother's discomfiture and her ineffectual start to prevent him, he threw the manuscript into the fire! ...

My first impression was that he had done it out of pique. But it was not. He really had been convinced, and this was his dramatic amend. When my mother and I both cried out at the folly of destroying the manuscript he justified himself vehemently. 'It was all wrong', he said. 'In trying to save some of it I should have got hopelessly off the track. The only way was to put temptation beyond my reach'.

Then ensued another three days of feverish industry on his part ... The culmination was the Jekyll and Hyde that every one knows ...

These incidents, culminating in a 'stupendous achievement' for anyone let alone a man who was haemorrhaging from the lungs at the time and so ill that 'his conversation [was] usually carried on by means of a slate and pencil' – have become part of the legend or folklore of *Dr Jekyll and Mr Hyde*. But, unfortunately, it did not really happen like that at all. A series of unpublished, and up-to-now unknown, papers kept in the National Library of Scotland (*Notes and papers of Sir Graham Balfour*) reveal how this legend came to be pieced together.

The nightmare itself certainly happened: Louis published his detailed essay about it a couple of years later, and two letters written exactly at the time (beginning of October 1885) confirm this part of the story. The first letter is from Fanny Stevenson to family friend and patron Sidney Colvin:

Again Louis is better, and possessed by a story that he will try to work at. To stop him seems to annoy him to such a degree that I am letting him alone as the better alternative; but I fear it will be only energy wasted, as all his late work has been. For the last few days he has, however, seemed much clearer in his mind about things, but has been suffering from dreadful nightmares and headaches at night.

The second is from her son Lloyd to Mrs Margaret Stevenson, transcribed by Graham Balfour. It is dated 4 October 1885:

Louis is doing very well tho' still very weak. He has been writing a most terrible story which he said occurred to him in the night. It is certainly one of the most ghostly and unpleasant stories I have every heard. He is still writing it.

But the incidents of the feverish first draft, Fanny's criticism and the consequent burning of the manuscript were not mentioned at all in any single document of the time. For these, we have to wait until the authorised biography, written under Fanny's close supervision ('if I had fault to find', she wrote to Balfour, 'nothing would or could keep my cat's claws out of the fire') in 1899-1901; the *Notes and Papers* are full of her detailed comments and corrections. While Balfour was compiling and negotiating, an article appeared

*R*elief medallion (1887) by the American sculptor Augustus St Gaudens, showing Stevenson working in bed, a cigarette in his right hand: by the time this medallion turned into Stevenson's memorial plaque in St Giles's Cathedral, the cigarette had become a more respectable quill pen.

(September 1900) in the American edition of *The Bookman* which gave a bald – and confused – outline of the writing of *Jekyll*:

> When Mr Stevenson finished [the first manuscript] he handed it over to his wife, and asked her what she thought of it. Two days elapsed, and Mrs Stevenson handed the story back to her husband, pointing out a few places which she thought were objectionable and ought to be changed. With that she left the room. When she returned a few minutes later, she noticed, to her horror, that the author had torn up the whole manuscript, and had thrown it into the fire.

This account was written, added the author, with help from Mrs Isobel Strong – that is, Fanny's daughter Belle who had become a close friend of Graham Balfour at Vailima (on Samoa) in 1892-94.

Evidently, Balfour had been a bit thin on material for this part of Louis' life, so he asked Fanny and Lloyd to fill in some gaps for him. Fanny replied (early in 1900) with 'my own answer to your list of questions'. This, of which the following is an extract, has never been published before:

> Louis wrote *Jekyll and Hyde* with great rapidity on the lines of his dream … He had had in his mind an idea of a double life story, but it was not the same as the dream. He asked me, as usual, to make no criticisms until the first draft was done. As he didn't like to get tired by discussing my proposed changes in his work it was the custom that I should put my criticisms in writing. In this tale I felt, and still feel that he was hampered by his dream. The powder – which I thought might be changed – he couldn't eliminate because he saw it so plainly in the dream. In the original story he had Jekyll bad all through, and working for the Hyde change only for a disguise. I wrote pages of criticisms, pointing out that he had here a great moral allegory that the dream was obscuring. I didn't like the opening, which was confused – again the dream – and proposed that Hyde should run over the child showing that he was an evil force without humanity. I left my paper with Louis, who was in his bedroom writing in bed. After quite a long interval his bell rang for me, and Lloyd and I went upstairs. As I entered the door Louis pointed with a long dramatic finger (you know) to a pile of ashes on the hearth of the fireplace saying that I was right, and there was the tale. I nearly fainted away with misery when I saw all was gone. He was already hard at work at the new version which was finished in a few days more.

This, then, was the first-ever reference to the (now) well-known version of events. But Balfour seems still to have been perplexed about exactly what Fanny's criticisms were. Was it, he asked, a question of the powders? She replied:

> No, my objection was that the story was an allegory and he had not made it so. I had an afterthought about the powder, but after the burning scene dared not mention it. He told me afterwards that he was so carried away by the dream that he wrote the thing just as it appeared to him in his sleep, but my criticism convinced him that it was an allegory, so he burned the first draft lest he [be] led astray by it.

So the legend was born, not only that the transcription of the dream was a piece of automatic writing (out of Louis' control, hence its nastiness), but that the manuscript was burned because he had completely missed the point of his own story – and Fanny, the guardian angel of his health *and* of his conscience, had supplied that point. The plot thickened, when Fanny's daughter Belle (Isobel Strong) – by now nearly ninety – dictated a formal note in April 1944, *fifty years* after Stevenson's death:

I heard RLS tell this story not only to me, but to several others ... When [Fanny Stevenson] came into the room RLS pointed to the fireplace and to her dismay she found that he had thrown the MS into the fire. She protested tearfully when he said 'No, you're right. It's a great story and I can do it.' He went at it day and night and in three days it was finished and again he gave it to her for her final criticism – this time she was apologetic. 'I have only one suggestion – when you describe Hyde you say he is evil. The reader should know some horrible deed to know how evil he is'. RLS replied, 'You write that yourself'. Louis told me that he did not change a word of her description of Hyde's evil deed.

So Fanny had not only criticised the first draft of *Dr Jekyll and Mr Hyde*, she had actually *written* one of the best-known sections of the book – Mr Hyde trampling over the child's body, leaving her screaming on the ground.

ccording to Robert Louis Stevenson's *Letters*, recently published in a new edition (1995), he was already 'pouring forth a penny (12 penny) dreadful' in late September 1885. On 20 October, he wrote to Fanny (who was staying in London) 'I drive on with *Jekyll*, bankruptcy at my heels'; and eight days later to Henry James, he added that his 'story' was 'done'. On 1 November, he wrote to his publisher Charles Longman (who had written to Stevenson, acknowledging receipt of the manuscript, on 31 October), 'It may interest you to know that the main incident occurred in a nightmare: indigestion has its uses. I woke up, and before I went to sleep again, the story was complete'.

Dr Jekyll had originally, it seems, been offered as a serial in *Longman's Magazine*, but it was decided to issue the story in book form as a shilling shocker, and on 3 November Stevenson signed a contract to this effect: royalties were one-sixth of the cover price, with an advance on 'the first ten thousand copies' (the publishers were evidently confident, assuming as they did that the book would be on sale before Christmas); plus half the proceeds of overseas sales.

By 12 November Stevenson was 'correcting the proofs'; by early December he was corresponding with Andrew Lang about the story's significance (Lang having read it in manuscript); and by the first week in January he was sending copies to his literary acquaintances. These are the only references he made to *Dr Jekyll and Mr Hyde*, between September 1885 and January 1886. There is no evidence of draft-burning, or collaboration with Fanny, but evidence of a period of writing, re-writing, and correcting which lasted just over a month.

In March 1886, Stevenson wrote that *Jekyll* was conceived, written and printed inside ten weeks (which was a bit of an exaggeration), and he told a reporter for the *San Francisco Examiner* in June 1888 that it was drafted in three days 'and written in six weeks' – a very long time instead to sustain a serious attack of 'feverish' automatic writing.

he surviving manuscripts of *Dr Jekyll and Mr Hyde*, which are known as 'The Notebook Draft' and 'The Printer's Copy', contain some evidence that Stevenson toned down his story, while he was re-writing it. Certainly, the first surviving draft seems to be a little more explicit in places. For example, the young Henry Jekyll, in the *Full Statement of the Case*, originally admitted that:

> From a very early age, I became (in secret) the slave of disgraceful pleasures … On the one side, I was what you have known me, a man of distinction, immersed in toils, open to generous sympathies, never slow to befriend struggling virtue, never backward in an honourable cause; on the other, as soon as night had fallen and I could shake off my friends, the iron hand of indurated habit plunged me once again into the mire of my vices. I will trouble you with these no further than to say that they were at once criminal in the sight of the law and abhorrent in themselves. They cut me off from the sympathy of those whom I otherwise respected.

And, instead of the saintly Sir Danvers Carew, MP, Mr Hyde murders a 'Mr Lemsome' who is 'dressed with that sort of outward decency that implies both the lack of means and a defect of taste … Mr Utterson knew him to be a bad fellow … an incurable cad'.

The *implications* of the story remained unchanged – but there was a steady move on the part of Stevenson away from sordid detail and towards generalities (which 'fits' his determination *not* to reduce the story to a case-study in sexual pathology). Maybe Fanny *was* concerned about Jekyll being 'bad all through'; and Lloyd *did* agree that the original draft contained 'contaminated' material. Maybe, as the article in *The Bookman* claimed, Fanny *did* think a few passages were 'objectionable and ought to be changed'. If so, the consequent changes are there in the surviving manuscripts – and there was not necessarily a first draft at all, let alone a first draft which was burned.

Why would anyone want to invent or embellish such a legend? Well, Fanny Stevenson was very aware of the fact that the market for Louis' work – up until *Jekyll* – wanted to see him as a writer of boy's books (such as *Treasure Island*), of poems for children, not of nasty or 'sensational' fiction. He had developed a public image as a gallant, charming, boyish and outward-bound sort of writer: a sickly, but adventurous spirit. She knew that he had a heart of darkness within him (especially when 'Bluidy Jack' was on the rampage), which could certainly spoil everything. She also had a strict moral code where publications were concerned (Adelaide Boodle called this 'noble-mindedness' and 'righteous indignation'). So, when the authorised biography came out, she became the guardian angel who protected him from himself, and what is more protected him *for the benefit of the public*. When Nellie Van de Grift Sanchez, her sister, wrote an authorised *Life of Mrs R L Stevenson* in 1920, she added a further gloss to the story:

> Their discussions over [his] work were sometimes hot and protracted, for neither was disposed to yield without a struggle. Speaking of this in a letter to his mother, Fanny says: 'If I die before Louis, my last earnest request is that he shall publish nothing without his father's approval. I know that means little short of destruction to both of them, but there will be no one else. The field is always covered with my dead and wounded, and often I am forced to compromise, but still I make a very good fight'. In this battle of wits they found intense enjoyment …

So, if Fanny was not to be the guardian angel, Thomas Stevenson – who had been so very upset by the freethinking of Louis' youth, and who had tried to bring him up as a good Presbyterian – was the angel in waiting. Luckily Fanny did not die before Louis, and so could continue to 'save him from temptation' – even, it seems, beyond the grave. Hence the legend of the burned manuscript, for which there is *no credible historical evidence*.

One remaining question is: why a story about a burnt manuscript? Was it because in the *story* Mr Utterson and Inspector Newcomen find 'a pile of grey ashes' in Mr Hyde's hearth, 'as though many papers had been burned'? Was the legend a transference from literature into life? It is more likely – and a more charitable interpretation – that Fanny Stevenson was confusing in her mind *Dr Jekyll and Mr Hyde* with another story by her late husband called *The Travelling Companion*. This story, which was *also* about 'man's double being', was started in summer 1881 and taken up again in November 1883 – at which time Stevenson referred to it as 'an unpleasant tale'. Three years later, in June 1886, after he had issued *Dr Jekyll*, he wrote to another publisher:

> I see my way to *The Travelling Companion* less and less clearly … It has good work, but it is ugly and incurable and instead of sending it to you I think I shall put it in the fire.

When he wrote his *Chapter on Dreams* the following year, Stevenson elided the two stories:

> I had long been trying to write a story on this subject … [and] had even written one, *The Travelling Companion*, which was returned by an editor on the plea that it was a work of genius and indecent, and which I burned the other day on the ground that it was not a work of genius, and that Jekyll had supplanted it.

No manuscript of *The Travelling Companion* has survived. It is the only work from the Skerryvore period (when Stevenson took it up yet again) for which there is contemporary evidence that the first draft was 'unpleasant' and 'ugly', 'a foul, gross, bitter, ugly daub' – and that it was burned by the author. Perhaps *this* was the memory which Fanny Stevenson transferred, in retrospect, to *Dr Jekyll and Mr Hyde* itself. All the evidence points that way.

When Graham Balfour's biography was published, Stevenson's old friend W.E. Henley (who had fallen out with Louis and especially Fanny in 1887) wrote a famously jaundiced article about it in the *Pall Mall Magazine*:

> I take a view of Stevenson which is my own, and which declines to be concerned with this Seraph in Chocolate, this barley-sugar effigy of a real man; that the best and the most interesting part of Stevenson's life will never get written – even by me; and that the Shorter Catechist of Vailima, however brilliant and distinguished as a writer of stories, however authorised and acceptable as an artist in morals, is not my old, riotous, intrepid, scornful Stevenson at all …

Stevenson himself had written to Henley, when they were still friends, to the effect that in any future authorised biography ' … "Youth in Edinburgh" is likely to be a masterpiece of the genteel evasion'. As it transpired, Balfour did indeed draw a veil over his student life in Edinburgh, his quarrel with his father Thomas (Fanny reminded the biographer in no uncertain terms that 'the whole affair had been forgotten by Louis'), the closeness of his relationship with Fanny before marriage – and the fact that Mr Hyde was as much a part of Stevenson's make-up as Dr Jekyll. The final fifth of the biography was devoted to life in exotic Samoa – which in fact occupied less than one tenth of Stevenson's life story. As Graham Balfour's son Michael has justly written, many of the biographer's problems – the watchful eye of Fanny Stevenson chief among them – 'were solved by leaving considerably more space between some lines than others'.

And there is no doubt that this carefully crafted image – 'barley-sugar effigy' is a *little* extreme – succeeded in taking hold. The rest of Fanny's family then pitched in as well, steadily embellishing the story of the creation of *Dr Jekyll and Mr Hyde*, always to Mrs Stevenson's advantage. She was right, they said: the crude horrors of this shilling shocker *did* need to be repressed. Louis *did* need saving from himself, at times. The story was told and re-told by her sister Nellie, her son Lloyd, her daughter Belle, her friend Adelaide Boodle – and by as many acquaintances and passers-by as could get hold of a publisher (which was a lot, in the Stevenson mania of the 1910s and 1920s). *Dr Jekyll* was an aberration, the product of a temporarily sick mind.

eanwhile, in the less rarefied atmosphere of mass culture, Thomas Russell Sullivan's dramatised version of *Dr Jekyll and Mr Hyde* – starring the actor Richard Mansfield (for whom it was written) in both roles – opened in Boston on 9 May 1887 and New York a week later, before touring the United States to packed houses until 25 June 1888 and transferring to Henry Irving's Lyceum Theatre in London on 4 August 1888.

Stevenson had warned Sullivan that, given the multi-layering of the book, adaptation 'appears to me a difficult undertaking', but when he eventually heard the play through – read by the understandably nervous adaptor early in 1888 – he professed to be satisfied with it: especially the transformation scene at the end of the third act, which had turned narrative into action. 'Good', he said, 'you have done precisely what that scene needed for stage effect. It is very strong'. He then added reassuringly that 'Mrs Stevenson liked it' (she had seen the play on the stage in New York). He also reminded Sullivan of how difficult it had been for him to write the original: '*Jekyll and Hyde* was written very slowly, and much material was discarded'.

The play seems to have disappeared, but it is possible to reconstruct it from early biographies of Richard Mansfield.

From the evidence of these, it is surprising that Stevenson enjoyed the play-reading so much. According to Sullivan, he exclaimed 'I might not have liked it, you know. But I do like it, all through. Now, let us go to luncheon'. It is surprising because the dramatised version did various things to the story which the author had studiously avoided. It gave Dr Jekyll a girlfriend and Mr Hyde a motive – he is so jealous of her that he murders her father. It turned Hyde into a noisy, and rakish villain of melodrama; added a supernatural dimension, and changed the scene at the window into a lovers' last farewell. Crucially, it expanded the story beyond the all-male world of Jekyll, Utterson, Enfield and Lanyon.

But the most important change arose from the fact that Mansfield himself played both Dr Jekyll *and* Mr Hyde – founding a tradition, *the* way of presenting the story, which survives even today. In the book, Hyde is smaller and younger than Jekyll, a different being who comes from inside the doctor and who looks grotesque partly because his clothes are too large. In the play, and ever since, he is the same person. And, to emphasise the contrast between the two – to make them more 'distinctively individual' – Mansfield made Jekyll much more saintly and Hyde much more of a villain.

It was, however, the transformation from Jekyll to Hyde, in Acts Three and Four, which attracted the most publicity. Mansfield started off as the fine, upstanding Dr Jekyll – fashionably pallid and ever-so-noble – and in full view of the audience, without hiding behind a pillar, going offstage or using a double, turned into the devilish Mr Hyde before their very eyes. How on earth did he do it? When interviewed (as he was, many times), Mansfield refused to divulge his trade secret. He seems to have altered his posture from an upright position, to an ape-like crouch; his sensitive fingers were curled into claws; his voice went from normal to guttural (or 'irritating') and the volume went up; and by use of coloured lights and make-up – especially magenta reflected on to green, with gells being slowly introduced to the electric lights – he managed to change the shape of his face. All of which took place behind a gauze curtain.

The most difficult aspect of the transformation for Richard Mansfield – one which apparently made him 'beside himself' with anxiety – was to be certain that the stage manager had done his job properly. He had no means of knowing whether the effect had actually worked. All he could do was look out at the audience and, as he once said, if they started fainting he knew the transformation had been a success.

When he read some of the reviews, Stevenson began to get upset: 'Hyde was the *younger* of the two' he wrote; Jekyll was 'not good looking'; and Hyde was *not* 'a mere voluptuary' who was jealous of Jekyll's attraction for Agnes Carew. But it was too late. Virtually every adaptation of *Dr Jekyll and Mr Hyde* since that time – including the film versions with John Barrymore (1920), Fredric March (1932), Spencer Tracy (1941) and Boris Karloff (1953 – in *Abbott and Costello meet Dr Jekyll and Mr Hyde*) – has followed the outlines of Sullivan's adaptation, with variations to suit the temper of the times. Mansfield's interpretation of Hyde as an embodiment of Jekyll's buried desires, an immature lout 'unable by reason of his hideous shape to indulge the dreams of his hideous imagination' (as the actor put it), has become the norm. And the doctor's name is now pronounced Jeckyll not Jeekyll.

A t the same time the academic 'commentators' to whom Stevenson preferred to give free vein, have interpreted the story in ways which he would not have understood – let alone recognised. He may have complained that people in the 1880s read sexuality into everything, but he hadn't seen anything yet!

In the last twenty years *Dr Jekyll and Mr Hyde* has been deconstructed as being really about the father/son relationship, the adolescent boy inside the grown man, homosexual panic, the eroticisation of the working man,

Actor Richard Mansfield, playing both the saintly Dr Jekyll and the devilish Mr Hyde in J.R. Sullivan's dramatised version of 1887: the play was running in London at the time of the Whitechapel murders.

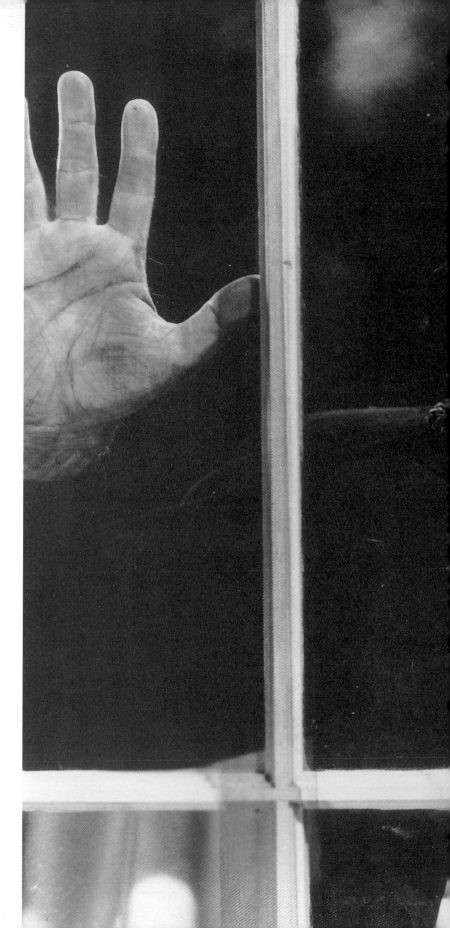

redric March as an ape-like Mr Hyde, an example of evolution in reverse, in Rouben Mamoulian's Hollywood film version of Dr Jekyll and Mr Hyde *(1932).*

impotence, misogyny and/or fear of women, the dark side of patriarchy, the rapist and – in general – anything that late Victorian single gentlemen could conceivably cram into their closets. Or else it was about the conscious and the unconscious. Or the capitalist and the proletarian. Or, long before its time, personality-changing drugs. And so on. One of the more convincing of recent interpretations sees the story as representing two sides of Stevenson's own personality: the man of action inside his head; the disabled artist he saw in the mirror. *Jekyll and Hyde* contains legions.

But in the public domain, the range of meanings encoded into the story was to be seriously curtailed by a series of real-life events which took place in the East End of London in the autumn of 1888. If readers of the shilling shocker felt short-changed by Mr Hyde's behaviour – as not bestial enough – and disappointed by the all-male ambience – as not 'Gothick' enough – they were about to re-write it as just the story they wanted to read.

Between 31 August and 9 November, a mere ten-week period, five unemployed women who had turned to prostitution – Mary Ann Nichols, Annie Chapman, Elizabeth Stride, Catherine Eddowes and Mary Jane Kelly – were murdered and savagely mutilated by an unknown killer the newspapers dubbed 'Jack the Ripper', in and around Whitechapel. It did not take long for these sordid events to be turned into an all-stops-out Victorian melodrama.

As it happened, the first of the murders occurred at precisely the same time as Sullivan's play was running in the West End, and the sixteenth edition of Stevenson's paper-covered story was on sale in the bookshops. The murders also happened at a time when the medical profession – the so-called 'new priesthood' which put health before morals – was getting a particularly bad press, with accusations of needless cruelty and high-handedness; of knife-happy surgeons taking advantage of vulnerable women in front of leering medical students. A novel had been published the previous year which told of an evil medical student who recklessly experimented with the living bodies of pauper women in a teaching hospital. The result of this combination of circumstances was that the story of *Dr Jekyll and Mr Hyde* became completely confused in public consciousness with the story of the Whitechapel murders.

One member of a neighbourhood watch committee wrote to the police suggesting that Richard Mansfield had to be the prime suspect, because his transformation and frenzied performance were so convincing. Others reckoned that the 'sensational' drama might have put ideas in Jack the Ripper's mind. How dare they put on a play which made women scared to walk home alone at night?

At the time these horrendous crimes occurred, the suggestion that Ripper might be a doctor – probably based at the London Hospital in the

THE MILLER-COURT MURDER, WHITECHAPEL; SITE OF MARY KELLY'S LODGINGS.

Cover of The Penny Illustrated Paper, *showing the surroundings of Jack the Ripper's murder of Mary Jane Kelly in November 1888: note how the murderer was presumed to have been wearing a top hat, and carrying a doctor's bag.*

Whitechapel Road – who had an obsession with destroying prostitutes, was by far the most popular, and accessible, explanation. 'Jack' was a soft-spoken surgeon who heard voices in the night; he was a medical student who had caught syphilis from a prostitute and wanted to revenge himself on the whole pack of them; he was a mad doctor in a teaching hospital who derived sexual satisfaction from inflicting cruelty on women.

Dr Jekyll and Mr Hyde – book and play – had provided a ready-made model of pathological behaviour, a model to explain the inexplicable. When the coroner at Annie Chapman's inquest suggested that the killer might have had some anatomical knowledge – 'might have known what he was doing' – the 'fit' seemed perfect.

Equally, the Whitechapel murders encouraged a particular 'reading' of Stevenson's story. Hyde is not a 'lust-murderer'; he does not consort with prostitutes; he lives in Soho in the West End; and his night-time beat is along dingy neighbourhoods just around the corner from smart residences. But from now on, all that would change: in every future adaptation of significance, Hyde would become a 'lust-murderer' (the lust being Jekyll's); a killer of prostitutes; and a fiend who haunts the fog-shrouded East End of London. The iconography of top hat, Gladstone Bag, silver-topped cane, and lovable Cockney 'sparrers' with large busts and tight bodices would become mandatory.

In Stevenson's book, although it is never made clear why Hyde should be cruising around those dingy neighbourhoods in the early hours of the morning, from autumn 1888 onwards there would no longer be any doubt. Although the setting is supposed to be London in the original – a London where 'a fog rolled over the city in the small hours' – the atmosphere, and the tone, is clearly the Edinburgh of Old and New Towns, as many commentators have observed: a place where Stevenson's 'Scotch Presbyterian preoccupation' made sense. But it turned into the West End (Jekyll) and the East End (Hyde); a journey into the abyss. By December 1894, a critic in *The Athenaeum* could write of the book as an example of 'Art following Nature':

> *Dr Jekyll* appeared in the midst of the Jack the Ripper terror, and I have often thought it was the artistic reflex of that mysterious series of crimes …
>
> In the background looms one aspect of the great problem of sex which Stevenson elsewhere evaded or avoided.

The following week, after someone had reminded him that *Dr Jekyll* in fact preceded the Whitechapel murders by over two-and-a-half years, he amended this to 'one of the instances where, as Mr Oscar Wilde has observed, Nature follows Art'. No-one questioned the point: *Dr Jekyll* had indeed *become* the 'artistic reflex' of Jack the Ripper. It was by now beyond its author's control. The experiment with the powders was irreversible.

hen, a decade after Stevenson's death, members of the Edinburgh establishment decided to erect a monument to his genius – as a sign that they had *almost* forgiven him – in the august, if slightly gloomy surroundings of St Giles's Cathedral, they commissioned a huge bronze relief sculpture of the saintly artist who suffered nobly – as was the fashion at the time – for his art.

If the good burghers had been completely convinced, they would perhaps have erected an elaborate public statue – like Walter Scott's – on Princes Street. The Stevenson sculpture, however, to the right of the main door, shows Stevenson sitting in a chaise longue, propped up on a pillow, covered with a tasselled rug – a bundle of papers in his left hand, and a quill pen, poised, in his right. He is looking into space, about to produce another masterpiece.

This image was, in fact, based on – and enlarged from – an earlier relief sculpture (or medallion), by the American artist Augustus St Gaudens, made while Stevenson lay in bed, coughing, having just survived a hero's welcome in New York about eighteen months after the publication of *Strange Case of Dr Jekyll and Mr Hyde*. In this original version, Stevenson was sitting up in a bed, covered with a blanket, the bundle of papers in his left hand – but in his right, a cigarette: a characteristic pose for receiving guests. For the Cathedral monument, the bed became a chaise longue, the blanket sprouted tassels, Stevenson put on a little weight – and there was that rather improbable quill pen. Great artists who made it into the Edinburgh pantheon evidently were not permitted to smoke in bed! And so, the man who was on record as stating that he could not write a word without the aid of a cigarette – despite the state of his lungs – and who was so good at rolling his own that an acquaintance said he could make roll-ups as thin as his arms (in other words, very thin indeed) had at last become respectable.

The trouble with the cult of the saintly Robert Louis Stevenson – fuelled by his wife Fanny, most of his friends and a small clique of adoring critics who had decided to suspend their critical faculties – is that it has actually affected his literary reputation. For when something as sickly sweet as the authorised version of RLS's life and works is rammed down your throat with the *Garden of Verses* in the nursery, *Kidnapped* and *Treasure Island* at school, and *Dr Jekyll* from the pulpit – you begin to gag on it.

In some ways, Stevenson has never recovered from this saintly image – Jekyll without Hyde is too one-dimensional, too squeaky-clean and sentimental a character to be taken entirely seriously. As Stevenson himself wrote of one of his characters, a Scotsman living in London, about 'as emotional as a bagpipe'. And he did not mean this as a compliment.

4

The Hound of the Baskervilles

The moon was shining bright upon the clearing, and there in the centre lay the unhappy maid where she had fallen, dead of fear and fatigue. But it was not the sight of her body, nor yet was it that of the body of Hugo Baskerville lying near her, which raised the hair upon the heads of these three dare-devil roisterers, but it was that, standing over Hugo, and plucking at his throat, there stood a foul thing, a great, black beast, shaped like a hound, yet larger than any hound that ever mortal eye had rested upon. And even as they looked the thing tore the throat out of Hugo Baskerville, on which, as it turned its blazing eyes and dripping jaws upon them, the three shrieked with fear and rode for dear life, still screaming, across the moor ... Such is the tale, my sons, of the coming of the hound which is said to have plagued the family so sorely ever since.

ARTHUR CONAN DOYLE

The 'dark form and savage face' of the Hound of the Baskervilles, observed through the Dartmoor fog by Holmes and Watson in Sidney Paget's illustration for the Strand (March 1902).

HE DEATH OF the world's first consulting detective, Sherlock Holmes of 221b Baker Street, was in the planning for nearly two years. In December 1892 his creator Arthur Conan Doyle had said 'a man like that mustn't die of a pin-prick or influenza. His end must be violent and intensely dramatic'. The following spring, he added 'I am weary of his name'. Holmes had to die, because 'he takes my mind from better things': he had to die 'even if I buried my banking account along with him'.

After *A Study in Scarlet* (first published Christmas 1887, book July 1888), *The Sign of the Four* (first published February 1890, book October), and *The Adventures of Sherlock Holmes* (twelve short stories which first appeared in the *Strand Magazine* 1891-2, book October 1892), the detective had become as tedious as the old man of the sea in Coleridge's poem who 'stoppeth one of three'; and 'if I don't kill him soon he'll kill me'.

The forensic details of his 'intensely dramatic end' were decided in August 1893, when Conan Doyle and his wife Louise – on their eighth wedding anniversary – travelled from Lucerne in Switzerland to the village of Meiringen, and via the 300-ft Reichenbach Falls a couple of miles outside the village, to the Rhône Valley. It was 'rather rough on an old friend who has brought you fame and fortune' to kill him off, suggested an ecclesiastical travelling companion, but Conan Doyle's mind was firmly made up. Sherlock Holmes's last journey, accompanied by his chronicler Dr Watson, had to extend beyond the foggy surroundings of Baker Street; it had to be a suitably grand tour: the boat-train to Newhaven, changing at Canterbury, the ferry to Dieppe, overland to Brussels and Strasbourg, then on to Geneva and 'a charming week' wandering up the Valley of the Rhône, and finally over the Gemmi Pass and 'so, by way of Interlaken, to Meiringen'.

Dr Watson's last view of Sherlock Holmes was of him standing with his back against a rock, arms folded, gazing down at the rush of the Reichenbach Falls in full flood – the Upper Falls, beyond the level of the viewing platform. After that, Watson went back down the path, to the left of the spectacular Middle Falls, to the village of Meiringen, while Holmes settled his account with 'Professor' James Moriarty – head of the most powerful syndicate of criminals in Europe.

> [The Reichenbach Falls] is, indeed, a fearful place. The torrent, swollen by the melting snow, plunges into a tremendous abyss, from which the spray rolls up like the smoke from a burning house. The shaft into which the river hurls itself is an immense chasm, lined by glistening, coal-black rock, and narrowing into a creaming, boiling pit of incalculable depth, which brims over and shoots the stream onward over its jagged lip ... We stood near the

*P*hotograph by Hoppé of Arthur Conan Doyle at work in the music room of his Sussex home in 1912. By this time, Sherlock Holmes had been 'resurrected' for over ten years.

edge peering down at the gleam of breaking water far below us against the black rocks, and listening to the half-human shout which came booming up with the spray out of the abyss.

The meeting between Holmes and Moriarty became it seemed (the event took place offstage) a hand-to-hand fight, which in turn led to them both reeling over the edge of the precipice, locked in each other's arms, and plunging into 'that dreadful cauldron of swirling water and seething foam'. Any

herlock Holmes and Professor Moriarty fight it out, on the path next to the 'tremendous abyss' of the Reichenbach Falls, in Sidney Paget's illustration to The Final Problem *(December 1893).*

attempt at recovering the bodies, wrote Dr Watson or rather Arthur Conan Doyle, was 'absolutely hopeless'. And there, somewhere among the rocks of the Reichenbach will lie 'for all time the most dangerous criminal and the foremost champion of the law of their generation'.

When the story *The Final Problem* was first published in December 1893 (describing fictional events which took place on 4 May 1891), it is said that black arm-bands and hat-bands were worn by usually sensible young businessmen in the City of London, and that shareholders in the *Strand Magazine* went into a state of shock – as well they might – because several thousand people cancelled their subscriptions to the *Strand* there and then.

'We have had this week to chronicle the death of Sherlock Holmes', reported the *St James's Gazette* on 16 December: 'He has well earned his retirement, and, unless the Queen shall command Mr Doyle to show Sherlock Holmes in love, he may perhaps be permitted to rest in peace.'

A few weeks later an advertisement appeared in the press, purporting to be 'the last letter from Sherlock Holmes' and asking for one large box of Beecham's Pills to be sent by first-class post to 'this benighted spot' – 'as my movements are uncertain'.

Meanwhile, Arthur Conan Doyle was alive and well, noting with evident relish, in his diary, 'killed Holmes'. True, he was writing to friends on black-bordered notepaper in the autumn of 1893, but that had nothing whatever to do with Sherlock Holmes. His father Charles Altamont Doyle (architect, surveyor, artist and long-term resident in Montrose Royal Lunatic Asylum – to cure him of alcoholism and epilepsy) had died in October.

Doyle was on good form because he had the sneaking suspicion – like his friend Arthur Sullivan – that the work he was best at, the work which had made his name a household word, was in some sense unworthy of an eminent Victorian. And now he was rid of it.

When Doyle later agreed to write a *Preface* to the Holmes stories (he had refused several times), he began with the words 'So elementary a form of fiction as the detective story hardly deserves the dignity of a *Preface*'. Just as Arthur Sullivan broke up his Savoy partnership with W.S. Gilbert, and went on to write ponderous and derivative sacred music, Conan Doyle killed off Sherlock Holmes to give himself more time to devote to his historical novels. Opinions differ as to the wisdom of this career move.

Nothing, however, could bring back the consulting detective now. Dr Watson had written positively 'the last words in which I shall ever record the singular gifts by which my friend Mr Sherlock Holmes was distinguished'. Nothing, that is, except a particularly ferocious black dog which haunted an ancient stretch of moorland in the wild West of England …

he story of how Arthur Conan Doyle came to hear of the legend of the hound began in and around a hotel in Cromer, Norfolk, seven years and three months after the publication of *The Final Problem*. The hotel was the Royal Links, an ace guesthouse with eighteen-hole golf course attached. It was 'Royal' because Cromer was one of Prince Eddie's favourite watering places. The Royal Links Hotel was to burn down in the 1940s: today, only a few bricks remain – in what is now a holiday chalet park.

Conan Doyle went to stay there in March 1901 for a short rest-cure, after a very demanding period in his life. He was feeling depressed. The month before, he had been asked to join Queen Victoria's funeral procession, and had involved himself in a controversy about unpleasant references to Roman Catholics in the coronation oath (he had been baptised a Catholic and educated by the Jesuits, but rejected the family faith – and all institutional religion – in his early twenties).

In October 1900 he had unsuccessfully stood in the so-called 'khaki' election as a Liberal Unionist candidate for Edinburgh Central. His defeat, following a smear campaign which included the putting up of posters in Protestant areas accusing him of being a Jesuit lacky, convinced him that electioneering was like 'a mud bath'.

To make matters worse, his domestic life was under considerable strain. His wife Louise Hawkins had for some time been bedridden with tuberculosis of the lungs (there had been early signs of the disease when they had visited the Reichenbach Falls together in summer 1893) and at the same time it was becoming more and more difficult for him to maintain a 'chivalrous' and Platonic attitude towards Jean Leckie, the woman he loved. He could not sleep, and he had a touch of fever – perhaps something he had brought back with him from South Africa where he had tried hard to enlist in the British army, but had been turned down (he was forty-one, with no army record) and instead worked as voluntary supervisor at Langmans Field Hospital in Bloemfontein, capital of the Orange Free State, for several months in 1900.

While there, he had also found time to write his controversial account of *The Great Boer War* and think about his *The War in South Africa. Its Course and Conduct* – a polemic justifying Britain's war against the Boers and defending both Kitchener's campaign and the behaviour of ordinary soldiers against widespread criticism from home and abroad.

The short holiday at the Royal Links was shared with Bertram Fletcher Robinson, a young journalist he had met – and struck up a friendship with – in 1901 while returning from Cape Town and the Boer War aboard the *SS Briton*. The energetic Robinson had been sent out as war correspondent by the newly founded *Daily Express*. A graduate of Jesus College Cambridge, ex-editor of *Granta*, and trained barrister, 'Bertie' or 'Bobbles' was beginning to make his name as a talented journalist.

One Sunday afternoon at the Royal Links Hotel, when the breeze from the North Sea was blowing too strongly for Conan Doyle and Fletcher Robinson to play their usual round of golf, they passed the time in a private sitting room. In the course of a long chat, Robinson told Doyle of the legend of a ferocious black dog which haunted the countryside.

The folklore of the British Isles is littered with legends of phantom black dogs (they are called 'black dogs' by professional folklorists, whatever colour they happen to be) – sometimes single ones, sometimes whole packs of them – and there are still 'Black Dog Lanes' and 'Black Dog Inns' in villages all over the place. Most of these dogs are fairly friendly creatures, which warn of impending disaster or haunt a location where something terrible happened to their owner or their owner's family. They are known by colourful local names such as 'padfoot', 'barguest', 'shrike', 'Moddey Dhoo', and 'the Gabriel Pack'. One big exception is Black Shuck or old Shuck of Norfolk – Shuck or Scucca meaning 'the demon' in Anglo-Saxon. Black Shuck was said to appear at dusk, a huge, shaggy creature 'the size of a calf, easily recognisable by his saucer-sized eyes weeping green or red fire'. And no-one who caught sight of him, or felt his icy breath in the night, survived till daybreak. Black Shuck was one of the most vicious dogs in British folklore – mindlessly vicious – and Cromer was on his beat.

According to an article written by J.E. Hodder Williams exactly a year later, 'Robinson ... mentioned in conversation some old country legend which set Doyle's imagination on fire. The two men began building up a chain of events, and in a very few hours the plot of a sensational story was conceived ... '

Max Pemberton was convinced that Robinson must have mentioned Black Shuck in the course of his conversation with Conan Doyle at the Royal Links. Indeed, Pemberton himself had recounted the gruesome legend to Robinson a little while before, when 'Bertie' was visiting him in Hampstead. This story had had a particular immediacy about it, because Pemberton had not read about it in a book of folklore, but had been told it firsthand by a Norfolk marshman – one Jimmy Farman – whose own dog had been terrified out of its wits by a manifestation of Black Shuck.

Conan Doyle, Pemberton added, would have been instantly fired up by this legend because 'it was ever the bizarre and the daring that drew [him] as a filing is drawn to its magnet'. This side of Dr Doyle's personality had, said Pemberton, been rather sidelined by his public association with the arch-rationalist Sherlock Holmes.

The legend, he might have added, would also have struck a chord because,

The Hound of the Baskervilles

THE STORY

Sherlock Holmes and Dr Watson receive James Mortimer MRCS in Holmes's room at 221b Baker Street. Mortimer reminds them of the sudden death three months before of his friend Sir Charles Baskerville, in the yew alley outside Baskerville Hall on Dartmoor, and reads an eighteenth-century manuscript which tells of the legend of the black hound of the Baskervilles and of its origins in the behaviour of the wicked Hugo at the time of the English Civil War. Sir Charles, it seems, died of a heart attack, and near his body were 'the footprints of a gigantic hound'. Sir Henry Baskerville (Charles's nephew and heir), on his arrival in London from Canada, reports to Holmes that he has been warned to keep away from the moor, and has lost one of his brown boots.

Since Holmes claims to be too busy to accompany Sir Henry to his estate on Dartmoor, Watson travels with him. When they reach Baskerville Hall, they learn that a murderer called Selden has escaped from the prison at Princetown and hear the sound of a woman sobbing in the night. The following day, Watson explores the moor, sees a pony drown in the treacherous Grimpen Mire, and meets Jack Stapleton, a specialist in flora and fauna, and his beautiful sister Beryl who live in nearby Merripit House. Sir Charles is instantly attracted to Beryl, but Stapleton is not pleased. John and Eliza Barrymore, servants at the Hall, are caught signalling to someone at night and it transpires that Mrs Barrymore is the sister of Selden the escaped convict. Watson and Sir Henry find Selden's hiding place, and see the silhouette of a man on a tor; Watson is told that Sir Charles had expected to meet a woman called Laura Lyons on the night of his death. Dr Watson then discovers that Sherlock Holmes has in fact been camping all along in one of the moor's neolithic stone huts - rather than working in London. Holmes has managed to deduce that Beryl is in fact Stapleton's wife, and that Stapleton is having an affair with Laura Lyons (who thinks he is a single man). On their way back to the Hall, they see Selden - dressed in Sir Henry's tweed suit - killed by the hound.

At Baskerville Hall, Holmes notices a resemblance between a 1647 portrait of the wicked Hugo Baskerville and Stapleton. He arranges that Sir Henry will walk alone across the moor from Merripit House, and, together with Watson and Inspector Lestrade from London, succeeds in shooting the huge coal-black hound, which is not only mortal but painted with phosphorus. Stapleton dies in the Great Grimpen Mire, where Sherlock Holmes finds Sir Henry's missing boot.

to judge by his published detective stories, Conan Doyle the writer had it in for dogs of *all* descriptions, never mind the huge shaggy variety which wept fire. In *A Study in Scarlet*, Holmes tests a deadly poison pill on Mrs Hudson's pet terrier – with the result that the hapless creature 'gave a convulsive shiver in every limb' and dropped down dead on the spot, while the callous detective uttered 'a perfect shriek of delight'; in *The Copper Beeches*, Dr Watson blows the brains out of 'the huge famished brute' of a mastiff which has buried its 'black muzzle … and its keen white teeth' in its master's throat.

Canines, in the Holmes stories, tend always to be 'brutes' and 'beasts' and 'devils' – and those are the *domestic* ones!

Anyway, in the heat of the moment, Conan Doyle wrote to his mother Mary (the woman he revealingly called 'The Ma'am') from the hotel:

> Fletcher Robinson came here with me and we are going to do a small book together … a real creeper. Your own, A.

It appears that there was no question of this 'real creeper' being an out-and-out horror story. The ghost-hound was to prove flesh and blood in the end, an approach which had already been tested by Conan Doyle in his short story *The King of the Foxes* (published in *The Windsor Magazine*, July 1898). This was the tale of a legendary spectral fox which turns out to be a grey Siberian wolf 'of the variety known as *Lupus Giganticus*' on the run from a travelling menagerie. The narrator is instantly cured of alcoholism by the experience of meeting an unlikely hunt saboteur:

> Some silly talk which had been going round the country about the king of the foxes – a sort of demon fox, so fast that it could out-run any pack, and so fierce that they could do nothing with it if they overtook it – suddenly came back into his mind … When he first caught sight of them the hounds were standing in a half-circle round this bramble-patch with their backs bristling and their jaws gaping. In front of the brambles lay one of them with his throat torn out, all crimson and white – and tan … [Another] one of them sprang with a growl into the bushes … there was a clashing snap like a rat-trap closing, and the howls sharpened into a scream and then they were still …

As the 'two men began building up a chain of events' for their book, it is also more than likely that copies of *The Strand* provided some of the key links. There must, for example, have been a copy of a very recent issue of *The Strand Magazine* – the issue for December 1900, to be exact – lying around the sitting-room of the Royal Links Hotel. This contained a short story called *Followed* – by the prolific Irish detective story writer Mrs L.T. Meade, assisted on medical details (as she often was) by Dr Robert Eustace – which is all about a crumbling manor house called Longmore on Salisbury Plain, with a sinister servant, an ancestral curse, and a devilish plot to disinherit a young girl. This story hinges on a monstrous black beast – which seems magic but isn't – in this case a venomous Tasmanian snake by the name of Darkey, *Pseudechis Porphyriacus*, whose bite causes certain death in six minutes.

The climax of *Followed* involves the snake (with 'its enormous glistening coil, polished as ebony') chasing the heroine – a young English rose called Flower Dalrymple – across the Plain to the slaughter stone of the ancient temple of Stonehenge, because the creature has been given one of her boots covered in a snake-attracting powder.

> Suddenly I paused and looked back … Whatever the thing was, it came towards me, and as it came it glistened now and then in the moonlight. What could it be? I raised my hand to shade my eyes from the bright light of the moon. I wondered if I was the subject of an hallucination. But, no … It was making straight in my direction. The next instant every fibre in my body was tingling with terror, for gliding towards me, in great curves, with head raised, was an enormous black snake!

In other words, Miss Dalrymple, they were the coil-prints of a gigantic glistening snake.

Eventually, the creature is shot just as it reaches Stonehenge – a moment illustrated by one of the *Strand's* house illustrators, Sidney Paget – and all except the villainous *chatelaine*, the Lady Sarah, live happily ever after.

Conan Doyle was particularly partial to stories about monstrous beasts which gave nightmares to the complacent folk of deep England, and if we substitute a hound for a snake, we virtually have the entire plot of *The Hound of the Baskervilles*.

In another issue of *The Strand* – July 1898 – the regular *Curiosities* slot (which Conan Doyle always enjoyed, for its puzzles) included a photograph of a letter written by an inmate of H.M. Convict Prison Millbank to her aunt, where each character had been 'cut separately out of a Bible, and the requisite words made up with much patience and perseverance'. This 'delightfully ingenious puzzle' bears a strong resemblance to another 'little puzzle' – the note received by Sir Henry Baskerville at the Northumberland Hotel: 'as you value your life or your reason keep away from the moor'.

When Conan Doyle's imagination was 'on fire', it is well known that the resulting story was often stimulated by recent articles, events and pieces of ephemera – as well as by plot suggestions and anecdotes from his friends and relations.

After his short holiday, Conan Doyle returned to London for a couple of weeks and then went to stay at Park Hill House, Ipplepen, near Newton Abbot in Devon, home of the Fletcher Robinson family. 'Bertie' had gone to school at nearby Newton Abbot grammar.

The coachman and groom at Park Hill was young Henry (or Harry) Matthews Baskerville, who had worked for Bertram's father, Joseph Fletcher Robinson, since the age of fifteen cleaning and 'boning' the boots, polishing the cutlery, chopping wood and looking after the croquet lawn. After his marriage, he lived just down the drive from the main house, in a small cottage called Park Lodge. Later, Harry Baskerville was to remember:

> Mr Doyle stayed for eight days and nights. I had to drive him and Bertie about the moors. And I used to watch them in the billiards room in the old house, sometimes they stayed long into the night, writing and talking together.

According to Robinson (in an article published in 1905):

> [Doyle] made the journey [to Devon] in my company shortly after I had told him, and he had accepted from me, the plot which eventuated in *The Hound of the Baskervilles*. Dartmoor, the great wilderness of bog and rocks that cuts Devonshire in two parts, appealed to his imagination. He listened eagerly to my stories of the ghost hounds, of the headless riders and of the devils that lurk in the hollows – legends upon which I had been reared, for my home lay on the borders of the moor. How well he turned to account his impressions will be remembered by all readers of *The Hound*.

Harry Baskerville – who sat, watched and listened attentively, while cleaning their boots and stuffing them into boot-trees – claimed in later life that his employer's son actually *wrote* substantial chunks of the *Hound* at Ipplepen: notably the manuscript of 1742 describing the curse of the Baskervilles and the devilish behaviour of Hugo of that ilk which forms much of chapter 2. He also claimed that both Conan Doyle and Fletcher Robinson thanked him for permitting the use of his name in the story.

So, according to Harry, Sir Henry Baskerville was based on himself, and his proudest possession was a copy of the first edition of *The Hound of the Baskervilles* in a brown paper jacket bearing the inscription 'To Harry Baskerville, with apologies for using the name, Fletcher Robinson'. That's *the* name, note, not *your* name.

Harry eventually came to argue that both he – and his master's son – had been written out of history, leaving the sainted Arthur Conan Doyle with all the credit. He had permitted his name to be used, and as his sole reward could read that the coachman who meets Dr Watson and Sir Henry at the station was a 'hard-faced gnarled little fellow'. Since his claims are still highly controversial – indeed, the great controversy surrounding the preparation of *The Hound of the Baskervilles* – they are worth examining in some detail.

In 1959, Hammer Films issued a publicity manual – 'written and compiled by Unit Publicist Colin Reid and Publicity Supervisor Dennis Thornton' – to promote its new release, *The Hound of the Baskervilles* (starring Peter Cushing and Christopher Lee). This was the first remake of *The Hound* since the Basil Rathbone/Nigel Bruce version of 1939, and the first ever in technicolour. Under the heading *special press features*, the publicists included a news story about Harry Baskerville:

THE STORY OF THE 88-YEARS-OLD COACHMAN (STILL LIVING)
WHO GAVE THE BASKERVILLE HOUND ITS NAME.

Now living at Ashburton in Devon is ... Mr Harry Baskerville, whose claim to some degree of immortality is the fact that he gave The Hound its name! And Harry Baskerville is convinced that young 'Bertie' Robinson, for whose father he worked as coachman and groom, had much more to do with the Sherlock Holmes Dartmoor adventure than many appreciate. Harry, employed by the Robinson family at Parkhill, their Ipplepen home, was once asked by 'Bertie' if he would object to his name being used in a story about Dartmoor. Harry said 'of course not'. The permission granted, the young groom thought no more about the matter ... Harry well remembers the day when he was sent to Newton Abbot railway station to welcome 'Dr' Conan Doyle to Devonshire. Then for several days afterwards he was ordered to drive 'Bertie' and the distinguished visitor over Dartmoor, while Doyle listened to Robinson's tales of local legend ... 'I often saw Dr Doyle and 'Bertie' writing together in the house', says Harry ... [When Fletcher Robinson died, in 1907] the howling of a dog was heard by many people on nearby Dartmoor. Superstitious folk nodded their heads and said it was The Hound mourning the departure of the man who had inspired Conan Doyle to immortalise its story ...

When a copy of this pressbook came into the hands of Adrian Conan Doyle – Arthur's third son and the eccentric literary executor of the Estate – he thundered back to publicity supervisor Dennis Thornton from Switzerland: 'Fletcher Robinson played no part whatever in the writing of the *Hound*. He refused my Father's offer to collaborate and retired at an early stage of the project (*vide* letters, Conan Doyle biographical archives).'

But, in the wake of the new film, there was no stopping the story – and it improved in the telling! Under the headline *This Man's Name Is Baskerville and what he says today brings a big argument over the Sherlock Holmes legend*, Peter Evans of the *Daily Express* picked up the scent on 16 March 1959:

Pink-faced and younger-looking than his 88 years, Baskerville told me in a firm, fine Devonshire voice:- 'Doyle didn't write the story himself. A lot of the story was written by Fletcher Robinson. But he never got the credit he deserved.' Baskerville ... told me that long before Doyle arrived at Park Hill, in Devon, Fletcher Robinson had confided: 'Harry, I'm going to write a story about the moor and I would like to use your name.' ... Shortly after his return from the Boer War, Bertie told me to meet Mr Doyle at the station. He said they were going to work on the story he had told me about ... Then Mr Doyle left and Bertie said to me 'Well, Harry, we've finished that book I was telling you about. The one we're going to name after you'. But last night, Baskerville's story was angrily denied by Sir Arthur Conan

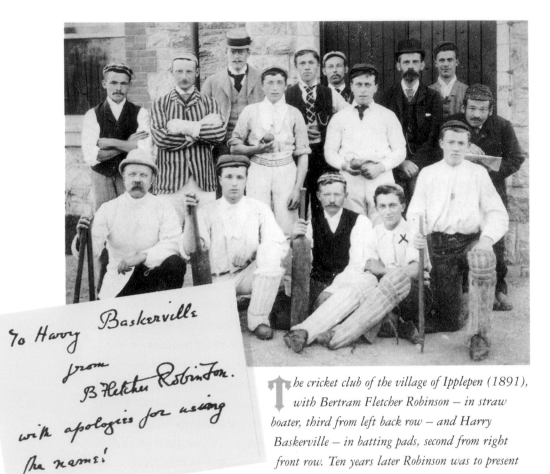

To Harry Baskerville
from
B Fletcher Robinson.
with apologies for using
the name!

The cricket club of the village of Ipplepen (1891),
with Bertram Fletcher Robinson – in straw
boater, third from left back row – and Harry
Baskerville – in batting pads, second from right
front row. Ten years later Robinson was to present
Baskerville with a signed copy of the first edition of The Hound:
his inscription (inset), written in the book apologises to Harry for having used 'the name'.

Doyle's son Adrian ... 'My father never stayed with Fletcher Robinson. He
stayed at the Duchy Hotel, Princetown. He accepted Robinson's offer of a
coach and went riding with him on the moors simply to get the atmosphere
of the place ... It was Robinson who told my father about a West Country
legend, but that was just about the extent of his contribution'.

The story in the Hammer pressbook had been based on an interview com-
missioned by publicist Colin Reid from a reporter on the *Western Morning
News*. And it was the West Country press which had first unearthed the
Harry Baskerville story eight years before, in Festival of Britain year. A short
article in *The South Devon Journal* of 13 June 1951 revealed that one Harry
Baskerville had visited some sheepdog trials at a fête near Ipplepen. Mr
Baskerville had, it seems been 'very interested in dogs' for some time, ever
since Arthur Conan Doyle 'was rather taken with the Coachman's name and
asked his permission to use it in a story he was writing at the time'. Four
months later, *The Journal* elaborated:

> [Harry] was a coachman at Parkhill House, Ipplepen, when Conan Doyle
> came to stay there to gather material for his books in the area, and it was as
> a result of the many long journeys over Dartmoor on which Mr Baskerville
> used to drive the author, that the location and background of scenes in
> *Hound of the Baskervilles* ... were created.

In these articles which laid the original scent, there was no mention at all
of Robinson *writing* the story, or of Conan Doyle taking the credit for work
which was not his. But they did cause Stuart Black – 'one of South Devon's
best-known photographic artists' – to seek Harry out, and take his picture.
This photograph, showing a tweed-jacketed and bespectacled old man
leaning on a stick, with a shock of white hair and a professorial look, became
known worldwide in Festival year when it was featured in the *Sherlock Holmes
Exhibition* in Baker Street (which subsequently toured America) and repro-
duced in the press. Harry's 'discovery' was one of the great research *coups* of
the show.

Stuart Black then wrote an article about Harry Baskerville and the portrait
for *John O'London's* (21 November 1952), in which he reiterated:

> The way it came about was this: Conan Doyle had a friend who was a
> country gentleman called Fletcher Robinson, living on the fringe of Dart-
> moor, with whom he stayed, and apparently Robinson told him the legend
> of the phantom hound, still very prevalent on the moor in various forms.
> Doyle was struck with the possibilities of the legend as the basis of a novel,
> but at first never thought of it in connection with Sherlock Holmes ... At
> that time young Baskerville was Robinson's groom and frequently drove his
> carriage, and so took Conan Doyle on many of his research trips, and long
> and arduous they must have been for Dartmoor covers a vast area, and Doyle
> covered most of it ...

It would seem, therefore, that Harry Baskerville – fêted as a national
treasure in Festival of Britain year, visited as a holy relic by international
Sherlockians, and hounded by the Hammer Films publicity machine –
improved his story (at least, the reported version) under the pressure of
events. This is no wonder, but his original memories, as recorded by his local
paper, were most likely the truth: that he *was* thanked by Robinson for 'using
the name' (that first edition proved it); that Robinson *did* give Conan Doyle
the idea of the legend of the hound; and that Doyle stayed at Park Hill,
Ipplepen *as well as* Rowe's Duchy Hotel, Princetown.

Why should Harry, this 'quiet and unassuming old gentleman', lie about
such things, to *The South Devon Journal*? What he had not realized (since,
apart from anything else, he had never read any Sherlock Holmes stories – let
alone the kind of newspaper hype which surrounded them) was the level of
public interest in his revelations – enhanced by the fact that he was the last

surviving link with the *Hound*. Could these circumstances explain why he embellished his stories?

There remains Adrian Conan Doyle's aside about '*vide* letters, Conan Doyle biographical archives'. Would that one *could* see them! Many have been dispersed; others are inaccessible to scholars, locked away somewhere in London. But the two *published* documents relevant to the case (from the *Sir Arthur Conan Doyle Foundation, Lausanne, Scrapbook 1*) in no way contradict Harry Baskerville's original account of what happened. One is the letter to 'The Ma'am' from the Royal Links Hotel; the other is a subsequent letter to 'Dearest of Mams' dated 2 April 1901, on the headed notepaper of Rowe's Duchy Hotel, Princetown (as we will see). That Conan Doyle did *not* happen to write to his mother from Park Hill, Ipplepen, does not of course mean that he did not stay there.

As Harry Baskerville's *obituary* in the *New York Herald Tribune* sensibly, and charitably, concluded (2 April 1962): 'Holmes students … attribute Mr Baskerville's [post-1959] claim to failing memory and zealous loyalty to an old employer'.

Plus, they could have added, to over-zealous publicists determined to find a new angle or resurrect an old one!

onan Doyle and Fletcher Robinson probably did use Ipplepen as a base for operations, when they explored – by horse-drawn coach – the eastern part of Dartmoor: the small towns of Bovey Tracey, Ashburton and Buckfastleigh, the larger town of Newton Abbot (already a tourist attraction, with the late Victorian fashion for visiting nearby Tor Bay), the massive Hound Tor and nearby Heatree House.

On the manuscript of *The Hound of the Baskervilles*, Conan Doyle originally wrote 'Newton Abbot', but subsequently changed this – throughout – to the fictional 'Coombe Tracey'. Harry Baskerville was convinced that the two-storey Heatree House near Manaton, with its long drive, porch and imposing first impression, was the original for Baskerville Hall:

> The avenue opened into a broad expanse of turf, and the house lay before us.
> In the fading light I could see that the centre was a heavy block of building from which a porch projected. The whole front was draped in ivy, with a patch clipped bare here and there where a window or a coat-of-arms broke through the dark veil. From this central block rose the twin towers, ancient, crenellated, and pierced with many loopholes. To right and left of the turrets were more modern wings of black granite. A dull light shone through heavy mullioned windows, and from the high chimneys …
>
> 'Welcome, Sir Henry! Welcome, to Baskerville Hall'.

Heatree has the avenue, the heavy block of building, the porch and the modern wings. It does not have any coats of arms, turreted towers or mullioned windows or an alley of old yew hedges, like the one where Sir Charles met his death. But perhaps Harry had special reasons for showing the guest this house: for, several generations before, it had actually belonged to his family, the Dartmoor Baskervilles; and because of the wheel of fortune 'instead of being master of Heatree House', Harry found himself 'touching his forelock to the masters of Park Hill, Ipplepen and their guests'. Maybe he told 'Bertie' and Conan Doyle this story, in which case the house would certainly have stuck in their minds.

Then, as a base from which to research the main locations for the story – the mire, the stone huts, the standing stones and stone rows, the prison and the Tors – Robinson and Doyle moved seventeen miles further west to Rowe's Duchy Hotel, Princetown, just down the road from Dartmoor prison on the moor proper. This hotel, a substantial stone structure, with a recently-erected gas lamp outside, columned porch, mosaic entrance hall ('welcome the traveller, speed the parting guest'), had the arms of the Duchy of Cornwall proudly emblazoned on its wall. One of *the* Dartmoor hotels of the time – not many mod-cons, but dependable and very well placed – it was later to become a hostel for HM Prison staff and is now an interpretation centre.

From Rowe's Duchy Hotel, Conan Doyle wrote the previously-mentioned letter to his mother on 2 April:

> Dearest of Mams,
>
> Here I am in the highest town in England. Robinson and I are exploring the moor over our ... book. I think it will work out splendidly – indeed I have already done nearly half of it ... it is a highly dramatic idea – which I owe to Robinson. We did 14 miles over the moor today and we are now pleasantly weary. It is a great place, very sad and wild, dotted with the dwellings of prehistoric man, strange monoliths and huts and graves.

Fletcher Robinson recalled this stay near 'the famous convict prison of Princetown', in an article he published a couple of years before his death:

> The morning after our arrival Doyle and I were sitting in the smoking room, when a cherry-cheeked maid opened the door and announced 'visitors to see you, gentlemen'. In marched four men, who solemnly sat down and began to talk about the weather, the fishing in the moor streams and other general subjects. Who they might be I had not the slightest idea. As they left I followed them into the hall of the inn. On the table were their cards. The governor of the prison, the deputy governor, the chaplain and the doctor had come, as a pencil note explained, 'to call on Mr Sherlock Holmes'.
>
> One morning I took Doyle to see the mighty bog, a thousand acres of

iew of the deserted huts of Whiteworks shallow tin mine, taken from Fox Tor Mire, which Conan Doyle and Fletcher Robinson visited in April 1901 and which became 'the great Grimpen Mire'.

quaking slime, at any part of which a horse and rider might disappear, which figured so prominently in *the Hound*. He was amused at the story I told him of the moor man who on one occasion saw a hat near the edge of the morass and poked at it with a long pole he carried. 'You leave my hat alone!' came a voice from beneath it. 'Whoi! Be there a man under the 'at?' cried the startled rustic. 'Yes, you fool, and a horse under the man!' From the bog we tramped eastward to the stone fort of Grimspound, which the savages of the Stone Age in Britain … raised with enormous labour to act as a haven of refuge from marauding tribes to the South. The good preservation in which the Grimspound fort still remains is marvellous.

Suddenly we heard a boot strike against a stone [outside the hut in which they were sitting] and rose together. It was only a lonely tourist on a walking excursion, but at sight of our heads suddenly emerging from the hut he let out a yell and bolted. Our subsequent disappearance was due to the fact that we both sat down and rocked with laughter: and as he did not return I have small doubt Mr Doyle and I added yet another proof of the supernatural to tellers of ghost stories concerning Dartmoor.

This was almost certainly the fourteen-mile trip 'over the moor' mentioned by Conan Doyle, which took place on 2 April: from Princetown to Fox Tor Mire (the 'mighty bog' with nearby tin mine which became Grimpen Mire in the novel), eastward to the stone huts of Grimspound (the hiding-place of Sherlock Holmes) and back to the hotel again; on foot it is actually nearer twenty-one miles than fourteen.

Fletcher Robinson's account of this trip is highly revealing in another way. The story of the moorman, the mire and the hat was not original to him, or even heard first-hand: it came from *A Book of Dartmoor*, published the previous year, by the Rev Sabine Baring-Gould – Rector of the remote Dartmoor parish of Lewtrenchard, situated some twelve miles northwest of Princetown. Baring-Gould (1834-1924) was a prolific writer: his output included some hymns, rather nasty novels, books of West Country folklore, legend and fairy tale, guides to the region, books of theology, as well as fat biographies of Napoleon Bonaparte and the Caesars.

He had to keep producing books by the yard – more than one a year on average – in order to sustain, remodel and extend his magnificent, huge late fifteenth-century stone manor house of Lew Trenchard and outbuildings, which had been constructed near the site of a Leuya manor mentioned in the *Devonshire Doomsday Book* of 1086. This house *did* incidentally have mullioned windows, a front draped in ivy, a stone porch, coats of arms, and its interior certainly resembled Dr Watson's description of 'the high, thin window of old stained glass, the oak panelling, the stags' heads, the coats-of-arms upon the walls, all dim and sombre in the subdued light of the central lamp ... '

Baring-Gould also had to write in order to fill Lew Trenchard to capacity with suitably large-scale *objets d'art*, period landscapes and portraits; and – *after* all that had been taken care of – he had to support his wife Grace (who was said to have been the model for George Bernard Shaw's *Pygmalion*), and fifteen children.

The energetic Rector wrote *A Book of Dartmoor* as a follow-up to his *A Book of Devon* (1899) at the request of the publishers Methuen because, as he put it, 'in their opinion this wild and wondrous region deserved more particular treatment than I had been able to accord to it'. In the first chapter, he told the story of a man who was trying to make his way through one of the Mires (*not* Fox Tor, as it happens) and mistook a horse for his hat:

> ... he came on a top-hat reposing, brim downwards, on the sedge. He gave
> it a kick, whereupon a voice called out from beneath, 'what be you a-doing
> to my 'at?' The man replied, 'Be there now a chap under?' 'Ees, I reckon'
> was the reply, 'and a hoss under me likewise'.

If *A Book of Dartmoor* provided Robinson with 'the story I told Doyle', it is equally evident that Baring-Gould's guide – perhaps a copy from Robinson's library at Ipplepen – was well thumbed by Conan Doyle when he wrote *The Hound of the Baskervilles*. It contained a wealth of material, most of it wreathed in 'fog, dense as cotton wool', which found its way more of less directly into the novel: material about the quaking bogs; about the neolithic stone huts at Grimspound which had recently been excavated by archaeologists; about the prison ('the only convict who really got away ... was last seen making a beeline for Fox Tor Mire'); and about local legends of English Civil War landowners who behaved badly.

In addition, *A Book of Dartmoor* would have told Conan Doyle about Hound Tor (the tower – or Tor – like rocks which 'have been weathered into forms resembling the heads of dogs peering over the natural battlements') and the distinctive silhouette of Black Tor at Meavy, a couple of miles south-west of Princetown – the same Black Tor on which Dr Watson sees 'the figure of a man' in the moonlight, outlined as clearly as an ebony statue. But, above all, he would have gleaned an *atmosphere* from Baring-Gould's book – the atmosphere of a primeval wilderness 'so vast, and so barren, and so mysterious' – which permeates the entire novel. An atmosphere so shrouded in fog that 'in half an hour we won't be able to see our hands in front of us'.

A Book of Dartmoor presents the moor as a place of mist, legend and antiquity. It is, in fact, a sustained plea for a certain kind of conservation. Baring-Gould does not like the people he calls 'wanton trippers' (and his views about them resemble the eccentric and litigious Mr Frankland's of Lafter Hall in the *Hound*) or 'enclosers' or 'restorers' or tin-miners who have 'scarred the face of the moor'.

The main working tin-mines of Dartmoor – Hexworthy, Birch Tor, Vitifer and Golden Dagger – were not deemed worth a mention in *A Book of Dartmoor*, presumably because their water-wheels, shafts, gantries, rails and surrounding cottages, and indeed their miners, would have been seen as 'scars' on the face of the moor. There was an attempt in Baring-Gould's time to get the shallow mines at Whiteworks up and running again, right next to Fox Tor Mire, but you certainly would not know it from his guide. Rather, Fox Tor Mire is the dark place where convicts and horses sink to their doom in the fog of the night; and Dartmoor a place of untamed wilderness – scarcely occupied, except in isolated pockets, since neolithic times – 'uncontaminated by the hand of man'. It was not a living, working landscape at all, but, as Baring-Gould wrote in his *Preface*, 'a wild and wondrous region', a place of mystery rather than industry – a place for romantics:

> There is an old mine-work, now filled with water. It covers nearly an acre, and the banks are in part a hundred feet high. According to popular belief, at certain times at night a loud voice is heard calling from the water in articulate tones, naming the next person who is to die in the parish. At other times what are heard are howls as of a spirit in torment. The sounds are doubtless caused by a swirl of wind in the basin that contains the pond … The 'wisht hounds' that sweep overhead in the dark barking are brent-geese going north or returning south …

Conan Doyle, too, was very drawn by the mystery, the romance and the superstitious peasants. Indeed, he made of these such a key symbol in

The Hound of the Baskervilles that the crime novelist P.D. James has justly called the book 'this atavistic study of violence and evil in the mists of Dartmoor'. Stapleton the villain, appropriately enough, gets some of the best lines about this benighted place:

> A long, low moan, indescribably sad, swept over the moor. It filled the whole air, and yet it was impossible to say whence it came. From a dull murmur it swelled into a deep roar and then sank back into a melancholy, throbbing, murmur once again. Stapleton looked at me with a curious expression on his face.
>
> 'Queer place, the moor!' said he.
>
> 'But what is it?'
>
> 'The peasants say it is the Hound of the Baskervilles calling for its prey. I've heard it once or twice before, but never quite so loud'.
>
> I looked round, with a chill of fear in my heart, at the huge swelling plain, mottled with the green patches of rushes …

From the moment Dr Watson arrives, this way of seeing through tinted romantic spectacles colours the view:

> To [Sir Henry Baskerville's] eyes all seemed beautiful, but to me a tinge of melancholy lay upon the country-side, which bore so clearly the mark of the waning year … Our wagonette had topped a rise and in front of us rose the huge expanse of the moor, mottled with gnarled and craggy cairns and tors. A cold wind swept down from it and set us shivering … the grim suggestiveness of the barren waste, the chilling wind and the darkling sky.

Stapleton, one of Baskerville's neighbours – who is a blow-in to the region of only two years' standing, but who is confident that 'there are few men who know it better than I do' – sees the environment in the same way:

> 'It is a wonderful place, the moor', said he, looking round over the undulating downs, long green rollers, with crests of jagged granite foaming up into fantastic surges. 'You never tire of the moor. You cannot think the wonderful secrets which it contains. It is so vast, so barren, and so mysterious'.

By the time Dr Watson meets 'Miss Stapleton', he feels confident in admitting:

> ' … ever since I have been here I have been conscious of shadows all round me. Life has become like that great Grimpen Mire, with little green patches everywhere into which one may sink with no guide to point the track'.

And when he writes of Fox Tor Mire and the Whiteworks tin mine – which we know that Conan Doyle visited with Fletcher Robinson on his great trek – Dr Watson excels himself:

> … the path zig-zagged from tuft to tuft of rushes among those green-scummed pits and foul quagmires which barred the way to the stranger …
> Somewhere in the heart of the great Grimpen Mire, down in the foul slime

*T**he circular inclosure of neolithic dwellings at Grimspound, which turned into Sherlock Holmes's secret hiding-place in* The Hound of the Baskervilles: *this area had been excavated, and partially restored, by archaeologists in the early 1890s.*

of the huge morass which had sucked him in, this cold and cruel-hearted man [Stapleton] is for ever buried. Many traces we found of him in the bog-girt island where he had hid his savage ally. A huge driving-wheel and a shaft half-filled with rubbish showed the position of an abandoned mine. Beside it were the crumbling remains of the cottages of the miners, driven away, no doubt, by the foul reek of the surrounding swamp …

Whiteworks shallow tin mine, then, has become a deserted village: Fox Tor has become a place of 'green-scummed pits and foul quagmires' – a nightmare place which has defeated the successive attempts of human beings – prehistoric people or modern tin-miners – to civilise and tame it. Likewise Baskerville Hall, and all that it represents – an 'old race', a title, a family home, a go-ahead young heir who has spent most of his life up to now 'in the States and in Canada', 'the prosperity of the whole poor, bleak countryside' even – must at all costs be saved (as Edgar Allan Poe's House of Usher could not) from sinking into the tarn or rather the mire. And if life itself has become 'like that great Grimpen Mire … with no guide to point the track', all the more reason to hope against hope that the civilised rationality of the great detective, the secular priest, will be able to provide salvation.

The poet W.H. Auden, in his essay *The Guilty Vicarage* (1948), argued that *the* classic detective story involved explaining away an ancestral curse, and re-establishing the fragile values of civilisation. P.D. James has added that *The Hound of the Baskervilles* remains one of the greatest examples of the form precisely *because* it pits 'the Great Detective, combining as he does a dominant intellect with bizarre personal eccentricity and the heroic virtues of triumphant individualism' against the atavism, violence and evil of the moor. No wonder T.S. Eliot – a devoted Holmes fan who, as a poet, particularly enjoyed the sound of the names in Conan Doyle's stories (he once rhymed 'musical sound' with 'Baskerville Hound') – associated Watson's moor with the waste-land. In *East Coker* he wrote:

> In the middle, not only in the middle of the way.
> But all the way, in a dark wood, in a bramble,
> On the edge of a grimpen, where there is no secure foothold.

Arthur Conan Doyle's image of Dartmoor was so strong, that today it *still* colours public perceptions of the place. The current conservation debate between 'the wilderness lobby' and 'the working landscape lobby' is at some level a debate between what Conan Doyle wrote and what he must have seen. Of course, his version of the topography of Dartmoor involved much compression, which has mightily confused literal-minded pilgrims. In *The Hound of the Baskervilles*, Baskerville Hall, the standing stones, the neolithic huts, and the mire are within relatively easy walking distance of each other, when in fact it would have taken Dr Watson the best part of a day – at a brisk pace – to reach some of them. And the prison at Princetown, which really *was* just down the road from where he was staying, was located for some reason 'fourteen miles' from Baskerville Hall – in which case it wasn't on Dartmoor at all! Equally, Conan Doyle's version of Baring-Gould's folk stories, which originated from widely different parts of the moor, involved much compression when they all became centred on the area around the Hall.

But we are not talking maps here – we are talking nightmares. Conan Doyle seems to have had a *thing* about drowning in a bog. In his historical novel *Micah Clarke* (1889), John Derrick perishes in a quicksand, and in *The Sign of the Four* (1890), Jonathan Small struggles to his death in Plumstead Marshes.

And while we are on nightmares, if Sir Henry Baskerville was the 'true descendent … in that long line of high-blooded, fiery and masterful men', there was another, rival claimant, who was threatening to disperse the estate for his own short-term gain and who was reckoned by Holmes to be the most 'dangerous man' he had ever helped to hunt down: a dark descendant of 'the cause of all the mischief, the wicked Hugo, who started the *Hound of the Baskervilles*'. When he notices the facial resemblance between Stapleton and the portrait of Hugo dated 1647, Sherlock Holmes observes:

> … it is an interesting instance of a throw-back, which appears to be both physical and spiritual. A study of family portraits is enough to convert a man to the doctrine of reincarnation. The fellow is a Baskerville – that is evident.

It is strange that Mr James Mortimer MRCS, whose special research interest is craniology, with published articles on *Some Freaks of Atavism* and *Do We Progress?*, had not managed to notice the facial resemblance before.

Anyway, this great revelation – the final piece in the *Hound of the Baskervilles* jigsaw – was to be found in *another* of Sabine Baring-Gould's books, also published in 1890, called *Old Country Life*. This contained a long chapter, *Family Portraits*, about the physical resemblances which could be traced through genuine collections of family pictures. His thesis was that in the current generation of a family, some facial characteristics might re-appear from the distant past, which had disappeared in the generations which came between.

> … One day I was visiting a friend when I was struck by the excellence of a portrait in his hall of a very refined and beautiful old lady; there was nothing characteristic in the dress … Moreover, it was a perfectly life-like 'presentiment' of my friend's wife. He and she were both old people. Said I to my friend, 'What an admirable likeness! The artist has not only made a good picture, but he has caught your wife's expression as well as features and peculiar colouring. Who is the painter? I did not know we had the man nowadays who could have painted such a portrait'.
>
> 'Oh', he answered, 'that is not my wife – it is her great-grandmother'. Thus the wife represented four united streams of two generations back, but she represented in face, and represented exactly, only one of them.

Baring-Gould goes on to cite 'a still more remarkable instance of atavism', complete with illustrations for handy comparison. It concerns a portrait he has found in an 'old manor-house', dated about 1672, of a certain Sir Edward, 'a dandy, in long flowing curls' (which seem to resemble the 'curling love-locks' of Hugo Baskerville in that portrait of 1647) with a 'haughty, somewhat dreamy' expression on his face. Next to it hangs a portrait of Sir Edward's elder brother James 'also with flowing hair' but more 'bluff and good-natured in appearance'.

Although the estate passed down the genial *James's* side of the family, the current descendant resembles the haughty Edward so closely that 'he might have been the same man' (if the Restoration curls, ribbons and velvet jacket were to be covered up – just as Holmes covers the curls, lace collar and black velvet jacket of Hugo's portrait). The facial characteristics remained latent for six of seven generations, argues Baring-Gould, only to re-appear in the current (1888) one.

At a time when physiognomy was still fashionable among criminologists, when what went on *behind* the eyes was only just beginning seriously to be studied, and when it was thought you could tell a degenerate criminal 'type' just by looking at him or her, Baring-Gould's thesis would no doubt have struck a chord with Arthur Conan Doyle. As if to acknowledge the debt, he makes a joke about it when Mortimer meets Holmes in 221b Baker Street at the beginning of *The Hound*:

> 'You interest me very much, Mr Holmes. I had hardly expected so dolicho-cephalic [extended] a skull or such well-marked supra-orbital [above the eye-line] development … I confess that I covet your skull'.

Mortimer follows this bizarre outburst with a reference to the latest researches of the French anthropologist Alphonse Bertillon – much admired by Holmes on other occasions – in the area of the measurement and classification of heads, or 'anthropometry'. The real villains of the piece – the 'throwback' Stapleton with his 'savage hound' – both represent biology run amok. So the nightmare is not just about nature-as-wilderness: it is about *human* biology as well.

When Conan Doyle wrote to his mother about his 'highly dramatic' new story from Rowe's Duchy Hotel, he revealed that he had 'already done nearly half of it'. So between his visit to Cromer in March and 2 April, he had put about 30 000 words down on paper. The surviving manuscript pages of *The Hound* show that they were written in a bold, clear, hand with very little revision – just the occasional tense, adjective, or piece of punctuation.

The single complete manuscript chapter to have survived – chapter 11, *The Man on the Tor*, now in the Berg Collection of New York Public Library, 16 pages – has some minor changes in the dialogue between Dr Watson and Mrs Laura Lyons ('a passage' for 'a postscript', 'wrote' for 'read'), describes Mr Frankland as 'red-faced' rather than the original 'choleric', deletes a repetitive reference to his telescope and substitutes the 'chequered light' for the 'dim light' of the prehistoric hut. Where Watson's state of mind is concerned as he waits for the mysterious man, the manuscript substitutes 'and yet … my soul shared none of the peace of Nature, but quivered at the vagueness and terror

The mysterious man on the tor,
silhouetted against the moon
on the wasteland of Dartmoor,
illustrated by Sidney Paget for the
Strand *serialisation (December 1901).*

of that interview which every instant was bringing
nearer' for the cruder 'and yet here was I waiting for some crisis,
waiting with my nerves in a quiver, knowing that ... ' It also
includes a paragraph which was deleted:

… disheartened. Either she was a accomplished actor and a deep conspir-
ator, or Barrymore had misread the letter, or the letter was a forgery – unless
indeed there could by some extraordinary coincidence be a second lady
writing from Newton Abbott whose initials were L.L. For the time my clue
had come to nothing and I could only turn back to that other one which lay
among the stone huts upon the Moor …

The passage 'Either ... L.L.' was crossed out, perhaps because it raised too many possibilities, and showed too much subtlety on Watson's part.

Apart from these, the most interesting corrections involve proper names: Conan Doyle originally included real places and people – the town of 'Newton Abbot', 'the Mayor of Plymouth' – then obviously thought better of it, and changed these to the fictional 'Coombe Tracey' and, instead of the Mayor, the fictional 'Sir John Morland'. It seems that he was turning his explorations of the moor, and his researches, into fiction and drama *during the actual process of writing*.

His second wife Jean was later to recall: 'I have known him write a Sherlock Holmes story in a room full of people talking ... he would write in a train or anywhere'. Which is one reason why Holmes enthusiasts the world over have managed to make a minor industry out of Conan Doyle's inconsistencies and inaccuracies. *Could* Stapleton have possibly heard 'a bittern booming' on Dartmoor, when the marsh bird was almost extinct? How on earth did Holmes empty 'five *barrels* of his revolver into the creature's flank'? How does Mrs Laura Lyons read about Sir Charles's death 'in the paper the next morning', when he died at midnight the night before? And so on.

There have been numerous 'chronologies' of the Holmes cases, as well as several 'biographies' of the detective, concordances, glossaries, Encyclopedias and even a Baker Street Songbook. One of the first moves in this game was an 'open letter to Dr Watson' written by Frank Sidgwick for *The Cambridge Review* (23 January 1902), which attempted in the name of 'literary morality' to establish a coherent chronology for *The Hound of the Baskervilles* – before the final instalments had even appeared in *The Strand*: the dates and days when the case took place, starting with Watson's first report on 13 October, seemed hopelessly confused. But the founding father of 'Sherlockology' (as it has come to be known) was Fr Ronald Knox, who, when he was an undergraduate at Oxford in 1911, wrote an essay on Sherlock Holmes which was intended to be a satire on the wilder excesses of biblical scholarship (and which was published in 1928, by which time he was a chaplain at the University):

> I must not waste time over other evidences (very unsatisfactory) which have been adduced to show the spuriousness of *The Hound of the Baskervilles*. Holmes's 'cat-like love of personal cleanliness' is not really inconsistent with the statement in the *Study in Scarlet* that he had pinpricks all over his hand covered with plaster ... A more serious question is that of Watson's breakfast hour. Both in the *Study in Scarlet* and in the *Adventures* we hear that Watson breakfasted late. But...

This essay set the tone for future contributions to 'Sherlockology': treating the Holmes stories as 'the Canon', and Holmes and Watson as real people –

and what began as a satire on scholarly conventions was to become itself a kind of scholarship. It began as a Senior Common Room joke: on another occasion, Fr Knox categorised 'The Hound of the Baskervilles' as one of his four types of preaching voice (the Threshing Machine was another). It has turned into a minor industry.

The manuscript of *The Hound of the Baskervilles* was dispersed in 1902, when the American News Company despatched it – as individual pages in frames – to bookstores across the States, to publicise the title in window-displays. Of the pages which somehow survived this process (which itself gives an idea of how casual Conan Doyle was about the business of drafting), one complete chapter and a page are in New York, while of the fifteen other single known pages from a variety of chapters four are in Universities and the remainder in private hands.

Apart from small drafting details, these reveal two things: that Conan Doyle did indeed write decisively and with the minimum of revision; and that the manuscript was entirely in his handwriting. Twenty-one words from 'The curse of the Baskervilles' have survived in manuscript. 'This from Hugo Baskerville to his sons Rodger and John, with instructions that they say nothing thereof to their sister Elizabeth' – and they are *not* written in the hand of Bertram Fletcher Robinson, which would tie in with what Conan Doyle wrote to Herbert Greenhaugh Smith, his *Strand* editor:

> I have the idea of a real creeper for the *Strand:* it is full of surprises, breaking naturally into good lengths for serial purposes. There is one stipulation. I must do it with my friend Fletcher Robinson, and his name must appear with mine. *I can answer for the yarn being all my own in my own style without dilution, since your readers like that.* But he gave me the central idea and the local colour, and so I feel his name must appear.

Conan Doyle had used the phrase 'a real creeper' to his mother from Cromer, so perhaps this letter predates the trip to Dartmoor. Perhaps it was sent from Dartmoor: Sir George Newnes of *The Strand* certainly knew about *The Hound* before Conan Doyle returned from Devon to London. We have seen how Fletcher Robinson helped his guest with 'the local colour' both in Norfolk *and* Devon. But what about 'the central idea' – the curse of the spectral hound/fiend dog? Was this based on Black Shuck of Norfolk or on a Devon variety of the species?

The Book of Dartmoor gives black-dog legends only the most cursory of mentions – just the reference to 'wisht hounds' cited above: apart, that is, from the story of the tailor from Plymouth who gets stuck in a bog near Merrivale Bridge and thinks he sees 'large, glaring-eyed monsters' staring at him

Chapter XI
The Man on the Tor.

The extract from my private Diary which forms the last Chapter has brought my narrative up to the 18th of October, a time when these strange events began to move swiftly towards their terrible conclusion. The incidents of the next few days are indelibly graven upon my recollection, and I can tell them without reference to the notes made at the time. I start then from the day which succeeded that upon which I had established two facts of great importance, the one that Mrs Laura Lyons of ~~Newton Abbott~~ had written to Sir Charles Baskerville and made an appointment with him at the very place and hour that he met his death, the other that the lurking man upon the Moor was to be found among the stone huts upon the hill side. With these two facts in my possession I felt that either my intelligence or my courage must be deficient if I could not throw some further light upon these dark places.

I had no opportunity to tell the Baronet about what I had learned Mrs Lyons upon the evening before, for Dr Mortimer remained with him at cards until it was very late. At breakfast however I informed him about my discovery and asked him whether he would care to accompany me to ~~Newton Abbott~~. At first he was very eager to come but on second thoughts it seemed to both of us that if I went alone the results might be better. The more formal we made the visit the less information we might obtain. I left Sir Henry behind therefore, not without some prickings of conscience, and drove off upon my new quest.

The first page, in Conan Doyle's bold handwriting, of the only complete manuscript chapter of The Hound of the Baskervilles *to have survived: note how 'Newton Abbott' becomes 'Coombe Tracey'.*

– which turn out to be stray sheep! Baring-Gould's *Book of Devon*, published in 1899, gives a little more information under the heading *Superstition*:

> There existed formerly a belief on Dartmoor that it was hunted over at night in storms by a black sportsman, with fire-breathing hounds, called the 'wish Hounds' [folklorists these days prefer 'whisht']. They could be heard in full cry, and occasionally the blast of the hunter's horn on stormy nights. One night a moorman was riding home from Widecombe ... The horse knew the way [through the thick vapour] perhaps better than his master. The rider had traversed the great ridge of Hameldon, and was mounting a moor on which stands a circle of upright stones – reputedly a Druid circle, and said to dance on Christmas Eve – when he heard a sound that startled him – a horn, and then past him swept without sound of foot-fall a pack of black dogs. The moorman was not frightened – he had taken in too much Dutch courage for that – and when a minute after the black hunter came up, he shouted to him, 'Hey! huntsman, what sport? Give us some of your game'.
>
> 'Take that' answered the hunter, and flung him something which the man caught and held in his arms. Then the mysterious rider passed on.

When eventually he gets back home, the moorman looks at the piece of 'game hunted and won by the Black Rider', and discovers it is his own baby, dead and cold.

Other references to black dogs in Baring-Gould's writings about the region all *postdate* the publication of *The Hound*. So Conan Doyle must have heard 'the central idea' from Robinson himself who had presumably been told it first-hand rather than gleaned it from a printed source. In his various dedications to the published book, Conan Doyle referred to Robinson's 'account of a West Country legend' (1901 & 2) and his remark 'that there was a spectral dog near his house on Dartmoor' (1929) as the inspiration for the project.

J.E. Hodder Williams elaborated (1902) that 'Robinson is a Devonshire man, and he mentioned in conversation some old country legend which set Doyle's imagination on fire'. Harry Baskerville was at first reported as saying there was 'no Baskerville legend' (1951), then that it was 'invented' by Bertie (1957), then – in the Hammer films publicity (1959) – that Robinson not only recounted many 'tales of local legend', but that one of them closely resembled the story of *The Hound of the Baskervilles*:

> There was one, in particular, which fired Conan Doyle's imagination. It was the tale of a legendary ghost-hound which was said to appear on a Tor over-looking the moor on the first night of every full moon. Superstitious folk on Dartmoor claimed to have seen the animal ... According to the legend, the dog once belonged to a girl who was murdered on the moor in the early eighteenth century by a jealous-crazed husband who suspected her of

infidelity. Fleeing for her life, she was overtaken on the Tor by her husband who killed her with a hunting knife. The woman's dog – a large hound – attacked her murderer and killed him. The dog itself, badly wounded in the fight, was found next day lying dead by the side of its murdered mistress.

The 'eighteenth century' reference is particularly interesting because that was the period in which *Hammer* set 'the curse of the Baskervilles' – nearer the Hell-Fire Club than the Great Rebellion.

Theo Brown, who spent much of her life collecting 'black dog stories' from all over Britain, calculated that there were more of them from Devon than almost anywhere else. Usually, these were stories of black dogs which appeared to commemorate 'a deed of horrible violence' or 'whenever something grim was about to occur' – along a stretch of road or trackway. Variant versions ranged from the black dog which walks past the spot in Newton St Cyres where a young girl was murdered, to the black dog of Uplyme 'with fiery eyes, which made the air cold and dark as he passed' and which went on swelling until he was as big as a forest and then turned into a cloud, to the pack of Whisht Hounds (or 'Yeth' hounds as they are known in North Devon) which chased the souls of unbaptised babies across Dartmoor or were themselves the souls of unbaptised babies pursuing their negligent elders. Hence the moorman, the Black Rider and the baby.

None of these black dogs attacked individuals or resembled the 'legend of the fiend dog which haunts the family': even the Whisht Hounds were – in Christian times at any rate – hunting 'for the good of men's souls'; the horse and hounds motif was used prominently on fonts 'to show the loving reclamation of innocent children'.

Brown concluded 'The Hound of the Baskervilles does not correspond with any of the black dogs known so far, and it is probably a hotch-potch of several': a cocktail of Jan Tregeagle of Bodmin Moor (with his pack of diabolical hounds) and the Whisht Hounds of Dartmoor – plus a large dash of Black Shuck of Norfolk. A black dog story with the usual 'commemorative' or 'haunting' function had been turned into something much more vicious.

So whatever it was that Fletcher Robinson told Conan Doyle in Cromer, from the point of view of the folklorist he must either have been confused – or good at making up a shaggy dog story of his own.

In 1932, a Mr C.J. Robb – possibly after reading Conan Doyle's then recent reference to the legend of a spectral dog which haunted an area near Ipplepen – wrote to *Devon and Cornwall Notes and Queries* (vol xvii) asking the editors about 'the origin of the theme' of *The Hound*. In the following issue, West Country folklorist F. Nesbitt replied that the legend 'probably' related to that of Richard Cabell (or Capel), lord of the manor of Brook in the parish of Buckfastleigh (which is about 8 miles from Ipplepen):

[He] was a gentleman of ill repute, and on the night of his death, black hounds, breathing fire and smoke, raced over Dartmoor and howled round his manor house. This legend is referred to by Baring-Gould *(Methuen's Little Guide to Devon)* and gives 1677 as the date of Sir Richard's death.

Since the *Little Guide* was first published in 1907, it cannot possibly have been the original source – although it *could* have been the source of Conan Doyle's reference in 1929 to 'a spectral dog near [Robinson's] home on Dartmoor'. Describing the churchyard of Buckfastleigh, Baring-Gould wrote:

Before the S. porch is the enclosed tomb of Richard Cabell, of Brooke, who died in 1677 [in fact it was 1672]. He was the last male of his race, and died with such an evil reputation that he was placed under a heavy stone, and a sort of penthouse was build over that with iron gratings to it, to prevent his coming up and haunting the neighbourhood. When he died, the story goes that fiends and black dogs breathing fire raced over Dartmoor and surrounded Brooke, howling.

According to Theo Brown, in her study of *The Fate of the Dead:*

[Cabell or Capel had a] woman-baiting reputation and is said to have kept his victims at Hawson Court, a mile or so the west of his home. There are two versions of his death-scene: either he was chased across Dartmoor by 'Whisht' hounds till he dropped dead, or he died in his bed and the 'Whisht' hounds howled round outside the house that night. Post-mortem trouble was anticipated, so he was buried very deep …

Maybe, she added in her article on *The Black Dog in Devon, The Hound* is a 'dramatically telescoped version of the pack that hunted Capel to death at Buckfastleigh in the seventeenth century'.

It has to be said that none of this has much to do with the legend contained in *The Hound of the Baskervilles*. It looks more like a variant on the Whisht Hounds – or on countless 'commemoration' stories – with some sectarian violence and post-Civil War settling of scores thrown in for good measure. According to Theo Brown, 'Black Dogs seem to show a marked preference for the Stuarts'.

The Hammer Films version of the legend – which has a 'jealous-crazed husband', a chase across the moor, murder by hunting-knife, a faithful hound destroyed and a manifestation whenever there is a full moon, *none of which was part of the original* – is the result of a quarter of a century of embellishment by over-eager Sherlockians: the legend of Cabell and the legend of *The Hound* have converged in a global version of the oral tradition.

Interestingly, the convergence seems to have begun in earnest in 1930s America when a Holmes buff and distant relative of the Cabell family – the writer Branch Cabell – claimed that the connection between Richard Cabell and Hugo Baskerville was an established fact, and when the Basil Rathbone version of *The Hound of the Baskervilles* was filmed and publicised by Hollywood in 1939. Basil Rathbone was later to recall a story which was going around the set at 20th Century Fox:

> According to Bertram Fletcher Robinson [said Rathbone] … the legend began in the seventeenth century with a large hound that had slain Sir Richard Cabell, Lord of the Manor of Brooke; a man of the West Country whose evil reputation was very well known by all the people living thereabouts. In Devonshire, driving by horse and carriage over the very same desolate moor regions where the Hound's real life legend began, Fletcher Robinson told Conan Doyle that Sir Richard Cabell was a very jealous creature and that one night at his home Cabell viciously accused his wife of having an affair with a man of Buckfastleigh. Lady Cabell denied this, but refusing to believe her, Cabell started thrashing her mercilessly. Finally, though, Lady Cabell was able to break away from him, and escaping their house, she began fleeing for her life across the bleak surrounding moors that were swept by the wild chill winds from the even bleaker regions of nearby Dartmoor. Moments later, however, Cabell overtook her, and in a rage murdered the woman with one of his hunting knives. Then came the Hound … [It] was Lady Cabell's own, a large faithful dog that had leaped after Lady Cabell when Cabell had gone chasing her across the moors … [A]fter a fierce and violent struggle, the hound slaughtered Cabell. In the struggle, however, the hound itself was fatally wounded by Cabell's slashing knife … Since that time, Fletcher Robinson recounted, local legend had it that the ghost of Lady Cabell's hound could often be seen stalking the moors, howling lonesomely for its slain mistress on nights of the full moon …

The elements picked up by the Hammer publicity people in 1959, and attributed to Harry Baskerville, are all there: the row with Elizabeth Cabell, the chase, the hunting-knife, and even the re-appearance of the faithful hound 'on nights of the full moon'. The only details to be added by Hammer were two small bits of publicity-speak: that the spectral creature tended to appear *'on a Tor overlooking the moor* on the *first night* of every full moon'. Clearly, someone involved in promoting Hammer Films' *Hound of the Baskervilles* had been reading the publicity for 20th Century Fox's *Hound of the Baskervilles*. So the convergence of the legends of Richard Cabell and Hugo Baskerville happened in the public relations offices of two film companies – films, perhaps, performing the function in the twentieth century of folk-myths in earlier centuries. Less a case of whisht hounds than wishful thinking.

It is, however, quite possible that Bertram Fletcher Robinson told Conan Doyle of the *original* legend of Richard Cabell (or one of them), which had been passed from Buckfastleigh to Ipplepen by word of mouth; and that Conan Doyle's vivid imagination could have done the rest.

From the folklorist's perspective, the key addition to the original in the novel is 'the daughter of a yeoman' who is imprisoned at Baskerville Hall, and runs across the moor for fear of being raped. The rest of the fictional curse, including the wicked squire, the night shepherd on the moor (who presumably thinks he has seen a pack of Whisht Hounds), and the hound of hell – which is *not* the girl's faithful dog, but a supernatural black dog – all had at least some folkloric roots in the region. But the 'young maiden ... of good repute' is a new addition – which is where Conan Doyle's imagination comes in. For – as some critics have noticed – there is an uncharacteristic, almost gloating, emphasis on brutality to women throughout *The Hound of the Baskervilles*: Hugo's cruelty to the yeoman's daughter in the curse; Mrs Laura Lyons's life of 'incessant persecution from a husband whom I abhor' and habit of putting her trust in men who abuse her; and above all Stapleton's sadistic treatment of his wife, who ends up with 'the clear red weal of a whip lash across her neck' and 'her arms ... all mottled with bruises'.

In the spring and early summer of 1901, Conan Doyle evidently had something on his mind which expressed itself through this needless, and needlessly detailed, punishment of women. Could it have been his guilt about having neglected his wife Louise, until it was too late (as has been suggested)? Or his confused feelings towards his beloved Jean Leckie? Whatever it was, the emotion was unusually strong and destructive – and it transformed the legend he was told by Fletcher Robinson into the curse of the Baskervilles.

In Conan Doyle's imagination, the black dog became the sharp end of the melancholy and baleful atmosphere of the moor in general – with Holmes and Watson not only protecting civilisation against a wilderness which is out of control, but also protecting 'the feminine' against the destructive impulses of uncontrolled (male) nature. Conan Doyle was concerned that too many works of literature of the time presented relations with 'the opposite sex' as 'the be-all and end-all' of life, when they should have been extolling the 'manly' virtues instead.

It is even possible that as part of their sightseeing from Park Hill, Ipplepen, Fletcher Robinson showed his guest Conan Doyle around the parish churchyard of Buckfastleigh. If so, Doyle would have seen much to confirm the local legend of Richard Cabell. To make sure that the wicked squire would *never* be able to come back from the grave, his coffin was buried deep below a heavy stone box or altar tomb with – it is said – a metal stake through his heart to nail him down. The box was encased in a kind of 'penthouse' or pagoda-like structure and this square little house was surrounded, on the north side facing the church porch, by sturdy iron railings, and on the south side by a small oak door with a large keyhole in it.

Even after all these precautions had been taken, the locals didn't feel entirely safe, because legend still has it that if you walk thirteen times (or three, or seven – it depends) around the grave-house and insert the tip of your little finger into the keyhole, it will be gnawed by the voraciously hungry vampire inside – a devil who is still trying desperately to escape. As recently as the Second World War, when iron railings were being collected for the war effort, the people of Buckfastleigh persuaded the authorities to leave the Cabell railings *in situ*, where they could continue to serve their original purpose.

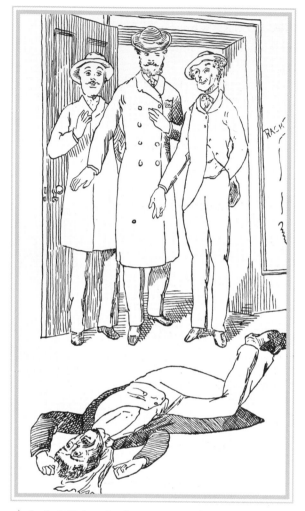

♦herlock Holmes (right) arrives at the scene of the crime, with Dr Watson and Inspector Lestrade, in one of Charles Doyle's illustrations to A Study in Scarlet *(1888): a portrait of the artist as a young detective.*

The pagoda structure, the iron railings, and the stone box can still be seen in Buckfastleigh churchyard. The oak door has come off its hinges, so one can enter the tomb and see the carving of the names of the seventeenth-century Cabells round the stone slab. In 1672, the stone-mason managed to carve just one word RICUS (for Richard) and then, for some reason, did not complete the second word CABELL. Was he interrupted in his work? Did the people of Buckfastleigh stop him? Did he perhaps catch sight of a pack of phantom hounds breathing fire and baying their anger – before running for his life?

If Robinson and Doyle *did* visit the churchyard at the end of March 1901, they must have had a whale of a time speculating in this kind of way.

n his note to his mother from Cromer, Doyle made no mention of Sherlock Holmes. At that stage, the spooky story he and Fletcher were concocting was not – presumably – to be a Holmes story. Yet, by 2 April, when he wrote again – from Rowe's Duchy Hotel – he added that 'Holmes is at his very best, and it is a highly dramatic idea – which I owe to Robinson'. So, some time between Cromer and Princetown,

Conan Doyle had made the historic decision to turn *The Hound of the Baskervilles* into a Sherlock Holmes novel. As J.E. Hodder Williams observed:

> When he came to working out the details, he found, however, that some masterful central figure was needed, some strong man who would influence the whole course of events, and his natural reflection was: 'Why should I invent such a character when I have him already in the form of Holmes?' So Sherlock Holmes came back into the *Strand Magazine* ...

Perhaps the decision was made at Ipplepen. For, to confront the evil of the legend which Robinson had recounted to him, Conan Doyle required a suitably larger-than-life master of destinies who could credibly stand up to it. If the legend was powerful, the antidote had to be even more powerful. Sherlock Holmes, it seemed, was about to make the most spectacular come-back since Lazarus.

He was of course just the man for the case. Partly because he had a hard-nosed attitude towards legends such as these:

> 'Do you find it interesting?'
> 'To a collector of fairy-tales'.

But Mortimer observes that Holmes puts 'the matter more flippantly than you would probably do if you were brought into contact with these things'. And indeed, once the detective actually reaches the moor, the flippant tone soon disappears:

> 'It is the greatest blow which has befallen me in my career'.
>
> 'But how could I know – how could I know – that he would risk his life alone upon the moor ... '
>
> '[Watson], as you value your life do not go across the moor in any direction save along the straight path which leads from Merripit House to the Grimpen Road, and is your natural way home'.

Holmes was also the man for the case because there was a streak of the romantic in him, which responded to the weird atmosphere of the moor. The early stories in which he features (up to and including *The Hound of the Baskervilles*) amount almost to a portrait of the artist as a young detective, treating science as an art while avoiding the hard slog of either activity. Although he called his method 'the science of deduction' and others have called it 'logical deduction', it was in fact a rich mixture of close observation, breadth of knowledge, 'reasoning backwards', free association; inspired guess-work and some great one-liners.

Holmes has a Bohemian disposition and an analytical mind – a 'duality' that was present to some extent in Conan Doyle: biographer Pierre Nordon speculates that the two sides of Holmes's personality reflect those of his creator (the man of action who needed to be involved in public 'causes' and the dreamer who sought a substitute for his family's Roman Catholicism).

So Holmes knows a Stradivarius from an Amati, writes arcane monographs, is fascinated by secret societies, is addicted to cocaine and is much given to pithy *mots justes* such as '*le mauvais goût mène au crime*. The French have a very neat way of putting these things'. The detective's 'extreme exactness and astuteness', writes Watson, were a 'reaction against the poetic and contemplative mood which occasionally predominated in him'.

What Watson calls Holmes's 'dual nature' served several purposes: it perhaps helped Conan Doyle to work his own confusions out of his system; it appealed to any latent romanticism in readers of *The Strand* who might still cherish the values of the aesthetic movement in art – without seriously undermining the stories' commitment to science; it contributed to Holmes's image as a genius, and made the thinking machine more interesting (later, after *The Hound of the Baskervilles*, Watson manages to wean the detective off cocaine, 'to the detriment of romantic interest, whatever the benefit to Holmes', as writer Vincent Starrett nicely put it); and it explained why Holmes indulges in *creative* thinking and seems to have second sight at the same time as justifying his method as the 'science of deduction'.

It also made sense of his attraction for cases which others thought 'supernatural': he yearned for intellectual problems which would transport him beyond the 'commonplace'. But the duality does not go very deep. Holmes doesn't smoke or drink opium, like Poe and his disciple the poet Charles Baudelaire: instead, he writes a monograph on 140 different kinds of tobacco ash. He does not explore the sensual possibilities of perfume, or use scent as the basis for aesthetic experiments, like Huysmans's character Des Esseintes, or Wilde's Dorian Gray: instead he prides himself on the fact that he can distinguish seventy-five different varieties of them.

When Dr Watson is confronted with the real thing he is appalled: referring to a man who had read Thomas De Quincey's *Confessions of an Opium Eater* at an impressionable age, and 'had drenched his tobacco with laudanum in an attempt to produce the same effects', he feels both 'horror and pity'; 'I can see him now, with yellow pasty face, dropping lids and pin-point pupils, all huddled in a chair, the wreck and ruin of a noble man' (what makes it far, far worse is that the man in question is the brother of the late Principal of the Theological College of St George's).

Holmes's decadence is never taken beyond bounds which were considered by Conan Doyle to be socially acceptable. The detective may profess to detest 'every form of society' (in fact, he never seems to get any invitations to refuse), but members of the aristocracy and even on one occasion Queen Victoria herself prefer to consult him rather than the full-time (and 'ferret-like') flat-feet of Scotland Yard, if they wish their problems to be dealt with discreetly: in the end they prefer the gentleman to the players.

S idney Paget's classic image of Sherlock Holmes – complete
with deerstalker and cape – in the first-class smoking
compartment of a train to Dartmoor, to solve the mystery of
Silver Blaze (December 1892).

When *A Study in Scarlet* was first issued as a separate book in 1888, the illustrations were made by Charles Doyle (Arthur's sickly father). The first of these – showing the detective's arrival at the scene of the crime, with Dr Watson and Inspector Lestrade – presents Sherlock Holmes as an almost Oscar Wildean figure, with curly hair, a fashionably cut jacket which does not quite fit his narrow, sloping shoulders, and a lived-in face. This image of Sherlock Holmes does not bear much resemblance to Conan Doyle's description of his *physical* appearance. Sidney Paget's more famous illustrations for *The Strand* come much closer to that. But it does capture the 'poetic and contemplative' side of his character.

For Sidney Paget, Holmes is austere and donnish – lean, with sharp eyes, a hawk-like nose, a prominent chin and a receding hairline. Of all the hundreds of drawings Paget did for *The Strand Magazine* (from 1891 to 1908, 201 for *The Adventures* and *The Memoirs* alone), only a few present the detective in the more 'decadent' pose preferred by Charles Doyle. The readers' mental image of Holmes – in Britain, at least – was constructed out of the more characteristic Paget drawings.

Conan Doyle himself was worried that they made the detective too good-looking (in place of the 'more powerful but uglier Sherlock' he had written about), like a matinée-idol. His 'original idea', he added, had been to make the detective taller, thinner, with 'a great hawk's-bill of a nose, and two small eyes, set close together on either side of it'. The model for Sidney Paget's work had been the artist's younger brother Walter, and Doyle observed 'perhaps from the point of view of my lady readers it was as well'.

Dignity and Impudence *(1839), a much-reproduced painting by Edwin Landseer which shows a bloodhound in his kennel next to a terrier: precursors, in canine form, of Sherlock Holmes and Dr Watson.*

Sidney Paget also added a deerstalker, an item of headgear that is never once mentioned in the stories: Conan Doyle just referred to a 'close-fitting cloth cap' and an 'ear-flapped travelling cap'. Yet Paget's illustrations of Holmes in a deerstalker and cape were to enter the visual bloodstream. Likewise, when Holmes was smoking in a Paget illustration, it was nearly always a pipe, but in the stories he is equally fond of cigarettes and cigars. So the two 'icons' we associate most readily with Holmes – deerstalker and pipe – come from the pictures as much as from the words.

Where American readers were concerned, the best-known artist's model was the actor-manager William Gillette – whose stern, solid features, even more matinée idol than Walter Paget's, were used by the illustrator Frederic

Dorr Steele. An amalgamation of the Charles Doyle, Paget and Dorr Steele versions (if such a thing were possible) might come nearer to the 'original idea' – part Wilde, part University don, part man of action.

Gillette it was who added another element to Holmes's public persona: in some early acting versions of his play *Sherlock Holmes*, the detective is made to say 'Elementary, my dear Watson' or 'Elementary, my dear fellow' – a phrase which, again, had never appeared in the stories. Following the success of Gillette's play in New York (1899) and London (1901), however, this was to become a catch-phrase in numerous parodies and pastiches.

When he was in the process of adapting Conan Doyle's first and last short stories (*A Scandal in Bohemia* for the love interest; *The Final Problem* for Moriarty and his gang), Gillette wired the author to ask 'May I marry Holmes?', to which Doyle replied that he 'might marry the detective, or murder him or do anything he liked with him'. In the event, the ending of the play – which Doyle reckoned had diminished Holmes, because the detective should never be 'thawed by love' – proved especially popular with audiences:

> HOLMES: ... Believe me, I meant no harm to you – it was purely business. For that you see I would sacrifice everything. Even my supposed friendship for you was a ... was a ... pretence ... a sham.
>
> ALICE: I don't believe you.
>
> HOLMES: Why not?
>
> ALICE: From the way you speak ... from the way you look ... from all sorts of things! You're not the only one who can tell things from small details.
>
> HOLMES: Your powers of observation are somewhat remarkable, Miss Faulkner ... and your deduction is quite correct! I suppose ... indeed I know ... that I love you. (*Holmes sits on edge of desk*). I love you. (*Alice starts to move towards Holmes but he stops her*). But, I know as well what I am ... and what you are ... I know that no such person as I, seared ... (*Alice turns away from him opening her handbag to take out the famous 'Sherlock Holmes' meerschaum pipe to give him as a present*) ... drugged, poisoned, should ever dream of being a part of your sweet life. There is every reason why I should say good-bye and farewell!! (*Alice turns to him offering him the pipe*) There is every reason ... (*Holmes takes the pipe, looks at it in ecstasy, then grabs Alice and kisses her on the mouth*).
>
> *Blackout and curtain*

So the way to Holmes's heart, it seems, was through his pipe!

In Britain, where William Gillette's play opened at the Lyceum on 9 September 1901 (just one month after the first instalment of *The Hound of the Baskervilles* had appeared in *The Strand*), there were four versions touring the provinces *before* the Lyceum run closed. And a parody co-written by the drama critic of the *Daily Telegraph* subtitled, inevitably, *Why D'Gillette Im Off?*

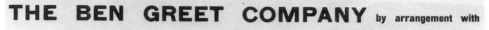

A 1902 poster for the touring production of Sherlock Holmes, *showing William Gillette as the great detective: the play ran at the Lyceum Theatre while* The Hound of the Baskervilles *was being serialised in* The Strand.

he final element in the public image of Holmes – his cluttered rooms at 221b Baker Street, which look more like one of the stately holmses of England than a set of bachelor digs – probably dates from the Sherlock Holmes exhibition of 1951, put on by the London borough of Marylebone. This featured a fully-furnished interior, designed by Michael Wright, which managed to cram just about every 'prop' mentioned in the stories around the fireplace – a collection of relics which was much appreciated by the house magazine *Justice of the Peace and Local Government Review* (1 September 1951):

> Here the physical eye can enjoy the Victorian interior pictured in the mind's eye of generations of admirers – the room where the Master lived and worked. Here is the famous dressing-gown, side by side with Dr Watson's stethoscope, hanging on the inside of the door; there are the retorts used in Holmes's chemical experiments, and a hundred other objects vividly recalling the fascinating pages of Arthur Conan Doyle ... Nor are the great man's foibles concealed his cigars in the coal-scuttle, his tobacco in the toe-end of a Persian slipper: and his unanswered correspondence transfixed by a jack-knife into the very centre of the wooden mantelpiece ...

Deerstalker, violin, knuckle-dusters and handcuffs, pipes galore, two arm-chairs, one sofa, a wickerwork chair, a plaster paw cast of *The Hound* and a 'faded' manuscript of its legend. Some of these had been illustrated by Paget, and all of them – it was claimed – were mentioned at least once in the stories. But they were never mentioned *all at the same time* – and as we know Conan Doyle wrote fast, as ideas came to him. The result of presenting *all* this clutter in one room was to extend 221b into a cinemascope Victorian drawing-room. No wonder pilgrims (not to mention Hammer Films) thought 221b Baker Street was the number of a *house* – and still do.

But in one important sense, the Festival exhibition got it right: Baker Street *was* Holmes's centre of operations, and he was by temperament a city man who needed to be wired in to the resources of a modern metropolis. In *The Adventures* and *The Memoirs*, he feels distinctly ill at ease in the country-side. It makes him feel 'in exile', he says, and fills him with 'a certain horror'. The countryside camouflages the activities of 'poor ignorant folk who know little of the law', activities which usually involve some form of detestable quadruped which is *literally* bestial. So in *The Hound of the Baskervilles*, Holmes sends Watson down to Dartmoor alone – to look after Sir Henry Baskerville – because, although he is prepared to go to the country 'if matters came to a crisis', he says he is unwilling to tear himself away from Baker Street for more than a day or two – an excuse which everyone accepts without demur.

Not only was this in character, but in plot terms it was one of the most important ingredients in the novel's overall success. For whereas in his previous full-length stories Conan Doyle had included extensive and exotic flashbacks – which did not involve either Holmes or Watson – to flesh out the narrative (the story of Jefferson Hope and the Mormons in *A Study in Scarlet*; the story told by Jonathan Small about the Agra treasure in *The Sign of the Four*), by sending Dr Watson to Dartmoor in *The Hound of the Baskervilles* he achieved for the first time the unity of a single narrative.

He also, by removing Holmes from chapters 6 to 11, avoided the problem of seeming to expand a short-story concept (with its by then familiar ingredients) into a full-length novel. Watson's reports from Dartmoor sustain the narrative tension, while providing Holmes with texts to analyse when finally he makes a personal appearance: his chronicler is at his furthest from the buffoon figure of Hollywood films in *The Hound*. In fact, Sherlock Holmes is hiding in a neolithic hut on Dartmoor all the time, but we (and Dr Watson) don't know that until the last lines of chapter 11. When he *does* find out, Watson is understandably miffed:

> 'I thought that you were in Baker Street working out that case of blackmailing.'
>
> 'That was what I wished you to think.'
>
> 'Then you use me, and yet you do not trust me!' I cried, with some bitterness. 'I think that I have deserved better at your hands, Holmes'.

ut the conscientious Dr Watson would have had a hard time unravelling the mystery of the hound itself, without the presence of Sherlock Holmes. For, after Black Shuck of Norfolk and the Whisht Hounds of Dartmoor, there was yet a *third* candidate for the 'original' of the legend. And it lived of all places in the countryside of the Welsh borders. This real-life mystery might have baffled the great detective himself, let alone Watson.

Less than a mile outside Clyro, near the village of Hay-on-Wye, there lived *another* branch of the Baskerville family – the main branch, in fact, descended from an ancient Norman line – in a huge country house called Clyro Court built in 1839, which bears a strong resemblance to the Baskerville Hall of the book. Yew alley, porch, pseudo-turrets, coats of arms, double stair in the hall, the lot. The Baskerville coat of arms shows a wolf's head erect (Theo Brown thought it was perhaps 'a wolf-hound' and it could easily be taken for one) with a broken spear pointing upwards through its mouth and five drops of blood. This was said by local people to refer to a family legend of a faithful hound who, at the time of the Wars of the Roses, warned the heir of the Baskervilles that the enemy was at the gates. Baskerville became so fed up with the hound's whingeing that he drove the shaft of his spear through the hapless creature's neck, before he realised his mistake. The enemy *was* at the gates. Or perhaps it was a wolf. Or ... From then on, whenever a Baskerville died, the hound would materialise at night, complete with spear.

This legend seems suspiciously like the popular parlour poem *Beth Gêlert or the grave of the greyhound* (1800) by William Robert Spencer, which tells the story of Llywellyn's Hound — one of the best-known folk tales of Wales. In the thirteenth century, apparently, Prince Llywellyn the Great mistakenly thought that his faithful hunting hound Gêlert was attacking his son, when in fact the dog was protecting the child from a wolf. The lachrymose poem became an evergreen at recital evenings:

> But when he gain'd his castle door,
> Aghast the Chieftain stood,
> The hound was smeared with gouts of gore,
> His lips, his fangs ran blood ...
> 'Hell-hound, my child's by thee devoured',
> The frantic father cried;
> And to the hilt his vengeful sword,
> He plunged in Gêlert's side.

The story goes that Arthur Conan Doyle stayed in the Welsh border country in 1897 or 1898 — at a house called Dunfield at Kington or a house called Caemawr — saw the painted coat of arms on an inn sign outside the Swan public house (since the 1950s The Baskerville Arms, complete with a plaster alsatian standing above the door), visited Clyro Court and subsequently asked the Baskervilles if they minded him using their name for his story. They agreed, it is said by the sole surviving relative, on the strict condition that he re-locate the book to the West Country — to avoid any stigma being attached to the family and to ward off tourists. The Hound of the Baskervilles was, it seems, bad for their image. From here on in, the plot thickens even further.

For the Baskervilles of Eardisley Castle in Herefordshire (the family moved to Clyro in 1837) had inter-married on various occasions in history with their neighbours the Vaughans of Hergest (usually pronounced Hargest) Court a few miles away. Today, only a farmhouse remains on the site of what was once a great medieval border castle. And the Vaughans most certainly had a legend of a black dog associated with their family — a much nastier one this time. The legend was attached to Thomas Vaughan, or Black Vaughan, who terrorised the local priests and farmers until his death in 1409. After that, the spectre of his equally vicious dog — the huge black boar-hound of Hergest, pulling on his chain — made an appearance in the neighbourhood, whenever there was about to be a death in the family.

In the south chapel of the early thirteenth-century church at nearby Kington, in Herefordshire, is Thomas's elaborate tomb – where there are life-sized figures of Black Vaughan and his wife Elena or Ellen Gethin, Ellen the Terrible, carved in alabaster. It has to be said that Thomas Vaughan does not *look* very sinister, but then again he wouldn't necessarily would he? On the wall opposite the tomb is the family memorial of the Vaughans (restored in 1846), which records the occasional inter-marriage of the Vaughans and the Baskervilles: 'Walter Vaughan of Hergest Esq, son of Thomas Vaughan, married Sibil, daughter of Sir James Baskerville of Eardisley Knt [who had a son James, who had a son] Charles Vaughan Esq who married first Elizabeth daughter of Sir James Baskerville Knt ... ' So Thomas Vaughan's son and great grandson both married into the Baskervilles round about the time of the Wars of the Roses, which might explain how the hound legend was transferred, over time, from one family to the other.

If Conan Doyle *did* stay near Kington (for which there is no documentary evidence), he could have heard the Vaughan legend, then chosen the Baskerville name because it was more romantic. (He probably knew it already, because the eighteenth-century *John* Baskerville was the man who invented the famous printing type-face – in which some of Conan Doyle's stories had been set). Certainly, the coincidence is extraordinary. As is the fact that while Harry Baskerville at Ashburton on Dartmoor (who said he had 'never heard tell' either of the Herefordshire Baskervilles *or* of their hound legend) was busy claiming that his name was used for the story, Major Geoffrey Hopton – grandson of Lady Dorothy Nesta Baskerville, was claiming that his side of the family provided the name but preferred not to acknowledge it: it was good for Harry's image, but bad for theirs. When Fletcher Robinson gave a signed copy of *The Hound of the Baskervilles* to Harry Baskerville, he wrote in it 'with apologies for using the name'. The name, not *your* name. Curioser and curioser.

Whether or not Conan Doyle really *did* stay in the Welsh borders three years before writing the story (some claim he actually *wrote* the story on Hergest Ridge), and picked up on the local legends of the Baskervilles or the Vaughans or both, there is some hard evidence of a connection which has recently been unearthed – and it comes from the editor of *The Strand Magazine* no less. Herbert Greenhaugh Smith wrote in a biographical article for his magazine (October 1930) that Fletcher Robinson's main contribution to the story had been 'to draw the attention of Conan Doyle to the tradition of the fiery hound *in a Welsh guide-book*'. So Conan Doyle did not *have* to have stayed there: Robinson told him all about the Welsh borders connection *at Cromer*.

What makes this evidence particularly interesting is that it *pre-dates* the researches and speculations of Sherlockians into the matter by over twenty

Ornate cover, designed by Alfred Garth Jones, of the first book
edition of The Hound of the Baskervilles (London, 1902).

years, and was unknown to them when articles such as Dr Maurice Campbell's *The Hound of the Baskervilles – Dartmoor or Herefordshire?* was written in 1953. So, not Black Shuck of Norfolk or the Whisht Hounds of Dartmoor, but the Hound of the Baskerville-Vaughans of Hergest Ridge. When Conan Doyle wrote to his mother from the Royal Links Hotel, saying 'we are going to do a small book together *The Hound of the Baskervilles*', he had already come across the name *before* he visited Dartmoor.

Most scholars assume that Fletcher Robinson must have mentioned Harry Baskerville to his golfing companion at some stage during their conversations, but it is equally plausible that he mentioned the name of a family which *did* have connections with a black dog legend, a name he had seen in 'a Welsh guide-book'. If so, Doyle's subsequent references to the legend of a spectral dog near Robinson's 'home on Dartmoor' were an attempt to cover his tracks – because the Baskervilles had asked him to. Part of a tale told in Cromer, and elaborated on Dartmoor, about a Welsh boar-hound, which was to become an international best-seller.

Much to the relief of the shareholders, *The Hound of the Baskervilles* was first published in *The Strand Magazine* in August 1901. Conan Doyle had returned to London via Sherborne, Bath and Cheltenham (where he watched the beginning of the cricket season), and completed the book by July at the latest. When first he wrote to Greenhaugh Smith about the project, he asked for 'my usual £50 per thousand words for all rights', but when he then decided to turn it into a Sherlock Holmes story he upped the figure to £100 per thousand because, as he put it, 'this is a very special occasion since as far as I can judge the revival of Holmes would attract a great deal of attention'.

But in his first letter he had stipulated something else as well: Fletcher Robinson's 'name must appear with mine'. Archibald Marshall, a good friend of Robinson's at this time, recalled in his memoir *Out and About* (1933):

> [Bobbles] loved a story, and was a great inventor of them. He gave Conan Doyle the idea and plot of *The Hound of the Baskervilles* and wrote most of its first instalment for the *Strand Magazine* [that is, the instalment which included 'the curse of the Baskervilles'] ... Conan Doyle wanted it to appear under their joint names, but his name alone was wanted, because it was worth so much more. They were paid £100 per thousand words, in the proportion of three to one. As I put it to Bobbles at the time, 'then if you write 'How do you do?' Doyle gets six shillings and you get two'. He said he had never been good at vulgar fractions, but it sounded right, and anyhow what he wrote was worth it.

If this *was* the arrangement, Robinson earned upwards of £2,500 from the deal. Three years later, he also added the sub-title 'Joint Author with Sir Arthur Conan Doyle in his Best Sherlock Holmes Story *The Hound of the Baskervilles*' to the serial version of his own short stories *The Chronicles of Addington Peace*, so permission from Doyle to advertise himself as 'Joint Author' was presumably also part of the agreed package. According to Marshall's account, *The Strand* wanted a Conan Doyle story, so Robinson had to settle for the next best thing – the generous fee and the by-line. According to Adrian Conan Doyle, Robinson actually *declined* 'my father's offer to collaborate'. Whatever the truth, Robinson's Addington Peace story *The Terror of the Snow* is about a ghostly wolf that haunts an alley of yew trees …

When the first instalment of *The Hound* was published – as 'another adventure of SHERLOCK HOLMES' – it bore an unusual note at the foot of the first page of double-column text: 'This story owes its inception to my friend, Mr Fletcher Robinson, who has helped me both in the general plot and in the local details – A.C.D.' The book version, published in 1902, changed this footnote into an open letter to Robinson – the wording of which was slightly but significantly different in the American edition:

> MY DEAR ROBINSON:
>
> It was to your account of a West-Country legend that this tale owes its inception. For this and for your help in the detail all thanks.
>
> Yours most truly, A. CONAN DOYLE

The above dedicatory letter, from the Newnes edition of 1902, has appeared in most subsequent British editions.

> MY DEAR ROBINSON:
>
> It was your account of West Country legend which first suggested the idea of this little tale to my mind.
>
> For this, and for the help which you gave me in its evolution, all thanks.
>
> Yours most truly, A. CONAN DOYLE

This letter, the manuscript of which is now in New York Public Library – dated 26 January 1902 – was written for the McClure Phillips edition of 1902, and has appeared in all subsequent American editions.

So, before Fletcher Robinson's death in January 1907 of typhoid fever at the age of thirty-five, Doyle was unsure about how to credit his contribution. Did he supply 'the central idea and the local colour' (as Doyle wrote to Greenhaugh Smith), the legend to which 'this tale owes its inception' as well as 'help in the detail', or the legend 'which first suggested the idea' and 'help … in its evolution'? Was he a collaborator or an originator? The dedications all appear to have been written by Conan Doyle himself. After Robinson's death, he was much clearer in his mind. His *Preface* to *The Complete Sherlock Holmes* (June 1929) states:

igel Bruce as Watson
and Basil Rathbone
as Holmes in the
studio-bound but highly
atmospheric 1939
Hollywood version of The
Hound of the Baskervilles.

[The Hound of the Baskervilles] arose from a remark by that fine fellow whose premature death was a loss to the world, Fletcher Robinson, that there was a spectral dog near his house on Dartmoor. That remark was the inception of the book, but I should add that the plot and every word of the actual narrative was my own.

So, no longer a collaboration: just a chance remark. No longer a plot: just a shaggy dog story. Later still, in his autobiographical *Memories and Adventures*, Conan Doyle did not mention Fletcher Robinson – or his contribution – at all. No wonder Harry Baskerville claimed that Bertie 'never got the credit he deserved' – *whether or not he actually wrote any of the story*.

One reason why Conan Doyle diminished Robinson's contribution with each of the dedications, may have been a series of articles which appeared in American *Bookseller* magazine – starting with the issue of October 1901:

The New Sherlock Holmes Story

Every one who read the opening chapter of the resuscitation of Sherlock Holmes in the September number of the *Strand Magazine* must have come to the conclusion that Dr Doyle's share in the collaboration was a very small one. *The Hound of the Baskervilles* opens very dramatically and promises to be a very good tale. But the Sherlock Holmes to whom we are introduced is a totally different personage from the Sherlock Holmes of *A Study in Scarlet, The Sign of the Four, The Adventures* and *The Memoirs* ... we have very little hesitation in expressing our conviction that the story is almost entirely Mr Robinson's and that Dr Doyle's only important contribution is the permission to use the character of Sherlock Holmes.

Then, in April 1902 – shortly before 'the completion of *The Hound of the Baskervilles*' in serial form:

... how much of the story is Fletcher Robinson's and how much Conan Doyle's? Discussion waxes hot. Both Editors are violently stirred. Both talk at the same time – interminable, impatient, dogmatic, delighted. They go out at last to finish the argument at dinner.

Finally, in June 1902, as part of a review of the book version by Arthur Bartlett Maurice:

... just how much Mr Fletcher Robinson did contribute to the inception and the working out of *The Hound of the Baskervilles,* the reviewer is neither inclined nor prepared to say. Only there is in this book much that is materially different from the former work of Dr Doyle in his detective stories, and the methods of Sherlock Holmes here are not entirely the methods of the astute, intellectual reasoner ... in *A Study in Scarlet* ...

The review went on to argue that *The Hound of the Baskervilles* was more of a horror novel than a detective story, that Sherlock Holmes was 'a compara-tively small factor' in the success of the narrative, and that when he *does* appear 'our belief in his infallibility and in his resemblance to the Holmes of Dr Doyle's earlier stories is severely shaken'. Furthermore, Holmes's explanations in the final chapter are 'woefully unsatisfactory and insufficient'. All of them good reasons, concluded Maurice, to suggest that Dr Doyle's contribution to *The Hound* was not as the main author.

We know that Conan Doyle read the February 1902 issue of the *Bookman* which commented on the story, because he in turn commented on some of its published theories and speculations. So it may well be that Conan Doyle toned down his dedication to the American edition in January 1902 – and thereafter – because speculation about the authorship of the book among American critics seemed to be getting out of hand.

onan Doyle's prediction that the new story would 'attract a great deal of attention' – and Hodder Williams's that the reading public 'had not entirely lost interest' in Holmes – were far too modest. For the one and only time in its history, *The Strand Magazine* went into seven printings. There were queues around the block outside the offices of the magazine as each instalment came out. In America, the publishers McClure had to keep postponing the publication date because there were so many thousands of orders for the first edition. Likewise, Gillette's play opened at the Lyceum to incredible box-office.

The writing was on the wall. Sherlock Holmes just *had* to rise from the grave. He would never be such an interesting personality again, but he would at least be on the bookstands.

The short stories which became *The Return of Sherlock Holmes* began publication in *The Strand* in October 1903: the book was issued by Newnes in March 1905. The novel *The Valley of Fear* followed in 1915 and the collection *His Last Bow* in 1917. Finally, *The Case-Book of Sherlock Holmes* was published in 1927, three years before the death of Arthur Conan Doyle.

Holmes's final case was solved at the beginning of August 1914, 'the most terrible August in the history of the world'. *His Last Bow* concludes with Holmes and Watson 'recalling once again the days of the past':

> … Holmes pointed back to the moonlit sea, and shook a thoughtful head.
>
> 'There's an east wind coming, Watson'.
>
> 'I think not, Holmes. It is very warm'.
>
> 'Good old Watson! You are the one fixed point in a changing age. There's an east wind coming all the same, such a wind as never blew on England yet. It will be cold and bitter, Watson, and a good many of us may wither before its blast. But it's God's own wind none the less, and a cleaner, better, stronger land will lie in the sunshine when the storm has cleared.'

I t was as a direct result of the trauma of the First World War that Conan Doyle became a devoted convert to – and crusader in the cause of – Spiritualism: the greatest personality the movement ever attracted. He had shown an interest in Spiritualism, with its apparently 'scientific' proof of the existence of an after-life, as early as 1887 – the year of *A Study in Scarlet* – when he attended table-rapping sessions in Southsea, a suburb of Portsmouth. In a letter to the magazine *Light*, published later that same year, he referred to himself as a Spiritualist. In November 1893 (shortly after the death of his father), he became an active member of the Society for Psychical Research and continued to take detailed notes on the séances he attended as well as writing the occasional story with mesmerism or psychometry (objects absorbing memories) as a theme. So at the time he wrote *The Hound of the Baskervilles* he was a committed researcher into paranormal phenomena and was keenly interested in debates surrounding them – if not yet a convert.

As Max Pemberton said of his state of mind in 1901, 'it was ever the bizarre and the daring that drew Conan Doyle'. But it took the horror of the trenches to convince him. In 1918, Conan Doyle wrote:

> In the presence of an agonized world, hearing every day of the deaths of the flower of our race in the first promise of their unfulfilled youth, seeing around one the wives and mothers who had no clear conception whither their loved one had gone to, I seemed suddenly to see that this subject with which I had so long dallied was not merely a study of a force outside the rules of science, but that it was really something tremendous … a call of hope and of guidance to the human race at the time of its deepest affliction. The objective side of it ceased to interest, for having made up one's mind that it was true there was an end of the matter.

Some have suggested that he continued to write Sherlock Holmes stories – which were, of course, centrally concerned by then with 'the objective side of it' – as an antidote to his spiritual interests; that they represented an equally strong side of his personality, the 'materialist philosophy' of the trained medical man – just like Dr Watson's comment on Sherlock Holmes. Others that he wrote *His Last Bow* and *The Case-Book* simply to finance his tireless crusade for the cause of Spiritualism.

When the question 'what would Sherlock Holmes have to say about Spiritualism?' was put to Conan Doyle in November 1918, he replied 'I suppose I am Sherlock Holmes, if anybody is, and I say that the case for Spiritualism is absolutely proved'. And yet, the nearest he came to introducing his psychical researches into the rational world of Baker Street was *The Hound of the Baskervilles*. After that, the 'romantic', open side of Holmes began to fade into the background. The game was over …

The Horror...

IN AUGUST 1914 the game was over not only for Sherlock Holmes, but for Victorian horror stories as well. The east wind which Sherlock Holmes predicted would blow on England would soon become a cataclysm.

At the Somme – a small river in Picardy, Northern France – two years later, half-a-million allied troops were killed or wounded in one engagement along a front of eighteen miles – 60 000 on the first morning, 30 000 in the first hour. The butchery of Saturday 1 July 1916 was – and still is – the greatest sacrifice in British military history – and all to gain *four miles* of ground at the expense of the German trench-lines.

These were the real-life horrors of the twentieth century, which made the great Victorian 'horror stores' – the nightmares of the nineteenth century – seem not only tame, but curiously re-assuring. Like your favourite box of chocolates. Frankenstein's creature, the vampire, Mr Hyde and the black dog – which had been in the mainstream of Victorian literature – became not very respectable components in the entertainment industry, ways of distracting the audience from the horrors of everyday life.

Originally, they were the products of nightmare and experience: they became landmarks in what has been called 'the geography of inexperience', with a minimal contact with the real world. In the process, they left the world of literature altogether to become *myths* – myths for the modern era. And, as a result, they changed their meaning beyond all recognition. As did the word 'horror'. Millions of people *think* they know these stories, but the stories they know are not the stories which were written. These Victorian horrors, these fantasies by gaslight, represent one of Britain's greatest and most lasting contributions to the global culture of the twentieth century, the era of mass production, mass consumption and of course mass destruction.

$\mathcal{S}$elect Bibliography

THE NIGHTMARE

Powell, Nicholas, *Fuseli – the Nightmare* (Allen Lane, 1973)
Schiff, Gert (ed), *Henry Fuseli* (Tate Gallery, 1975)
Shulman, S, *Nightmare* (David & Charles, 1979)
Starobinski, Jean, *Trois Fureurs* (Gallimard, 1974)
Todd, Ruthven, *Tracks in the Snow* (Greywalls Press, 1946)
Varnedoe, J. (ed), *Graphic Works of Max Klinger* (Dover Publications, 1977)

FRANKENSTEIN
Unpublished

Corrected rough draft manuscript of *Frankenstein,* in the collection of Lord Abinger at the Bodleian Library (Abinger Dep. c.477/1)
Fair copy manuscript of portion of *Frankenstein* (Abinger Dep. c.534/1)
Geneva police records for summer 1816 (Archives d'état de Genève; cote Jur Pen Juin et Juillet 1816)
Permissions to reside in Geneva (Registre de permis de séjour; cote D, Etrangers)

Published

Baldick, Chris, *In Frankenstein's Shadow* (Clarendon Press, 1987)
Beer, Gavin de, *Byron's French Passport* (in *Keats-Shelley Memorial Bulletin*, 20, 1969)
Beer, Gavin de, *Meshes of the Byronic Net in Switzerland* (from *English Studies*, XLIII, 5 October 1962)
Bishop, Franklin, *Polidori* (Gothic Society, Kent, 1991)
Byron, Lord (ed Marchand, Leslie), *So Late into the Night – Letters and Journals 1816-17* (John Murray, 1976)
Cantor, Paul A., *Creature and Creator* (Cambridge University Press, 1984)
Clairmont, Claire (ed Stocking, Marion Kingston), *The Journals* 1814-27 (Harvard University Press, 1968)
Engel, C.E., *Byron et Shelley en Suisse* (Dardel, Chambéry, 1930)
Fatio, Guillaume, *Milton et Byron à la Villa Diodati* (in *Nos Anciens et Leurs Oeuvres*, Recueil Genevois d'Art, Genève, 1912)
Fleenor, Juliann E., (ed) *The Female Gothic* (Eden Press, 1983)
Florescu, Radu, *In Search of Frankenstein* (New English Library, 1977)
Forgan, Sophie (ed), *Science and the Sons of Genius* (Science Reviews, London 1980)
Grylls, R. Glynn, *Mary Shelley* (Oxford University Press, 1938)
Hausermann, H.W., *Shelley's house in Geneva* (in *English Miscellany*, ed Mario Praz, edizione di 'storia e letteratura', 1950)
Holmes, Richard, *Shelley – the Pursuit* (Quartet Books, 1976)
Jennings, Humphrey, *Pandemonium* (Picador, 1987)
Joseph, Gerhard, *Frankenstein's Dream* (in *Hartford Studies in Literature*, vii, 1975)
King-Hele, Desmond, *The Essential Erasmus Darwin* (MacGibbon & Kee, 1968)
Levine, George and Knoepflmacher, U.C. (eds), *The Endurance of Frankenstein* (University of California Press, 1979)
Lyles, W.H., *Mary Shelley – an annotated bibliography* (Garland, 1975)
Mellor, Anne K., *Mary Shelley* (Routledge, 1988)
Moers, Ellen, *Literary Women* (Women's Press, 1978)

Nitchie, Elizabeth, *Mary Shelley* (Rutgers University Press, 1953)

Pirie, David, *A Heritage of Horror* (Gordon Fraser, 1973)

Polidori, J.W. (ed Rossetti, W.M.), *The Diary, 1816* (Elkin Mathews, 1911)

Pollin, Burton, *Philosophical and Literary Sources of Frankenstein* (in *Comparative Literature*, 17, 1965)

Poovey, Mary L., *The Proper Lady and the Woman Writer* (University of Chicago Press, 1984)

Rieger, James, *Polidori and the Genesis of Frankenstein* (in *Studies in English Literature*, 3, 1963)

Shelley, Mary, *Frankenstein, or the Modern Prometheus* (3 vols; Lackington, Hughes, Harding, Mavor and Jones, 1818)

Shelley, Mary, *Frankenstein, or the Modern Prometheus* (1 vol; Colburn and Bentley, 1831)

Shelley, Mary, (ed Butler, Marilyn), *Frankenstein, or the Modern Prometheus* (1818 text) (Oxford University Press, 1994)

Shelley, Mary, (ed Hindle, Maurice), *Frankenstein, or the Modern Prometheus* (1831 text) (Penguin, 1992)

Shelley, Mary, (ed Joseph, M.K.), *Frankenstein, or the Modern Prometheus* (1831 text) (Oxford University Press, 1980)

Shelley, Mary, (ed Lyons, Paddy), *Frankenstein, or the Modern Prometheus*) (1818 text) (J. M. Dent, 1994)

Shelley, Mary, (ed Macdonald, D.L. and Scherf, K.), *Frankenstein, or the Modern Prometheus* (1818 text) (Broadview Press, 1994)

Shelley, Mary, (ed Rieger, J.), *Frankenstein, or the Modern Prometheus* (1818 text) (Bobb's Merrill, 1974)

Shelley, Mary, (ed Wolf, L.), *Frankenstein, or the Modern Prometheus* (1818 text) (Plume Book, 1993)

Shelley, Mary (ed Feldman, Paula and Scott-Kilvert, Diana), *The Journals – vol one 1814-22, vol two 1822-44* (Clarendon Press, 1987).

Shelley, Mary (ed Bennett, Betty T.), *The Letters* (2 vols; John Hopkins Press, 1980-88)

Shelley, Percy (eds Ingpen, R. and Peck, W.), *The Complete Works* (Ernest Benn, 1926-30)

Skal, David J., *The Monster Show* (Plexus, 1994)

Small, Christopher, *Ariel Like a Harpy* (Gollancz, 1972)

Spark, Muriel, *Mary Shelley* (Constable, 1988)

St. Clair, William, *The Godwins and the Shelleys* (Faber, 1989)

Sunstein, Emily W., *Mary Shelley* (Johns Hopkins University Press, 1991)

Tropp, Martin, *Mary Shelley's Monster* (Houghton Mifflin, 1977)

Vasbinder, S.H., *Scientific Attitudes in Frankenstein* (UMI Research Press, 1976)

Veeder, William, *Mary Shelley and Frankenstein* (University of Chicago Press, 1986)

DRACULA
Unpublished

Original manuscript notes and data for *Dracula*, in The Rosenbach Museum and Library, Philadelphia.

Published

Booth, Michael R., *Victorian Spectacular Theatre* (Routledge & Kegan Paul, 1981)

Caine, Hall, *Bram Stoker – the story of a great friendship* (in *Daily Telegraph*, 24 April 1912)

Dalby, Richard, *Bram Stoker – a bibliography of first editions* (Dracula Press, London, 1983)

Deane, Hamilton and Balderston, John L., *Dracula – the vampire play* (Samuel French, 1960)

Dijkstra, Bran, *Idols of Perversity* (Oxford University Press, 1986)

Drummond, James, *Bram Stoker's Cruden Bay* (*Scots Magazine*, April 1976)
Drummond, James, *Dracula's Castle* (*The Scotsman*, 26 June 1976)
Drummond, James, *The Mistletoe and the Oak* (*Scots Magazine*, October 1977)
Farson, Daniel, *The Man Who Wrote Dracula* (Michael Joseph, 1975)
Frayling, Christopher, *Vampyres – Lord Byron to Count Dracula* (Faber, 1992)
Haining, Peter (ed), *The Dracula Centenary Book* (Souvenir Press, 1987)
Leatherdale, Clive, *Dracula – the novel and the legend* (Aquarian Press, 1985)
Leatherdale, Clive, *The Origins of Dracula* (William Kimber, 1987)
Ludlam, Harry, *A Biography of Dracula* (Fireside Press, 1962)
McNally, Raymond T. and Florescu, Radu, *In Search of Dracula* (NY Graphic Society, 1972)
Moretti, Franco, *Signs Taken for Wonders* (Verso, 1983)
Nandris, Grigore, *The Historical Dracula* (*Comparative Literature Studies*, 3,4, 1966)
Richards, Jeffrey, *Gender, Race and Sexuality in Bram Stoker's Other Novels* (in *Gender Roles & Sexuality in Victorian Literature*, ed C. Parker, Scolar Press, 1995)
Skal, David J., *Hollywood Gothic* (Deutsch, 1992)
Stoker, Bram, *Dracula* (Constable, 1897)
Stoker, Bram, *Dracula* (Constable sixpenny edition, 1901)
Stoker, Bram, Extracts from the original typed setting copy of *Dracula* (The Book Sail 16th Anniversary Catalogue, McLaughlin Press, California, 1984)
Stoker, Bram, (ed Hindle, Maurice), *Dracula* (Penguin, 1993)
Stoker, Bram, (ed Wilson, A.N.), *Dracula* (Oxford University Press, 1986)
Stoker, Bram, *Personal Reminiscences of Henry Irving* (2 vols; Heinemann, 1906)
Summers, Montague, *The Vampire – His Kith and Kin* (Kegan Paul, 1928)
Twitchell, James B., *The Living Dead – a Study of the Vampire in Romantic literature* (Duke University Press, 1981)
Viets, Henry, *The London Editions of Polidori's The Vampyre* (in *Papers of the Bibliographical Society of America*, 63, 1969)
Wolf, Leonard, *The Annotated Dracula* (New English Library, 1975)
Wolf, Leonard, *A Dream of Dracula* (Little, Brown & Co, 1972)

DR JEKYLL AND MR HYDE
Unpublished

Manuscript letters of Mrs R. L. Stevenson, autumn 1885, in the Edwin J. Beinecke Collection at Yale University; also typescript 'Mrs R. L. Stevenson's part in the writing of Dr Jekyll and Mr Hyde' dated 12 April 1944 and signed Isobel Field.
Manuscript correspondence and notes collected by biographer Graham Balfour, 1899-1901 (*Balfour Notebooks* 9903; 9895; 9906) in the National Library of Scotland.

Published

Adcock, A. St J. (ed), *Robert Louis Stevenson – His Work and His Personality* (London, 1924)
Balfour, Graham, *The Life of Robert Louis Stevenson* (2 vols; Methuen, 1901)
Balfour, Michael, *How the biography came to be written* (in *Times Literary Supplement* 15 & 22 Jan 1960)
Bell, Ian, *Dreams of Exile* (Henry Holt Owl Book, 1995)
Boodle, Adelaide, *RLS and His Sine Qua Non* (John Murray, 1926)
Calder, Jenni, *RLS – a life study* (Drew, Glasgow, 1990)
Calder, Jenni (ed), *The Robert Louis Stevenson Companion* (Paul Harris, Edinburgh, 1980)
Cunningham, Alison (ed Skinner, Robert), *Cummy's Diary* (London, 1926)
Davies, Hunter, *The Teller of Tales* (Sinclair-Stevenson, 1994)
Dudley Edwards, Owen, *Burke and Hare* (Mercat, Edinburgh, 1993)
Eigner, Edwin M., *Robert Louis Stevenson and Romantic Tradition* (Princeton University Press, 1966)

Elwin, Malcolm, *The Strange Case of R. L. Stevenson* (Macdonald, 1950)

Frayling, Christopher, *The House That Jack Built* (in *Rape, an historical and cultural enquiry*, ed Porter, R. & Tomaselli, S., Blackwell, 1989)

Furnas, J.C., *Voyage to Windward* (Faber, 1952)

Geduld, Harry M., *The Definitive Jekyll & Hyde Companion* (Garland, 1983)

Gibson, John S., *Deacon Brodie – father to Jekyll & Hyde* (Edinburgh, 1977)

Hammerton, John (ed), *Stevensoniana* (Grant, Edinburgh, 1910)

Heath, Stephen, *Psychopathia Sexualis; Stevenson's Strange Case* (in *Critical Quarterly*, 28, 1986)

Lucas, E.V. (ed), *The Colvins and their Friends* (Methuen, 1928)

Mackay, Margaret, *The Violent Friend* (J. M. Dent, 1969)

Maixner, Paul, *Robert Louis Stevenson, The Critical Heritage* (Routledge & Kegan Paul, 1981)

Masson, Rosaline (ed), *I Can Remember Robert Louis Stevenson* (Chambers, Edinburgh, 1922)

McLynn, Frank, *Robert Louis Stevenson – a biography* (Pimlico, 1994)

Miyoshi, Masao, *The Divided Self* (University of London Press, 1969)

Osbourne, Lloyd, *An Intimate Portrait of RLS* (New York, 1924)

Patterson, David (ed), *Thomas Begbie's Edinburgh* (John Donald, Edinburgh, 1992)

Rankin, Nicholas, *Dead Man's Chest* (Faber, 1987)

Rumbelow, Donald, *The Complete Jack the Ripper* (Penguin, 1988)

Sanchez, Nellie, *Life of Mrs Robert Louis Stevenson* (Chatto, 1920)

Showalter, Elaine, *Sexual Anarchy* (Virago, 1992)

Scally, John, *Pictures of the Mind* (Canongate Press/National Library of Scotland, 1994)

Steuart, John A, *Robert Louis Stevenson* (2 vols, London, 1924)

Stevenson, Robert Louis, *A Child's Garden of Verses* (Puffin, 1952)

Stevenson, Robert Louis, *Complete Works* (Tusitala edition, 1924; Skerryvore edition, 1924-6)

Stevenson, Robert Louis, (ed Harman, Claire), *Essays and Poems* (J. M. Dent, 1992)

Stevenson, Robert Louis, (ed Booth, B.A. and Mehew, E.), *The Letters – volume five (July 1884-August 1887) and six (August 1887-September 1890)* (Yale University Press, 1995)

Stevenson, Robert Louis, *Strange Case of Dr Jekyll and Mr Hyde* (Longman, Green & Co, 1886)

Stevenson, Robert Louis (ed Calder, Jenni), *The Strange Case of Dr Jekyll & Mr Hyde* (Penguin, 1979)

Stevenson, Robert Louis (ed Harman, Claire), *The Strange Case of Dr Jekyll & Mr Hyde* (J. M. Dent, 1992)

Strong, Isobel, *Robert Louis Stevenson* (Stevenson Society of America, Saranac Lake, 1920)

Sullivan, T. R., *Robert Louis Stevenson at Saranac* (Scribner's Magazine, New York, August 1917)

Swearingen, Roger C., *The Prose Writings of Robert Louis Stevenson* (Macmillan, 1980)

Twitchell, James B., *Dreadful Pleasures* (Oxford University Press, 1985)

Veeder, William & Hirsch, Gordon, *Dr Jekyll & Mr Hyde after One Hundred Years* (University of Chicago Press, 1988)

Wilstach, Paul, *Richard Mansfield, the Man and the Actor* (Chapman & Hall, 1908)

Winter, William, *Life & Art of Richard Mansfield* (vol 1; Greenwood Press, Connecticut, 1910)

THE HOUND OF THE BASKERVILLES
Unpublished

Manuscript of Chapter XI (The Man on the Tor), in the Berg Collection at New York Public Library; also single page ('may fall in with ... purpose I must now') in Rare Books and Manuscripts Division.

Published

Anon, articles in *The Bookman* (New York, October 1901, Feb, April, May 1902)

Baring-Gould, Sabine, *A Book of Dartmoor* (Methuen, 1900)

Baring-Gould, Sabine, *A Book of Devon* (Methuen, 1899)

Baring-Gould, Sabine, *A Book of the West* (Methuen, 1899)

Baring-Gould, Sabine, *Old Country Life* (Methuen, 1890)

Baring-Gould, W.S. (ed), *The Annotated Sherlock Holmes* (Wings Books, New York, 1992)

Baskerville, Harry (interviews), *South Devon Journal* 13 June and 17 Oct 1951; *John O'London's* LXI, 21 Nov 1952; *Western Times and Gazette*, 1 Nov 1957; *Daily Express*, 16 Mar 1959; *NY World-Telegram*, 28 Mar 1959; *NY Herald Tribune*, 2 April 1962

Bigelow, S. Tupper, *The Singular Case of Fletcher Robinson* (Baker Street Gasogene, 1, 2, 1961)

Bleiler, E.F. (ed), *The Best Supernatural Tales of Arthur Conan Doyle* (Dover, 1979)

Brown, Theo, *The Black Dog in Devon* (Transactions of the Devonshire Association, XCI, 1959)

Brown, Theo, *The Fate of the Dead – a study in folk eschatology in the West Country* (Folk-lore Society, London, 1979)

Cabell, Branch, *Ladies and Gentlemen* (McBride, 1934)

Campbell, Maurice, *The Hound of the Baskervilles – Dartmoor or Herefordshire?* (Guys Hospital Gazette 67, 30 May, 1953)

Carr, John Dickson, *The Life of Sir Arthur Conan Doyle* (Carroll and Graf, 1990)

Chapman, Matthew, *The Fiendish Hound of the Baskervilles* (Western Mail, 28 July 1992)

Cox, Don Richard, *Arthur Conan Doyle* (Ungar, New York, 1985)

Dakin, D. Martin, *A Sherlock Holmes Commentary* (David & Charles, 1972)

Down, H.J.W., *Arthur Conan Doyle – an appreciation* (Associated Sunday Magazine, 26 Nov 1905)

Doyle, A. Conan, *The Hound of the Baskervilles – another adventure of Sherlock Holmes* (in *Strand Magazine*, August 1901-April 1902)

Doyle, A. Conan, *The Hound of the Baskervilles – another adventure of Sherlock Holmes* (Newnes, 1902)

Doyle, A. Conan (ed Fowles, John), *The Hound of the Baskervilles* (John Murray, 1974)

Doyle, A. Conan (ed Robson, W.W.), *The Hound of the Baskervilles* (Oxford University Press, 1993)

Doyle, A. Conan, *The King of the Foxes* (in *The Conan Doyle Stories*, Murray, London, 1929)

Doyle, A. Conan and Gillette, William, *Sherlock Holmes – a play in two acts* (Samuel French, 1976)

Eco, Umberto and Sebeok, Thomas A., *The Sign of Three* (Indiana University Press, 1983)

Green, R. Lancelyn, *The Uncollected Sherlock Holmes* (Penguin, 1983)

Green, R. Lancelyn, *The Sherlock Holmes Letters* (Secker & Warburg, 1986)

Green, R. Lancelyn and Gibson, John Michael, *A Bibliography of Arthur Conan Doyle* (Oxford, 1983)

Greene, Hugh (ed), *The Rivals of Sherlock Holmes* (Bodley Head, 1970)

Greenhaugh Smith, H., *Some Letters of Conan Doyle* (Strand Magazine, LXXX, October 1930)

Greeves, Tom, *Tin Mines of Dartmoor* (Devon Books, Tiverton, 1993)

Haining, Peter (ed), *Sherlock Holmes Scrapbook* (New English Library, 1974)

Hall, Trevor H., *Sherlock Holmes and his Creator* (Duckworth, 1978).

Higham, Charles, *The Adventures of Conan Doyle* (Hamish Hamilton, 1976)

Holroyd, James Edward, *Baker Street By-ways* (Allen and Unwin, 1959)

Hodder Williams, J.E., *Arthur Conan Doyle* (Bookman, April 1902)

James, Clive, *Sherlockology* (New York Review of Books, 20 Feb 1975)

Jones, Kelvin, *Conan Doyle and the Spirits* (Aquarian Press, 1989)

Jones, Kelvin, *The Mythology of the Hound of the Baskervilles* (Sir Hugo Books, Cheltenham, 1986)

Knox, Ronald A., *Essays in Satire* (Sneed and Ward, 1928)

Kissane, James and John, *Sherlock Holmes and the Ritual of Reason* (in *Nineteenth Century Fiction*, 17, 4, March 1963)

Klinefelter, Walter, *Sherlock Holmes in Portrait and Profile* (Syracuse University Press, 1963)

Maurice, Arthur Bartlett, *Seven Novels of Importance* (*The Bookman*, NY, June 1902)

McNabb, Janice, *The Curious Incident of the Hound on Dartmoor* (Bootmakers of Toronto, 1984)

McQueen, Ian, *Sherlock Holmes Detected* (David & Charles, 1974)

Marshall, Archibald, *Out and About* (John Murray, 1933)

Nesbitt, F., *A Reply* (*Devon and Cornwall Notes & Queries*, xvii, Jan 1932-Oct 1933)

Norden, Pierre, *Conan Doyle* (John Murray, 1966)

Purves, Shirley (ed), *Hound and Horse – a Dartmoor Commonplace Book* (Sherlock Holmes Society of London, 1992, with key articles by Howlett, A. and Green, R. L.)

Reid, Colin and Thornton, Dennis, *The Hound of the Baskervilles publicity manual* (Hammer Films, 1959)

Ruber, P.A., *Sir Arthur Conan Doyle and Fletcher Robinson* (*Baker Street Gasogene*, 1, 2, 1961)

Sidgwick, Frank, *The Hound of the Baskervilles at Fault* (Cambridge Review, 23 Jan 1902)

Weller, Philip, *The Dartmoor of the Hound of the Baskervilles* (Sherlock Publications, London, 1992)

PICTURE CREDITS

BBC Books would like to thank the following for providing photographs and for permission to reproduce copyright material. While every effort has been made to trace and acknowledge all copyright holders, we would like to apologise should there have been any errors or omissions.

Page 2, from Max Ernst *Une Semaine de Bonté ou les Sept Eléments Capitaux Roman* (Troisième Cahier, Mardi). Societé des Edition Jean-Jacques Pauvert, Paris, 1963 ©SPADEM/ADAGP, Paris & DACS, London 1996/photo: Eileen Tweedy; 7, The Detroit Institute of Arts. The gift of Mr. & Mrs. Bert L. Smokler and Mr. & Mrs. Lawrence Fleischman; 9, from *Vom Tode* (Zweiter Teil) Opus XIII,1889. Courtesy Simon Reynolds (Fine Paintings) London SW13/photo: Eileen Tweedy; 10, BFI Stills, Posters & Designs/©1931 by Universal City Studios Inc. Courtesy of MCA Publishing Rights, a division of MCA Inc. All rights reserved; 15, Mary Evans Picture Library; 17, National Portrait Gallery, London; 20, David South; 23, Bodleian Library, Oxford; 27, National Portrait Gallery, London; 36, Kunstalle, Hamburg/Bridgeman Art Library; 39, David South; 42, Musée d'Art et d'Histoire de la Ville Neuchâtel; 46, from Francisco Goya *Los Caprichos*, 1799/photo: Eileen Tweedy; 47, The Kobal Collection/as page 10; 51, David South; 55, photo by Francis Frith. Frayling Collection; 58, Mander & Mitchenson; 61, BFI Stills, Poster & Designs/The Edison Company; 63, BFI Stills, Posters & Designs/as page 10; 67, Frayling Collection; 69, Mander & Mitchenson; 73 & 74, National Portrait Gallery, London; 76 & 79, Frayling Collection; 87, The Sutcliffe Gallery, Whitby; 91, Rosenbach Museum & Library, Philadelphia, USA; 94, *Tatler*, October,1902; 97, David South; 102, The British Library/photo: Eileen Tweedy; 110–11, BFI Stills, Posters & Designs/Friedrich Wilhelm Mornau Steftung/Transit Films; 112, The Kobal Collection/Hammer Films/©1958 as page 10; 115, Mary Evans Picture Library; 117, ©The Writers' Museum, Edinburgh City Museums; 123, The Trustees of The National Library of Scotland; 127, David South; 130 & 131, City Art Centre Edinburgh; 135, The Trustees of The National Library of Scotland; 137, The Writers' Museum, Edinburgh City Museums; 138, John Hay Whitney Collection, New York/The Bridgeman Art Library; 147, The Writers' Museum, Edinburgh City Museums; 155, Mander & Mitchenson; 156–7, The Kobal Collection/ Paramount Pictures/©Turner Entertainment Co. All rights reserved; 159, British Library (Colindale); 163, Lancelyn Green Collection/photo: Eileen Tweedy; 165, The Mansell Collection; 166 & 175, Lancelyn Green Collection; 179 & 183, ©Christopher Frayling; 187, Lancelyn Green Collection/photo: Eileen Tweedy; 190, Berg Collection, New York Public Library; 196 & 199, from Walter Klinefelter *Sherlock Holmes in Portrait and Profile*, Syracuse University Press, 1963; 200, The Mansell Collection; 202 & 207, Lancelyn Green Collection; 210–11, The Ronald Grant Archive/ 20th Century Fox.

*I*ndex

Page numbers in italic
refer to illustrations

Abinger Shelley
 Collection 30
Albertus Magnus 38
Alien 6
Arnold, Matthew 118
atavism 182, 184–5
Auden, W.H. 184
Austen, Jane 30
automata 41–3

Balfour, Graham 146–7, 152
Baring-Gould, Rev Sabine 180–1,
 184–6, 191
Baskerville family, main branch
 204–8
Baskerville, Harry 172–8, *175*
Baskerville, Hugo 185–6, 189, 194
Bath, 5, Abbey Churchyard *55*, 55–7
Baudelaire, Charles 81
Beardsley, Aubrey 90–1, 106
Bérard, Cyprien 75
black dog legends 189–95, 204–8
Black Shuck 169, 189, 204, 208
The Body Snatcher 133, *135*
Bond, Dr John 7–8
Boner, Charles 98
Boodle, Adelaide 151–2
Book of Dartmoor 180–1, 189
The Book of Were-Wolves 99–100
The Bride of Frankenstein 62
Brodie, William 128–9
Brown, Theo 192–3, 204
Bruce, Nigel *210–11*
Burke, Edmund 10–11
Burke and Hare, bodysuppliers 133
Burne-Jones, Edward 83
Byron, Lord
 death 64
 ghost story 30
 reputation 48–9
 Switzerland 16–18, 22, 25,
  28–9, 35
 vampires 72–3, *73*, 74–5

Caine, Hall 93, 103, 105, 113
Carmilla 82, 97, 104
Carpathian Mountains 86, 98–100,
 102, 104
Castle Dracula *67*, 68, 104–5
Castle Frankenstein 35–6, *39*
Charcot, Jean Martin 141
Childe Harold's Pilgrimage 18–19,
 25, 28
Christabel 26
Clairmont, Jane (Clare) 16–17, 19,
 25, 28, 48–50, 54–7
Coleridge, Samuel Taylor 13, 26,
 54
Cooke, Thomas Potter 60, 63
critics, *Dracula* 106–7
Cunningham, Alison (Cummy)
 125–6

Dartmoor 178–81, 184, 189–91,
 204
Darwin, Erasmus 8–10, 24, 29, 38,
 41
Davy, Humphrey 37–8, 40, 56
Dead Mother 9, 12
Dignity and Impudence 200
doppelganger 143
double personality 116, 140–1,
 143, 151
Doyle, Arthur Conan 162–214, *165*
 authorship controversy 174–7,
  208–13
 Cromer 168–9, 171
 Dartmoor 177–88, 195
 dogs 169–71
 letters to his mother 171–8,
  186, 189, 196
 marriage 168
 Spiritualism 214
Dr Jekyll and Mr Hyde 114–61
 see also *Strange Case of Dr Jekyll
  and Mr Hyde*
 cover illustration *123*
 critics 117
 dramatised version 153–4, 158
 film versions 154, *156–7*
 publication 118, 149–50
 reviews 119–21, 122–4
 sexual pathology 141–3, 150,
  154–8
 story 118
 writing of 144–9, 152

Dracula 66–113
 critics 106–7
 Cruden Bay influence 94–7
 films 109, *110–11*, *112*, 113
 publication 105
 story 70
 Whitby influence 83–8, 89–90,
  95
 working notes 87
Dracula, Count 66, 67, 102, 108
Dracula, Vlad *see* Vlad the
 Impaler
Dublin society 82
Dumas, Alexandre 76–7

Ebing, Krafft 141
Edinburgh *127*, 127–8, *130*, *131*,
 160
electricity, *Frankenstein* 37–8,
 45–6
Eliot, T.S. 184
Enlightenment, French 41–3
Ernestus Berchtold 25
eroticism, female 81
Eyriès, Jean Baptiste Benoit 24

Faust legend 34, 40
Festival of Britain, Sherlock Holmes
 exhibition 203
films
 Dr Jekyll and Mr Hyde 154,
  156–7
 Dracula 109, *110–11*, *112*, *113*,
  113
 Frankenstein 10, 44–5, 46–7,
  60–2, *61*
 The Hound of the Baskervilles
  173–5, 192, 193–4,
  210–11
The Final Problem 166, 167, 168
First World War 214, 215
Fletcher Robinson, Bertram
 175
 authorship controversy 174–7,
  189, 208–13
 black dog legend 168–9, 171,
  191–2, 197, 206
 Dartmoor visit 178–80, 195
 Harry Baskerville 172–3
folklore 85–6, 169, 189–93, 195,
 204, 208
Fox Tore Mire 179–81, *179*

Frankenstein 14–65
  1818 edition 30, 31–2, 40, 57–9
  1831 edition 14–*15*, 22, 30, 59
    introduction 22–4, 28
  adaptation difficulties 62
  films 10, 44–5, 46–7, 60–2, *61*
  first edition preface 21–2
  first illustration *15*
  laboratory 1931-style *63*
  manuscript draft *23*
  science 37
  story 18
Frankenstein, Fate of 58
Frankenstein, Victor
  character development 40, 59
  death of Elizabeth 31–2
  education 38, 56
  his creation 44, 50–2, 54
  life story 18
Freud, Sigmund 9, 11, 68, 141
Friedrich, Caspar David 12, 35
Fuseli, John Henry 6–12, 31, 44,
  60

Galvani, Luigi 29, 45
Garnerin brothers 37–8
Gautier, Théophile 81
Giger, Hans Rudi 6
Gillette, William 200–1, 213
godlessness 41
Godwin, Mary W. *see* Shelley, Mary
  Wollstonecraft
Godwin, William 28, 34, 53, 56,
  59, 62, 64–5
Goethe, Johann Wolfgang von 54,
  74
Gothic novels 30
Goya 44, 47

Hamlet 69, 91
Harker, Jonathan 69, 71, 83, 96,
  98–9, 104
Hodder Williams, J.E. 192
Hoffman, E.T.A. 43
Hollywood
  Dr Jekyll and Mr Hyde (1932)
    156–7
  Dracula 109
  Frankenstein 10, 44–5, 46–7,
    60–2
  The Hound of the Baskervilles
    193–4, *210–11*

Holmes, Sherlock
  death 164–7
  dogs 169–71
  illustrations *166, 196, 199*, 200,
    202, 210–11
  personal attributes 184, 195,
    197–8, 200–1
  resurrection 196–8
  'Sherlockology' 188
horror stories, origins 13
The Hound of the Baskervilles
  162–214
  authorship controversy 174–7,
    208–13
  films 173–5, 192, *193–4,
    210–11*
  first book edition cover *207*
  first instalment 209
  Holmes' resurrection 196–8
  manuscript 189, *190*
  moor location 179–80, *179*
  plot 171–3
  publication 208
  story 170
  Strand illustration *163*
  writing of 186
Hyde, Mr
  see also Dr Jekyll and Mr Hyde
  aura 121–2
  transformation 143
hypnosis 141
hypocrisy 131
  Dr Jekyll 121–2, 142
hysteria 141

Ibsen, Henrik 106
Interpretation of Dreams 11
Intimate Portrait of RLS 145
Irving, Sir Henry 69, 91–3, *94*, 97,
  108–9, 113

'Jack the Ripper' 158–60, *159*
Jacquet-Droz brothers 41–3
James, Henry 149
James, P.D. 182, 184
Jekyll, Dr
  see also Dr Jekyll and Mr Hyde
  first experiment 130
  hypocrisy 121–2, 142
  transformation 143

Karloff, Boris 44, 47, 60, 62

Klinger, Max 9, 12
Knox, Fr Ronald 188–9

Lang, Andrew 116–17
Lang, Fritz 45
Lawrence, Dr William 33, 37
Le Fanu, Sheridan 82, 97,
  104
Leaves of Grass 70–1
legends, phantom black dog 169,
  189, 191, 192–3, 195
Life of Mrs R L Stevenson 151
The Life of Robert Louis Stevenson
  144
Lord Ruthwen ou les Vampires
  75–6
Lyceum Theatre 68–9, 71, 82, 92,
  94, 108–109

Macbeth 69
The Man on the Tor 186, *187*
Mansfield, Richard 153–4, *155*,
  158
mara 6, 8, 11
March, Fredric *156–7*
marriage
  Arthur Conan Doyle 168
  Bram Stoker 82–3
  Percy and Mary Shelley 57
  Robert Louis Stevenson 133–4,
    136–9
Marschner, Heinrich August 78
Mazeppa 30, 75
Memoirs of Himself 126
Mer de Glace, Mont Blanc 50–2, *51*,
  56
Mérimée, Prosper 81
Metamorphosis 32
Milton, John 54
Mona Lisa 82
monster, Frankenstein's 13, 41, 44,
  46–7, 59
Moriarty, 'Professor' James
  164–7
Munch, Edvard 12
myths
  horror story origins 13
  Prometheus 13, 32–3

neolithic dwellings, Grimspound
  183
The Nightmare 6–12, *7*, 31, 44

nightmares
    Arthur Conan Doyle 172
    Bram Stoker 68–9, 72, 82, 83,
      88, 92–3
    Mary Shelley 29–30, 32, 34, 43,
      57
    Robert Louis Stevenson 124,
      140, 143, 144, 146
Nodier, Charles 75–6
Northanger Abbey 30
Nosferatu (1922) 109, *110–11*
Novalis 8
novels, Gothic 30

Oedipus Complex 106
Osbourne, Fanny Vandergrift
  133–4
Osbourne, Lloyd 145
Ovid 32

Paget, Sidney 199–202
Paracelsus 38
Paradise Lost 54
Pemberton, Max 169, 214
Planché, James Robinson 76–8
Plutarch 54
Polidori, Dr John 64, *74*, 74–5, 80,
  102
    Journal 17, 24, 26, 29
    Switzerland 16–18, 22, 30, 49
    The Vampyre 77–8
    vampire story 72
Presumption! see Frankenstein, Fate of
Prometheus 13, 18, 32–3, 37, 41
Psychopathia Sexualis 141–3

Rathbone, Basil 193–4, *210–11*
Reichenbach Falls 164–7, *166*
Rhine boat trip, Mary Shelley 35
Romantics 8, 11–12, 49, 53, 64
Rossetti, Dante Gabriel 102–3
Rousseau, Jean-Jacques 53
Royal College of Surgeons 37
Runge, Philipp Otto 12
Rymer, James Malcolm 78–81

St Gaudens, Augustus 147, 161
Sargent, John Singer *138*, 138–9, 140
science, *Frankenstein* 37
Scotland 93–7
Scott, Sir Walter 64
The Scribe automaton *42*, 43

sexual pathology, *Dr Jekyll and Mr
  Hyde* 141–3, 150, 154–8
Shelley, Harriet Westbrook 25, 56
Shelley, Mary Wollstonecraft
  14–65, *17*
    childbirth 33–4
    Journal 21, 33–4, 35, 38,
      49–52, 54
    marriage 57
    nightmare 29–30, 32, 34, 43,
      57
    Rhine boat trip 35
    Switzerland 16–30, 48–52
Shelley, Percy Bysshe
    Bath 54–6
    contribution to *Frankenstein* 21,
      27–9, 30, 35–6, 59
    illness 33–4, 37
    Marlow 57, 65
    Switzerland 16–21, 25, *29*,
      48–50
Sherlock Holmes, poster 201, *202*
Sherlockians 188–9, 193, 206–7
shipwrecks 85–6
Skerryvore 136–7, *137*, 139–40
Slains Castle 95–6, *97*
The Snake's Pass 68–9
The Sorrows of Young Werther 54
Southey, Robert 40
Spencer, William Robert 205
Spiritualism 214
Stevenson, Fanny 136–9, *138*,
  144–50
Stevenson, Louis and Fanny, double
  portrait *138*
Stevenson, Robert Louis 114–61,
  117, *138*
    Bournemouth 134–40, *137*,
      151–2
    childhood 125
    engineering studies 130–1
    illness 140
    Letters 149
    marriage 133–4, 136–9
    memorial plaque *147*, 161
    nightmare 124, 140, 143, 144,
      146
    as undergraduate 132–3
Stoker, Bram (Abraham) 66–113,
  69, *94*
    marriage 82–3
    nightmare 68–9, 72

research notes 95, 100, 104
Scotland 93–7
self-assessment 70–1
sexuality 69, 106–8
Whitby 83–8, *84*, 89–90, 95,
  97
Stoker, Florence 82–3, 109
The Strand Magazine 171–2, 206,
  213
*Strange Case of Dr Jekyll and Mr
  Hyde* 118, 124, 129, 143–4, 161
A Study in Scarlet 170, *196*, 200,
  204, 214
Sullivan, Thomas Russell 153, 158

The Tempest 40
transformation scenes, *Dr Jekyll and
  Mr Hyde* 143–44
Transylvania 68, 97–8, 100–1

The Vampire 76–8
Le Vampire 75–6
vampires
    Byronic 72–5, 80, 81, 104
    dramatic 75–8
    folkloric 71, 80, 103–4
    literary 72
The Vampyre 72, 74–5, 78
*Varney, the Vampire or the Feast of
  Blood* 78–81, *79*, 105
Vlad the Impaler 88, 101–2, *102*
Voltaire 71–2

*The Wanderer Over the Sea of Clouds,
  36*
Watson, Dr *196*, *199*, 210–11
    Dartmoor 182
    death of Holmes 164–7
    drugs 198
    'Sherlockology' 188
    The Copper Beeches 170
were-wolves 99–100
Westenra, Lucy 103
Whitby, Bram Stoker 83–90, *87*,
  95, 97
Whitechapel murders 158
Whitman, Walt 70–1
Wilde, Oscar 82, 91, 106
Williams, Hodder 213
Wohlbrück, Wilhelm August 78
Wollstonecraft, Mary 19, 28, 33,
  53, 64, 65